GENDER, THE STATE, AND SOCIAL REPRODUCTION:
HOUSEHOLD INSECURITY IN NEO-LIBERAL TIMES

KATE BEZANSON

Gender, the State, and Social Reproduction

Household Insecurity in Neo-liberal Times

UNIVERSITY OF TORONTO PRESS
Toronto Buffalo London

© University of Toronto Press Incorporated 2006
Toronto Buffalo London
Printed in Canada

ISBN-13: 978-0-8020-9065-2
ISBN-10: 0-8020-9065-6

Printed on acid-free paper

Library and Archives Canada Cataloguing in Publication

Bezanson, Kate
Gender, the state and social reproduction : household insecurity in
neo-liberal times / Kate Bezanson.

Includes bibliographical references and index.
ISBN 0-8020-9065-6
ISBN 978-0-8020-9065-2

1. Structural adjustment (Economic policy) – Ontario.   2. Ontario –
Social policy.   3. Women – Ontario – Economic conditions – 20th
century.   4. Poor – Ontario – Economic conditions – 20th century.
5. Neo-liberalism – Ontario – History – 20th century.   6. Ontario – Politics
and government – 1995–2000.   I. Title.

HC117.O5B49 2006   330.971'04   C2006-902657-2

This book has been published with the help of a grant from the Canadian
Federation for the Humanities and Social Sciences, through the Aid to
Scholarly Publications Programme, using funds provided by the Social
Sciences and Humanities Research Council of Canada.

University of Toronto Press acknowledges the financial assistance to its
publishing program of the Canada Council for the Arts and the Ontario
Arts Council.

University of Toronto Press acknowledges the financial support for its
publishing activities of the Government of Canada through the Book
Publishing Industry Development Program (BPIDP).

In memory of my mother, Alice Marian Mutrie Bezanson

Contents

Tables and Figures

Tables

Figure

Preface

The impetus for this book came originally from my training in international development studies. Having lived and studied in Latin America in the mid–1980s and again in the early 1990s, I witnessed first-hand some of the severe social dislocation and poverty brought about by the debt crisis and the subsequent adoption of neo-liberal structural adjustment policies. I also saw that the effects of 'adjustment' were borne differently by men and women. Indeed, international development scholars studying the effects of structural adjustment policies on developing countries have concluded that neo-liberal approaches burden the poor – and poor women in particular – as states retreat and capital is deregulated (Elson 1998; Kabeer 2003).[1] Politically and intellectually, I sought to understand both the economic philosophy behind structural adjustment, and the reasons why neo-liberal policies bore with such severity on women and the poor.

The path taken by many advanced welfare states (especially liberal ones such as the Canada, United States, the United Kingdom, New Zealand, and Australia) since the 1980s borrows heavily from the economic philosophies associated with 'adjustment.' The federal state in Canada embraced a neo-liberal philosophy beginning in the late 1980s and escalating in the mid–1990s. The process of welfare state change, often called economic 'restructuring,' resulted in a less universal, more targeted set of social entitlements for Canadians and reduced transfers to the provinces to deliver social services and supports. The election in Ontario in 1995 of a staunchly neo-liberal government echoed the structural adjustment models which had significantly affected poor women in many developing and other Anglo-American countries for almost two decades. The Ontario Progressive Conservatives closely followed the examples of neo-liberal policies in the United Kingdom and the United States, learning from some of their failings and adding to these their own particular brand of neo-conservatism to produce an extensive and transformative welfare state restructuring.

Based on a study of the Conservative government's neo-liberal experiment in Ontario between 1995 and 2000, this book represents an effort to capture the dynamics of a particular economic and political approach: neo-liberalism. It is an attempt to detail the process of redesigning an advanced liberal welfare state and to document how this reformulation affects the ability of citizens as members of families and households to get by on a day-to-day basis. Put differently, it is a study of how the tension between the accumulation of capital and the work of social reproduction are mediated in a period of neo-liberalism.

This book straddles several areas of study. It takes a political economy approach to understanding the distribution of power and resources among citizens and states. It is also concerned with debates in welfare state theory and policy about the extent and depth of changes in income and social entitlements. As well, it is a sociological study of the ways in which individuals negotiate changes in labour markets, income support and protections, gender relations, and family arrangements. As such, it links broad patterns in the regulation or deregulation of capital and changes in state form with debates about social protections and redistribution at the level of nations, regions, and households.

The writing (and rewriting) of this book would not have been possible without the assistance of family, friends, and colleagues. From York, I wish to thank Isabella Bakker, Barbara Cameron, Meg Luxton, Lisa Philipps, and Ester Reiter. From Brock, I thank Cheryl Athersych, Viola Bartel, Ellen Carter, June Corman, Sara Cumming, Jill Debon, Ann Duffy, Jane Helleiner, Linda Landry, Mary-Beth Raddon, Michelle Webber, Joanne Wright, and Don Wright. I also thank my students in the graduate seminar on labour and family and in the fourth-year seminar on social policy for weekly insights on the nature of welfare state change and continuity. From the Caledon Institute, I thank Susan McMurray, Michael Mendelson, Sheila Neysmith, Louise Noce, Anne O'Connell, and Fraser Valentine. I thank the Atkinson Charitable Foundation for funding the project. A special thanks to Jane Springer for editing assistance and to Bonnie Fox for advice on revisions.

For their ongoing support, I thank Amy Baele, Christian Baxter, Kerry Bebee, Alain Belair, Chris Beyers, Eileen Burke Bezanson, Sarah,

Keith, Julia, Monique, and Lynne Bezanson, Vee Farr, Jackie Jolliffe, Gerald Kernerman, Ruth Klahssen, Meg Luxton, Sue-Ann MacDonald, Grace Cowan Mutrie, Eric T. Mutrie, Katherine Side, Jackie Solway, and Leah Vosko. I am grateful to the excellent staff of the Rosalind Blauer Centre for Child Care at Brock University, whose quality child care afforded me the time and the peace of mind to complete this book. Good scholarship depends on financial support. I wish to thank the Ontario Graduate Scholarship and the Helena Orton Memorial Scholarship for financial assistance in graduate school.

I wish to thank as well three anonymous reviewers whose thoughtful suggestions made a significant difference in the transformation of this study from a thesis to a published book. I wish to deeply thank the members of forty-one households, who, over the course of three years, allowed my colleagues and me into their homes and their lives, and shared their stories with us. Most importantly, I thank my spouse, Jan Campbell-Luxton, and our son Joshua Bezanson, whose love and laughter make all things possible.

GENDER, THE STATE, AND SOCIAL REPRODUCTION:
HOUSEHOLD INSECURITY IN NEO-LIBERAL TIMES

1 The Neo-liberal Experiment in Ontario, 1995–2000

Friends, during the last three years our province has started to put itself back on track. It took strong leadership by the government. But mostly, it took hard work and sacrifices by the people of Ontario. As a result, families are better off.
  – Former Progressive Conservative Premier of Ontario, Mike Harris, 1999[1]

We are worried about the future. We don't think we will ever be able to afford to buy a house or have enough money and stability to have children ... right now, we are just living hand-to-mouth. We are not able to save anything ... it just backfires because some unexpected expense comes along.
  – Ron, a computer programmer and study participant, 1999

In May 1995, a majority Progressive Conservative government led by Premier Mike Harris was elected in Ontario. With the Conservatives' re-election in 1999, they formed the provincial government until 2003.[2] This government imposed major changes based on neo-liberal policies. In both of their election campaigns, the Conservatives had promised to decrease taxes, reduce the debt and deficit, streamline social services, cut 'overspending,' and reduce the role of government (Progressive Conservative Party of Ontario 1994). In particular, they promised to cut social spending, especially public income transfers, and to restrict the public sector in general, in order to cut costs and regulations and to decrease barriers to private sector growth. Their 1994 platform document, *The Common Sense Revolution,* underlined the need to increase individual responsibility, which they contended had been eroded by excessive social spending and state regulations. Their approach to social provision was based on the idea that the wage is the best form of welfare (Grover 2005).

Once elected, the Harris government made major changes in most areas of public life, ranging from withdrawing equity legislation to rewriting labour legislation to reduce protections for workers, and cutting low-income supports such as social housing and social assistance. One of the first acts of the Ontario government in 1995 was to cut social assistance rates in the province by 21.6 per cent, signalling a shift in both the scope of the welfare state in the province and the government's view of the causes of and solutions to poverty and unemployment.[3] The government's insistence on individual responsibility rested on a deeply familialist discourse about gender, kinship ties, and community life.[4] The Ontario government asserted that people should purchase the goods and services they needed for themselves and their families through the market. Where the market was not an option, 'community, family, and friends' and not the state, were the appropriate providers of social and economic support (see Neysmith, Bezanson, and O'Connell 2005).[5]

Welfare states, and particularly liberal ones like Canada, have historically depended on family caregiving, particularly on women's unpaid labour, as a crucial but unrecognized part of social reproduction; that is, the daily and generational reproduction of the working population (see Lewis 1992; O'Connor, Orloff, and Shaver 1999).[6] It is important to note that the work of social reproduction is not gender-specific per se: feminist scholars attempting to understand sex-gender divisions of labour have long noted that aside from the biological and time-limited functions of pregnancy, childbirth, and breastfeeding, there is nothing inherent in caring work that requires it to be assigned to women. Gender divisions persist, however, and the work of social reproduction continues to be performed largely by women. State policies have generally assumed that families serve as the main providers of welfare, leaving family members to work out their own solutions to the problems of combining paid employment and unpaid domestic labour. Women have typically borne the primary responsibility for doing so (see Cameron 2006). The extent to which state social provisions improve standards of living for the majority, or undermine them, varies historically and from country to country. The Ontario Conservative government's neo-liberal policies exacerbated the tension between social reproduction and paid work. It reduced labour market and other regulations along with taxes, and imposed increasing responsibility for social reproduction on individual households at a time when many found it difficult to earn incomes sufficient to support their households adequately.

In Ontario, as in other liberal welfare states, the 1990s were marked by increased female labour force participation (particularly for women with very young children), because both more and more households depended on women's earnings and more and more women sought the status and relative security of employment (Statistics Canada 2000b). At the same time, economic restructuring eliminated many of the well-paid jobs, especially in manufacturing (Luxton and Corman 2001) and government cut backs eliminated many well-paid jobs, especially for women (Brodie 1996; Cossman and Fudge 2002). Combined with changes in labour regulations, the result was an increase in typically low-paid contingent and non-standard work (Statistics Canada 1999; Vosko 2003). In this context, government cuts to social services raised important questions: How do people manage if all adults are (potential) workers, if most people cannot afford to pay for care, and few provisions are made to support care work? Given existing divisions of labour that allocate primary responsibility for caregiving to women, to what extent did these changes have different impacts on women and men?

In his campaign for re-election in 1999, Harris claimed credit for the economic boom in Ontario, and said that as a result of his government's policies, 'families are better off.' Lived experiences of the Harris regime did not support this claim. Ron, one participant Ontario family member, said: 'We are just living hand-to-mouth.' Ron's household was affected by the changes enacted by the Harris Conservative government between 1995 and 2000 in multiple ways. Unable to afford their own home, he and his partner, Heather, rented an apartment in Heather's mother Melanie's home in the Greater Toronto Area, and the three pooled expenses. Ron worked full time with a great deal of overtime in the private sector, but his income did not exceed $40,000. He and Heather owed a combined $18,000 for student loans. They deferred starting a family for financial reasons. Both Heather and Melanie worked in the broader public sector, where women have historically had access to greater job mobility and pay. This sector was a significant target for spending cuts and layoffs. Heather was laid off in 1997 from her job at an arts organization because the provincial government cut funding to the arts. In the same year, Melanie's annual income dropped by 14 per cent because the province cut her paid hours as an English as a Second Language teacher. Her employer then began to lay her off each summer because the province decreased the funding for social assistance recipients to attend language training classes. This family's situation differed substantially from the image conveyed by Premier Mike Harris, demonstrating that the Conservatives' neo-liberal policies were not necessarily beneficial. What were the implications of the policies implemented by the Conservatives for women and men, and for families/households, their divisions of labour, and their standards of living? More generally, what are the implications of neo-liberalism for the lives of people living under such regimes and through such changes?

This book investigates these questions. It presents a case study of Ontario, the most economically strong and populous Canadian province. It outlines the implementation and effects of the neo-liberal restructuring experiment that took place under the Progressive Conservative government of Mike Harris between 1995 and 2000. It combines a detailed investigation of the legislative, regulatory, and spending changes introduced by the government with the findings from a longitudinal study of selected Ontario households I conducted with three other researchers.[7] Between 1997 and 2000 we conducted four rounds of in-depth interviews (a total of 158) with 127 members of 41 households to investigate the effects of the restructuring of Ontario's welfare state.[8] The experiences of the various households illustrate the impact of the neo-liberal restructuring experiment, a process which dramatically altered the scope of the welfare state, labour market protections and conditions, and people's abilities to manage and plan their lives. The book investigates both the changing economic and policy context of the period *and* the changing circumstances of the participant households in order to examine how neo-liberalism affects daily lives, particularly of low-income people, and especially of women. Taking social reproduction as a key lens of analysis, it considers the state-labour market-family/household nexus as a central site in the restructuring of Ontario's welfare state.

More broadly, the book captures the dynamics of a particular economic and political approach: neo-liberalism. It details the process of redesigning an advanced liberal welfare state and documents how this reformulation affects the ability of citizens as members of families and households to get by on a day-to-day basis. Put differently, it is a study of how the tension between capital accumulation and the work of social reproduction is mediated in a period of neo-liberalism.

This book makes three principal arguments. First, I argue that neo-liberalism exerts downward pressure on standards of living and social protection and provision for the majority of the population, while permitting significant increases in wealth for the minority. The Conservative government's policies were particularly hard on low-income households in general and on women in those households in particular. Second, I argue that the concepts of social reproduction and gender orders/regimes offer important ways of understanding the relationship between states, markets, and households; their sex-gender divisions of labour; and the ways in which these shape the day-to-day and generational survival of the population. Third, I suggest that, at a policy level, a social reproduction framework must be incorporated into policy analysis in order to create a sustainable and workable organization of the reproduction of the labouring population and its capabilities on a daily and generational basis.

Conceptual Issues

Two concepts flow through this book: neo-liberalism and social reproduction. The first represents the ideological and economic canvas upon which the vast changes to welfare states, and indeed to governance, have taken place over the 1990s. The second represents a theoretical attempt to situate the work that goes into maintaining and reproducing people at the very centre of discussions about political economy generally, and public policy specifically. Each is introduced below and considered in detail in the following chapters. Both are crucial elements in understanding the broad changes taking place as economies deepen their global integration, as paid work arrangements undergo transformation, and as social infrastructures are stressed.

Neo-liberalism

The shift from a relatively universalist (rights-based) to a residualist (needs-based) welfare state began in Canada, as in most other advanced industrial welfare states, in the late 1970s and escalated through the 1990s (Marsland 1996; Pierson 1996, 2001; Rice 1995; Myles and Pierson 1997; Prince 1999; McKeen and Porter 2003).[9] The defeat of the Mulroney Progressive Conservatives by the Chrétien federal Liberals in 1993 heralded an intensification of the process of retrenchment and saw a massive realignment in federal-provincial relations, in social spending, and in philosophical commitment to the goals of the Keynesian welfare state (Bashevkin 2000, 2002a).[10] A focus on debt and deficit reduction, a devolution of responsibility for program and service delivery, and a 'remixing' of responsibility for social welfare among the state, families/households, the third/voluntary sector, and the private sector characterized the 1990s (for a good overview, see Myles and Pierson 1997). An emphasis on employability in social policy was also central to the emerging neo-liberal welfare state. In an employability framework, 'the role of the state is ... to lower the costs of labour and the expectations of the population with respect to living standards' (Cameron 2006: 35).[11] Further, federal and provincial governments sought to weaken the policy-making process by drastically reducing funding to third-sector organizations, especially lobby organizations advocating for vulnerable groups, by altering parliamentary and regulatory processes and by concentrating policy/decision-making power in ministries of finance (Rice 1995; Rice and Prince 2000).

Many of the federal policy initiatives undertaken in the 1990s in an effort to reduce the scope and size of the Canadian welfare state were swift and far-reaching. In the very early part of the 1990s, the Canada Assistance Plan (CAP) was dismantled and replaced with the Canada Health and Social Transfer (CHST). The CHST effectively eliminated federal-provincial cost-sharing for social assistance and social services. It eradicated national standards related to the social rights of poor Canadians associated with social transfers.

In addition to further cutting and decreasing eligibility for Employment Insurance (EI), the federal government cut the total cash transfers to the provinces by a third in 1995 (Rice and Prince 2000). Although the 2000 and 2003 health care meetings between the first ministers and the federal government promised to restore transfers for health care, federal cuts have had a significant effect on the provinces' ability to deliver health care services (Prince 1999; Madore 2001; MacKinnon 2003; Grant et al. 2004). The emphasis at the federal level rested on active social policies which fostered incentives for labour market participation. The lumping of federal funding for social assistance, health, and post-secondary education into the CHST block transfer, in combination with an employability model of social policy delivery, permitted the introduction of punitive workfare-style policies at the provincial levels and increased targeting for other social programs (see Day and Brodsky 1998). Moreover, a preference for negative income tax policies (tax credits rather than service provision) altered the capacities of Canadians to access public services.

Over the course of the 1990s, the Canadian welfare state escalated its retrenchment process. The ascendancy of neo-liberalism, with its philosophical emphasis on free markets, little state intervention, and an approach which sees the individual rather than the market as blameworthy for poverty and unemployment, resulted in a dramatically overhauled Canadian welfare state and allowed for provinces to move further towards more punitive, needs- and means-tested welfare states (Peck 2001). Federal neo-liberal policies in the 1990s created fertile ground for the success of the Progressive Conservatives in Ontario.

The economic policies associated with neo-liberalism find their origins in liberal philosophy and neo-classical economics. The neo-liberal approach to economic policy, whose influence grew sharply beginning in the early 1980s, is generally associated with Hayek and Friedman (McGraw 1984). The neo-liberal paradigm represents a significant ideological shift away from the Fordist-Keynesian consensus, which saw the state playing an active role in market regulation and social provisioning.

The neo-liberal paradigm encompasses the economics of capitalist market economies and is characterized by consumer sovereignty, profit maximization, laissez-faire policies, private enterprise, and perfect competition. The major focus is on the efficient allocation of scarce resources through the price system and the forces of supply and demand (Todaro 1994). A strong notion of individualism dominates this theory. Despite claims to be pro-free market and anti-regulation, in practice neo-liberal policies tend to concentrate power in the hands of a core group of decision makers. In Ontario, the Conservatives blended morally conservative imperatives with the economics of efficiency to produce a state form that increased surveillance of certain members of society, notably the poor (Evans 1996; Little 2005; Braedley 2006). Walker (1992:12) notes that the 'market liberal dimension is concerned with the conditions necessary for a free economy, while the neo-conservative dimension gives priority to the maintenance of authority particularly in civil society.' This results in the promotion of a free economy *and* a strong state.

The term *neo-liberal* is often confused with neo-conservatism. In Anglo-American polities, neo-liberalism is associated with the 'rolling back' of the state (state social provisioning and the regulation of capital) by Thatcher in the United Kingdom, Reagan in the United States, and Mulroney/Chrétien in Canada (see Bashevkin 2002a; Vosko and Clement 2003). This rolling back is twinned with an intensified individualist ideology, which views those who are not self-reliant in market terms as suspect. Neo-conservatism focuses on moral positions around personal life and 'the family' (Brodie 1996; Luxton 1997). Neo-conservatism and neo-liberalism can coexist, and governing styles, ideology, and economic policies often draw from each strand. This coexistence can also result in tensions among ideological positions. The dramatic attempts to redesign social assistance in various sub-national provinces/states (such as Ontario, Alberta, New York, New Jersey, and Wisconsin) under 'New Right' (though not monolithic) neo-liberal governments often resulted in *higher* costs for these programs, an outcome which runs contrary to the stated aims of efficiency and fiscal responsibility (Shragge 1997; Baker and Tippin 1999). Yet, the moral imperatives of neo-conservatism around family forms and labour market attachments result in a need for greater scrutiny of, and control over, those at the margins of the labour market. The individualist revivalism associated with neo-liberalism is, then, matched with a contradictory need for a strong (not a laissez-faire) state (Martin 1993).

Social Reproduction and Gender Systems

States and families/households mediate the conditions of social reproduction.[12] A gender system, namely a gender order, reflects a historically specific configuration of state-labour market-family/household relations so that the work of maintaining and reproducing people on a daily and generational basis is accomplished (see Connell 1990). A gender order refers to a 'set of social relations characterized by a sexual division of labour and a gender discourse that support that division' (Cameron 2006:84). A gender order is the sum of the gender regimes operating in various institutions, such as the state, the labour market, and the family/household (Connell 2002). In the Fordist period (1945–late 1970s), the work of social reproduction was ideally organized and performed by women doing unpaid work in their homes, while some men earned sufficient wages to support themselves and their families.[13] In addition, the welfare state underwrote some of the work of social reproduction in this period, as this work was an acknowledged, albeit unequal, component of the state-market-family/household relationship (Cossman and Fudge 2002). Thus, this gender order represented a fairly stable state-market-family/household entente about divisions of labour in paid/unpaid work and in state/employer supports.

With the dramatic increase in female labour force participation and the shift towards non-standard work, the decline of the Fordist model, and the corresponding welfare state supports attached to it, the ways in which gender relations were organized to meet the needs of caring for people also shifted (see Cameron 2006). The emergence of a neo-liberal emphasis in Canada, specifically in Ontario, meant that instead of public moneys underwriting some of the work of social reproduction, these services shifted to unpaid work in families/households, to the third sector, and to the market to provide for a price. The neo-liberal gender order that began to emerge in Canada in the early 1980s was hence less stable in the Fordist sense, as labour market demands and unpaid work demands increased, while welfare state supports decreased.

The neo-liberal thrust of the 1990s deepened the need for dual earner households, while withdrawing or failing to provide supports for social reproduction (see Daly and Lewis 2000). The work of social reproduction – that is, the work that goes into maintaining and reproducing people and their physical and emotional capacities needs on a daily and generational basis – mediates the tensions inherent in the labour market and social service provision while absorbing its insecurities (Picchio 1992). In a neo-liberal context, the tasks associated with social reproduction are individualized and privatized. Feminist analyses of political economy and power relations place the work that is largely invisible – such as caregiving and the provision of basic needs – at the centre of social and political processes, and, as a result, offer an exceptionally useful lens for understanding transitions in welfare states and the effects of such transitions on gender relations. The failure of economic theory to include the work of social reproduction means that social reproduction is not adequately understood in relation to social policy.[14] The analysis of social reproduction as developed by feminist scholars maintains that the work which is done in the home as a privatized labour of love underwrites much of the work done in the sectors of the market and the state. Because the work of social reproduction relies on access to particular items – food and food production, shelter, time, clothing, and other socially and historically determined needs – the inputs into social reproduction in capitalist economies generally come from some kind of exchange. Social reproduction depends on some form of income, which is typically in the form of wages, government transfers, access to arable land, or other forms of money inputs (Picchio 1992). Social reproduction, then, shifts the concept of the economic away from merely market measures to a more ample and dynamic understanding of the economy. Many of the insecurities that are inherent in the labour market, and to some extent in other forms of access to money, are absorbed and mediated at the household level. The degree to which households are able to bear the effects of a market downturn, in turn, affects the ways in which economic growth occurs.

This book takes the lens of social reproduction as a starting point for an examination of the effects of the overhaul of the welfare state in Ontario. It considers the interrelationships among states, labour markets, and families/households. It demonstrates how social reproduction is organized and structured at the micro-household level bears on social policy, economic planning, and gender orders at the macro level. It asserts that states play a powerful role in shaping the conditions of social reproduction, and that failure to support social reproduction has consequences both at and beyond the family/household level. Centrally, this book asks: What happens in families/households, particularly poor ones, as economies restructure towards a neo-liberal model? Who 'takes up the slack' for shortfalls in subsistence provisions, income, or for an absence of services? How is this done and at what cost?

Methodological Issues

Methodologically, the book attempts to pull together three themes: a macro-level perspective on the tensions between neo-liberal capitalism and the need for the reproduction of people; a meso-level perspective on the role of states, in this case a welfare state in a Canadian province, as it delimited its scope and thus redefined the conditions for capital and social reproduction; and a micro-level perspective of the consequences of this tension and redesign on the lives of people in households. These three themes demanded different methodologies and research approaches. The macro-level perspective required theoretical investigation. Using the lens of social reproduction it offers a historical review of the dynamics of capitalism and reproduction in different periods. It is detailed in Chapter 2, but serves as a lens for the book as a whole. The meso-level perspective involved a careful tracking and review of the vast and often very rapid budgetary, legislative, and regulatory changes enacted in the province between 1995–2000. It included reviewing Hansard, Ontario's Statutes and Regulations, Legislative Assembly Committee proceedings, and Ministry of Finance documents and budgets. It also involved secondary analysis of statistical data and trends in areas such as the labour market, household composition and spending patterns, health care, and education access and usage. The findings pertaining to the legislative and regulatory process of restructuring the Ontario welfare state are found in Chapter 3, and the secondary analysis is woven throughout. Finally, the micro-level component involved interviews conducted over three years. The data from 158 interviews offer an important picture of the effects of the process of implementing neo-liberal restructuring. Members of households were interviewed repeatedly, and thus interactions among policy and regulatory changes along with the complexities of lived experiences could be documented. Further, strategies for managing changes were captured. Chapters 4 to 6 weave together the three methodological approaches to show the interactions among policies and the lived experiences of household members.

Evidence from other experiences of restructuring suggested that those with low incomes were most affected by welfare state change and 'adjustment' (see Toynbee 2003; Luxton and Corman 2001; Burman 1996). Further, the Ontario Conservatives' election platform and many of their reforms between 1995 and 1997 (when the interviews began) targeted those with low incomes, particularly those receiving social assistance. For this reason, households with low incomes are well represented among the total interviewed for this book (just over 60 per cent in 1997).[15] Single mothers, visible minorities, and First Nations are over-represented in the low-income category in Canada in general (see Statistics Canada 2000b; HRDC 1996), and are well represented in this study as well. Yet neo-liberal restructuring does not affect only those with low incomes, nor does it merely target income programs. The remaining members of households represent middle and high-income categories (see McMurray 1997 and Appendix C in this volume). They experienced significant fluctuations in their incomes (especially those in the broader public sector), services, and supports throughout the period under study. The household interviews were designed to capture if and how some benefited from restructuring. Randy, a participant in this study and a father of three, summarized the complexities of living through conservative times:[16] 'We're doing better. We're getting by. We're the working poor again.'

The Speaking Out Project

The interview data presented in the following chapters stem from a research project funded by the Atkinson Charitable Foundation and managed by the Caledon Institute of Social Policy. The Speaking Out project was established in January 1997 to document the effects of the Conservative's Common Sense Revolution on the lives of people in Ontario, and particularly on the lives of people with low incomes. Speaking Out aimed to look at what happens to individuals, families, households, and communities over time as they respond to isolated and cumulative changes. It also monitored and documented policy changes. Because the government had drastically limited public consultation on legislation, even introducing time allocations on bills so that they were passed quickly,[17] the study also set out to give a voice to Ontarians affected by the changes. My role in the project was as a research associate and policy analyst.[18] Along with three other research associates, I interviewed the same household members four times over a three-year period.[19]

The study tracked 127 members of 41 households from across the province from January 1997 to January 2000. In-depth interviews meant that participants determined the content of their replies rather than responding to a predetermined set of categories; and the three-year length of the study meant that the data are longitudinal rather than cross-sectional. The sample size of 41 households from across the province provides a picture of the effects of particular policy initiatives on different groups of people over time. The resulting data catalogue the multiple unequal effects of policy, program, and taxation change on predominantly low-income households from a range of ethnic and geographic locations (see Tables 1.2 and 1.4 below). They also capture how individuals within households (predominantly women) have been picking up – or failing to pick up – the shortfall for dramatic reductions in the provision of public services. Policy reports published as part of the Speaking Out project considered education, health care, income insecurity, governance, and jobs.

The selection of households was purposive rather than representative. Households were chosen which reflected a range of income levels and a variety of household structures and demographic characteristics. These included:

- Low-, medium-, and high-income households;
- Geographic diversity (northern, eastern, central, and south-western Ontario, Metro Toronto, and the Greater Toronto Area);
- Varieties of household structures (two-parent families, single-parent families, single people, singles living with roommates or friends, couples, three-generation households);
- Different sources of income (people receiving social assistance, people with various types of jobs, retired people, and those with other sources of income such as federal employment insurance, workers' compensation, and rental income); and,
- Other characteristics, such as race and ethnicity, physical disability, sexual orientation, housing status, age, and gender.

The Speaking Out project deliberately selected low-income households with a range of income sources (see Table 1.1).[20] The focus on low-income households was important to the project: an initial hypothesis of the research was that those with lower incomes would be more affected by changes in social spending and taxation policies than those with higher incomes.[21] With income level and source of income as broad organizing categories, the research team selected participant households that reflected the other characteristics sought (see Appendix B for a description of the recruitment and selection process).[22]

Household members were interviewed together where possible.[23] This decision was taken to capture diverse policy experiences occurring within one household and because our funding permitted 40 total interviews per round.[24] However, the team noted from the outset that group interviews present a series of problems, particularly in relation to power and voice between household members based on gender or generation. Despite efforts to mitigate the effects of group interviews, they did have consequences for the data. For example, in situations where the (usually male) spouse dominated the interview, we would ask him (or her) to make tea or tend to other household chores in order to have a chance to discuss the other spouse's job and household responsibilities. This approach did not always alter the tone of the interview. One participant, Kate, remarked after she and her spouse Carl had separated: 'Carl kind of intimidated me in the interviews because he knew so much about education and about the government and about all kinds of stuff. That is why ... a lot of the time I'd just sit there. He knows about that kind of stuff, he reads the paper every day.'

Inclusive interdisciplinary research models were used to design and write the interview schedule.[25] Informed by sociological, political science, feminist, and social work research methods and a broad commitment to research for social change, the interview questions attempted to capture the range of experiences of households in Ontario, being sensitive to their particular social location.[26] The interviews can be characterized as both semi-structured and open-ended; in each round, 'benchmark' questions were asked (see Appendix C). The benchmark questions were semi-structured so that consistent data on changes in household configurations and coping mechanisms could be gathered across households over the period of the study. The benchmark questions tracked changes in income, paid and unpaid work, service use, and intra-household power relations over time. This longitudinal data was particularly important in capturing household changes in inputs into social reproduction, which is a central consideration of this book. A series of open-ended questions explored various aspects of specific policy issues.

The study was designed to accommodate changing configurations of households as people moved in and out of them, and as relationships formed and dissolved. It was anticipated that some household participants would move or drop out. Surprisingly, only two households dropped out over the course of the study, but the number of participant household units actually increased (from 38 in 1997 to 41 in 2000) as relationships dissolved and household units split (see Appendix D).[27]

The People in the Study

Collectively, the households selected were geographically diverse; had many sources and levels of income; cut across age, gender, racial, and ethnic categories; held diverse political and social beliefs; and related in many different ways to their families, friends, and communities (McMurray 1997). Throughout the course of the study, people moved, gained or lost income, and changed household membership. Their sources of support also changed significantly.

Appendix C shows the names (pseudonyms) of the 64 adults in the 38 original households first interviewed in mid–1997; their gender, racial, and ethnic categories; their location in the province; the composition of their households (including number and ages of children); and their household income at the start of the study in 1997.[28] In 1997,

Table 1.1
Primary Income Sources of Participant Households, 1997

Primary source of income	No. of households	Percentage of households
Employment	23	60.5
Social assistance	9	23.6
Other:		
Employment Insurance,		
Workers' Compensation,		
Ontario Student Assistance Plan,		
rental income, etc.	6	15.7
Total	38	100.0

Table 1.2
Geographic Location of Participant Households, 1997

Household characteristics		No. of households	Percentage of households
Geographic diversity	Toronto/GTA	23	60.5
	S. Ontario	8	21
	N. Ontario	4	10.5
	E. Ontario	3	7.8
	Total	38	100.0

the majority of the households – 23 (60 per cent) – were low-income, while 13 (37 per cent) were middle-income and only 1 (over 2 per cent) was high-income. For the province more generally, the distribution was significantly less skewed to low income, with just under 18 per cent in the low-income category in 1995.[29]

The range of household types in 1997 (38 households) is shown in Table 1.3. Two-parent households included common-law and married couples who had co-residing, dependent children. Some two-parent households were blended or step-families, and included dependent children. Lone-parent households, which in 1997 were all female-headed, were made up of an adult and her dependent children. Those who were single resided alone and had no children. Mixed-generation households comprised more than two generations of the same family, usually parents, adult children, and grandchildren. Couple households included married, common-law, and same-sex couples without co-residing dependents. Housemates were in households where individu-

Table 1.3
Household Type, 1997

Household type	No. of households
Two-parent	15
Lone-parent	8
Single, no children	6
Mixed-generation	3
Couples, no children	
opposite sex	2
same sex	1
Housemates, no children	3

als lived with others, sharing economic and social activities. The sample also included households where these activities were separate. This approach recognizes a diversity of living arrangements and captures changes in household configurations over time.

Table 1.4 outlines the characteristics of household participants. It shows that 60 per cent of the adult participants are women and 40 per cent men. Almost a third (30 per cent) of all participants, including children, are visible minority or First Nations people. This compares to roughly 13 per cent for Canada as a whole – Ontario is home to the largest number from each category, at over 50 per cent of visible minorities and 18 per cent of First Nations (HRDC 1996). These two groups are over-represented among those with low incomes in Canada and in this study. Moreover, for Canada as a whole, they are located primarily in large urban centres in Ontario. This study drew a large number of its participants from two urban centres, thus accounting for the strong representation of visible minority and First Nations participants. Four per cent of participants, including children, are disabled. English is not the first language of over 12 per cent, and 8 per cent of adult participants identify themselves as homosexuals.

My Use of the Speaking Out Data

The Speaking Out project produced a comprehensive database. Several reports published over the period of the project covered specific policy issues. This book draws on material that was not fully explored in the Speaking Out publications. My use of the interview data develops the

Table 1.4
Characteristics of Household Members, 1997

Individual characteristics	No. of participants	Percentage of participants
Adult members of visible minorities*	13	20
Adult persons with disabilities	4	6
Adult First Nations*	5	8
Adult gays or lesbians	5	8
Adult speakers of English as a second language	8	12.5
Children	57	47
Men	26	21
Women	38	31

*For two adults, information was not given pertaining to ethnic/racial origin.

social reproduction issues and the gender dynamics of putting together a living in this period of social and economic turmoil.

Gender is a central lens through which I examine the consequences and tensions of a reduction in the scope of the welfare state, but it is mediated by, and mediates, race and class. I begin my analysis in the following chapters with the assumption that social relations are dynamic, that gender is a constituent element of analysis that allows for a consideration of the factors and identities in tension within households across time, and that household configuration is not a given but subject to change. I am attentive to the various elements that affect financial, emotional, and social support. Inter-household relations are important sources of both support and tension and are infused by power relations hinging on gender, race, and class. Extended kin networks and friendships are in many cases critical factors in the smooth functioning of a household. In other cases, extended kin responsibilities can overwhelm already strained household members. The presence or absence of a male wage, employment for men or women, and the generosity or stigma of social welfare spending are constitutive factors in household formation, cohesion, and dissolution.

This study considers all 158 interviews and each round of data. It highlights the process of policy change in relation to household-based coping strategies to reveal the ways in which households mediate the tension between capital accumulation and social reproduction.

Outline of the Book

Chapter 2 examines the utility of social reproduction as a lens for understanding the relationships among changing welfare states, labour markets, and families/households. I elaborate the concept of gender regimes/gender orders as a way to understand the organization of social reproduction in different periods, with particular attention to its configuration in advanced welfare states. I contend that the work of social reproduction – which is almost always gendered – is usually unrecognized in examinations of state-market-family/household relations, but that it is called upon to absorb the shocks and tensions resulting from economic change.

Chapter 3 chronicles the Ontario experience of neo-liberal economic restructuring and its attendant welfare state retrenchment. It offers an examination of the speed and scope of changes in legislative and regulatory measures enacted in Ontario since 1995. Starting from the premise that capital accumulation and social reproduction are in tension with one another, chapter 3 shows how states can limit the inputs into social reproduction, while making conditions more favourable for the pursuit of profit.

Chapters 4 through 6 present findings from the interviews, twinned with policy and secondary analysis. Chapter 4 examines the ways in which members of the households who participated in this study put together a living. Most households combined income sources. Many relied on some kind of government transfer while they worked for wages, either at one point or on a continual basis. This chapter highlights the centrality both of government policies vis-à-vis the labour market in the province, and of income support provisions for households from a range of income groups. As the labour market became more insecure for many participants, so too did programs and policies aimed at supporting people through economic insecurity.

Chapter 5 considers the ways in which study participants managed the extent and breadth of social policy changes in the province. Health care, education policy, child care, and social assistance figure centrally among the areas in which households experienced significant changes. However, because social assistance is an income source and a social policy area, and is directly tied to labour market initiatives on the part of the province, a discussion of social assistance straddles Chapters 5 and 6. The case of social assistance is particularly well-suited to the lens of social reproduction because the basic goods needed to maintain people on a daily and generational basis are at the heart of this program. In Ontario, its redesign reflected a shift on the part of the provincial government towards an individualistic worker model of the welfare state.

All of the major policy areas interact with one another, and participants did not experience them as discrete areas. The cumulative effects of major policy changes in a variety of social policy areas had a significant impact on people's abilities to access services and manage the effects of dramatic redesign. Policy redesign had feedback effects to the larger economic and social framework.

Chapter 6 pulls together the theoretical lens of the book with the case study data in order to examine how people coped – or failed to cope – with insecure and/or small incomes, and with insecure social services and transfers. It shows that the restructuring significantly affected low-income people, particularly women.

The concluding chapter revisits the idea of gender orders. It argues that neo-liberal restructuring results in a general reliance on the gendered work of social reproduction and often an escalation of paid and/or unpaid work. It considers whether or not a neo-liberal gender order heralds a crisis in social reproduction. If so, what do the experiences of members of households in Ontario suggest in terms of social policy development to counter these mounting tensions?

2 Struggles over Social Reproduction in a Neo-liberal Era

The concept of social reproduction captures the varied processes involved in maintaining and reproducing people, specifically the labouring population, and their labour power on a daily and generational basis (Laslett and Brenner 1989; Clarke 2000). It involves the formation and transfer of skills, knowledge, social and moral values, identities, and cultures (Picchio 1992; Elson 1998; Bakker and Gill 2004; Cameron 2006). The questions and dilemmas that the concept addresses have a long history, reflecting broad concerns about how children are raised and cared for, how families and households are organized, how people secure a living, how workers are produced for a capitalist labour market, and how the work of caring for people is organized. Building on an extensive and wide-ranging literature dating back to at least the late eighteenth century, a renewed analytical effort has emerged since the 1980s in feminist scholarship to articulate the central role of the work that goes into producing and provisioning for people in economies and societies (see Luxton 1980; Fox 1980; Beneria and Roldan 1987). The rise of neo-liberal economic policies on an international level has intensified the work that goes into putting together a living and caring and provisioning for people, and has eroded gains made by progressive actors in socializing some of this work through state and workplace policies (Crompton 1999; Elson and Cagatay 2000; Bakker 2001; Daly 2001; Daly and Rake 2003). Neo-liberal policies are forging a new gender order, which reflects the kinds of social relations that develop and are developed alongside a particular regime of accumulation and mode of regulation. This gender order is made up of the gender regimes of various institutions, including the 'family,' the labour market, and the state (Connell 1987; Vosko 2006).

Central to this gender order are the ways in which the work of caring and provisioning for people takes place, either through the market for a price or in the home as increased unpaid labour (Connell 1990, 1995; Cagatay, Elson, and Grown 1995; Young 2001). Social reproduction is thus a primary site of contestation in a neo-liberal era.

In this chapter, I elaborate on the key theoretical thread that runs through this book: social reproduction and capital accumulation are in tension and often in contradiction with one another. Thus, the relationship between social reproduction and capital accumulation must be mediated and stabilized by the social institutions of the state, the market, families/households, and, to a lesser extent, the third, or voluntary sector.[1] Taking gender as a central lens of analysis, I lay out the roles that these social institutions play in managing changes in the organization and regulation of capitalism in a neo-liberal regime. First, I present the argument that social reproduction is dynamic, involving complex processes of human relations interacting with all levels of economic systems. Second, I consider the shift from a Fordist-Keynesian welfare state regime to a neo-liberal one.[2] I suggest that neo-liberal regimes create new hierarchies of gender, class, and race. Finally, I argue that the emerging gender order in Canada reflects the contradiction that while women are now fully integrated into the labour market, they retain responsibility for much of the private work of social reproduction. This occurs in a context where workers generally have to work longer hours for less remuneration and fewer benefits while, simultaneously, they face cuts to social services and supports. Neo-liberal states show a preference for labour markets regulated in favour of capital and social policies that elevate individualism, private responsibility for social reproduction, and restricted social and labour market supports. A key contention of this book is that neo-liberal states, such as Ontario in 1995–2000, create crisis tendencies in social reproduction for low-income people in particular. These crises have specific implications for women.

The Dynamics of Social Reproduction

Throughout the history of the development of industrial capitalism, the relationship between the processes of capital accumulation (profit-making) and the subsistence of the labouring population (standards of living) has been contentious, both in the actual struggles people engaged in, and through the related theoretical debates. Classical polit-

ical economy in the eighteenth and early nineteenth centuries was pre-
occupied with the production of populations, how subsistence needs
were met, and with the organization of kinship, marriage, and family
forms in the emerging social relations of early industrial capitalism
(see Smith 1969 [1776]; Marx 1996 [1867]; Engels 1990 [1884]). However, the neo-classical economic theory that came to dominate twenti-
eth-century thought based on supply and demand (McCulloch 1954
[1854]; Hayek 1963; Friedman 1964), and complemented by functional-
ist analyses of family forms (Parsons 1956), was not concerned with
these issues. An understanding of marriage, family, and subsistence in
relation to the larger economic production of people and populations
was marginalized and naturalized.[3]

The feminist movement of the late 1960s and 1970s, particularly its
Marxist and socialist feminist streams, challenged the tendency to nat-
uralize the nuclear family form and the gender divisions of labour it is
based on (for a good review, see Luxton 2006). Feminist activists and
scholars insisted that domestic labour contributed to the reproduction
of labour power and hence was an essential and socially necessary
labour (Benston 1997 [1969]; Seccombe 1974; Beechey 1979; Barrett
1980; Armstrong and Armstrong 1986). The women's and labour
movements mobilized a range of political demands reflecting that
argument. Some called for wages for housework (Dalla Costa and
James 1975) while others called for the socialization of domestic labour
(Vogel 1984). Most settled for a range of social democratic policy interventions (such as maternity and personal leaves, child care, and shorter
working hours) designed both to reduce the individual responsibility
for domestic labour and to reduce the conflict individual women experienced between the demands of paid and unpaid work (de Wolff 2006).
In the 1980s, neo-liberalism (emphasizing economic self-interest and
supply-side economics) and neo-conservatism (emphasizing moral life
and familial values) emerged, partially in reaction to the relative gains
of progressive social movements. Neo-liberalism focuses on an individualization of economic life and a privatization to the market or the
family/household of provisioning and care, obscuring the processes
of reproduction that feminist scholars and early social scientists
advanced.

While the concept of social reproduction illuminates the dynamics of
the social relations among families/households, subsistence, markets,
and state forms in the face of changing economic regimes and moral
orders, the exact meaning and boundaries of the concept of social

reproduction are not self-evident. There is a consensus in most literature that because this work is so intimately related to women's child-
bearing, child rearing, and interpersonal familial relationships, it is
both marginalized and made more or less invisible (depending on state
form and level of worker's organizational strength). Beyond this consensus, however, there is some terminological confusion. A wide range
of terms is employed in trying to define and quantify the concept –
domestic labour, reproduction, unpaid work, the care economy, household or living standards, natural and market price of labour – to name
but a few. This has created some misunderstandings about the meaning and application of social reproduction.

Part of the confusion around social reproduction can be explained by
the ways in which different disciplines approach it. Efforts to study the
production of populations and daily subsistence have used different
terms, depending on their disciplinary background and political or
theoretical orientations. Those focusing specifically on women's work
in the home have used domestic labour, unpaid work, and reproduction (Oakley 1974; Ward 1990; Luxton and Corman 2001). Others,
expanding beyond households, have considered care work (both paid
and unpaid) and concepts such as the care economy (Sparr 1994; Elson
1995a; Gardiner 1997; Folbre and Weisskopf 1998; Humphries 1998;
Folbre 1999). Efforts to link household labour and economics to the
labour market and the broader economy have explored standards of
living, natural and market prices of labour, and human capital (Elson
1998; Kabeer 2003; Picchio 2003). The term social reproduction has thus
been used by feminist scholars to encompass a broad range of activities, in an array of locations, which combine to ensure the daily and
generational reproduction of the population.

Another source of confusion about the term *social reproduction* is that
it applies to a *process* as well as to specific *tasks*. As a process, it refers to
class relations in a particular period (Cameron 2006). Social reproduction is about standards of living and reflects the balance of power
between capital's pursuit of profit and people's access to income, other
money, and in-kind inputs. As a process, it also embodies an enormous
amount of labour, a particular configuration of gender relations, and
resistance/agency. As specific tasks, it reflects the components of trans-
forming wages and other inputs into reproduction, in a physical,
social, and psychological sense. It reflects negotiations and (im)bal-
ances in gender and other relations. Social reproduction involves the
state and state provisioning (such as health care and education); house-

hold processes related to providing for social, emotional, and physical needs; and efforts to secure an income which can be transformed into basic needs provisioning (Ferguson 1999; Arat-Koc 2006). It is af-fected by structural inequalities such as gender- and race-segmented labour markets and the social construction of skill (Acker 1988; Fudge and Cossman 2002). Social reproduction thus operates simultaneously at the levels of the market, state, and family/household (Lewis 1992; Orloff 1993), sometimes called the economic, political, and domestic (Elson 1998).

Social reproduction involves the day-to-day work of maintaining and reproducing people and their labour power, including creating space for the building of their capacities such as learning, caretaking, and playing (Nussbaum 1999, 2000). It involves internalizing the inse-curity of putting together a living in a capitalist labour market. Espe-cially for people of colour and marginalized ethnic groups, it often involves internalizing and coping with discrimination and racism (Glenn 1992; Arat-Koc 2002). Social reproduction is usually carried out in homes and involves the teaching of social norms, which are social assets and which are integral in coordinating the activities of an econ-omy (Elson 1998; Figart, Mutari, and Power 2003). It involves negotia-tions over power and resources within households, usually between men and women (see Finch and Mason 1993). It is often characterized by an unequal division of labour and a gender-specific socialization process. It also includes provisioning beyond individual households through volunteer work, intra-household care work, and local initia-tives pertaining to shared social space or services. Social reproduction involves pooled-risk services and programs, such as getting access to income via citizenship-based entitlements such as those that have been provided through the welfare state (Beneria 1999; Ungerson 1997). In short, social reproduction encompasses the work that must be done in order to ensure that people at least survive and ideally thrive and develop, as well as to ensure that the economic system is perpetuated.[4] This is not to suggest that it is merely utilitarian for capitalism; social reproduction happens across economic systems as a means of survival and human development. But in capitalist economies, and particularly in neo-liberal regimes, this work is separated, made largely invisible, and assumed to be done regardless of the cost to the persons undertak-ing these tasks.[5]

Social reproduction is dynamic and is one part of the process of cap-

Struggles over Social Reproduction   27

ital accumulation (Picchio 2003; Cameron 2006). It is in conflict with the drive for the accumulation of capital because profit maximization and standard-of-living maximization are rarely compatible. Standards of living are historically and culturally determined, so the work of social reproduction is likewise not automatic, but is politically, socially, and culturally determined (Picchio 1992; Tilly and Scott 1978; Glenn 2000). The tension between accumulation and social reproduction is constant but changing. Capital requires a skilled and socialized workforce along with consumers of the goods and services produced. Capital also seeks to maximize profits and therefore wishes to direct as little as possible into social reproduction. The contradictions and conflicts between accumulation and social reproduction require mediation, the function of institutional sites such as the state. The state plays a central role in mediation, as regulator (Picchio 1992). The family/household is also central, and its role can be understood as alternator (Picchio 1992).[6]

The family and the state are not neutral sites; the amount of input into social reproduction each is willing or able to absorb reflects nego tiation that is conditioned by the balance of power relations between labour and capital, and between men and women.[7] The complex structure of social reproduction gives it a high degree of flexibility, allowing the family to absorb 'the costs of flexibility and internalize its conflicts' (Picchio 1992:120). This is particularly the case under conditions where atavistic sentiments about familial life and work ethics form part of mainstream political discourse.

The relationship between the state and the family in social reproduction is one in which the state intervenes at different historical moments to offset or offload the high costs of social reproduction onto or away from the family. The state's role in social reproduction involves stabilizing and institutionalizing a gender order (Connell 1990; Fudge and Cossman 2002). The state thus plays a substantial role in establishing the *conditions* under which social reproduction takes place by regulating capital and the labour market and providing socialized services. It also enforces financial obligations on the part of families (Brodie 1997). The family functions as an alternator in adjusting to demands: women's labour within and outside the household takes up the slack for reduced state spending, labour market insecurity, and weakened legal protections for workers and the poor. This alternator role is, however, politically, socially, and culturally given, rather than an automatic adjustment mechanism to external conditions.

Social reproduction is thus a central aspect of the capitalist economic system:

1. at the level of *production*, because labour is considered a produced input to production but one that is produced outside that sphere
2. at the level of *distribution*, because savings on the costs of social reproduction of the labouring population lead to higher profits
3. at the level of *circulation*, because the consumption of wage goods is the largest component of the aggregate demand.
4. at the *institutional* level, because insecurity of access to the means of reproduction is the fundamental source of command over work processes
5. and at the *political* level, because the process of social reproduction implies a radical conflict between profit and the living standards of the whole labouring population (Picchio 1992:88; emphasis mine)

Because of the central friction in capitalism between production and social reproduction, the crisis tendencies in capitalism are systemic.[8] There are, however, shifts in forms of capitalism and related modes of social regulation that force changes in the regime of accumulation. The need to mediate the central tension does not disappear, but the kinds of institutional interventions required or employed may be altered. What needs to be specified, then, is the kind of economic order framing the dynamics of social reproduction in the contemporary setting, the role that state and families/households play in mediating this tension, and the particulars of the aggregate gender relations, or gender order, in the neo-liberal regime.

Mediating Social Reproduction

Since the 1970s, a substantial shift has occurred in the ways in which states and other institutions can mediate either for or against capital, and foster particular types of accumulation. This is most apparent in patterns of household/family structure, and in the types of employment relationships becoming normative in many Organization for Economic Cooperation and Development (OECD) countries. Women's participation in the labour market and existing supports vis-à-vis social provisioning have undergone substantial change. Both the neo-liberal welfare state and its predecessor, the Fordist-Keynesian one, involve more than accords between capital and labour; they also involve settlements between men and women over paid and unpaid work (Lewis 2001). In Canada, as in most other OECD countries, the response to the 1970s stagnation of growth in the world economy was to begin to dismantle Fordist-Keynesianism, a process that transformed the conditions under which social reproduction takes place. Specifying the parameters of Fordist-Keynesianism and its demise illustrates how a neo-liberal regime reconfigures the relations of social reproduction.

Fordist-Keynesianism as a Class and Gender Settlement

The way in which capital accumulates, or the regime of accumulation, does not remain constant over time. There are factors which influence the ways in which capital can move (such as technological innovation), how the employment structure is organized (e.g., full-time, full-year employment in a workplace or just-in-time, contracted-out work), the extent to which capital is free to pursue the aim of profit maximization without regulatory intervention (such as environmental regulations), the extent to which cycles of boom and bust are buffered by institutional arrangements, and the extent to which societies are prepared to accept certain degrees of inequality. There are specific gender and class settlements associated with various regimes, reflecting negotiation and compromise in the relationship between social reproduction and capital accumulation (Picchio 1992; Cameron 2006). Regimes of accumulation are accompanied in different historical periods by modes of regulation that impose, or fail to impose, limits on the pursuit of profit.

National states, and, to an increasing extent, international agreements, play a significant role in regulating the ways in which capital accumulates in a given society and historical moment. In the Fordist-Keynesian model, the compromise between dramatic accumulation and social progress was mediated for a period of about 30 years (1945 on) by national states in the form of a *relatively* normative male breadwinner wage associated with social mobility and attendant state social provisions. This model buffered the earner and the entrepreneur from many of the vagaries of accumulative crises. The labour-capital accord afforded some workers a high degree of labour market security, access to a mix of public and private insurance, and a good standard of living. For governments, this postwar entente compelled them to build a welfare state infrastructure that supported a male social wage. The Fordist-Keynesian regime rested on a particular configuration of gender, race, and class dynamics which disproportionately benefited a select group of white male workers in the high value added and high-wage sectors, particularly those in core industries (see Vosko 2000, 2002).

Capital and labour stood at different ends of the class spectrum in Fordist-Keynesianism, but the compromises they created, which in turn informed social policy development, reflected a convergence of interest in maintaining a patriarchal male breadwinner family structure (Young 2001; Fudge and Cossman 2002). The development of Canada's liberal welfare state in the post-Second World War era was based in large measure on a presumption of full-time, full-year male waged employment and a dependent wife responsible for social reproduction. Benefits attached to this type of labour market affiliation only marginally assisted women and those whose employment relationships were different from this standard employment relationship. Most women were constructed as being primarily responsible for unpaid care work, whose access to a living was to be ideally delivered through a 'standard' male wage. White working men were more fully citizens, while these rights and privileges were only extended under very limited circumstances to women and non-white men (Williams 1995; Hobson and Lister 2002). Women's social citizenship claims could thus be made on the basis of their family role, and *not* as individuals (Lewis 1992; Sainsbury 1996; Daly 2001).[9]

The Fordist gender compromise was based on nuclear families with rigid gender divisions of labour, which provided some married women with access to income and some entitlements only via a relationship with a man. Yet even in its 'golden age,' the male breadwinner norm was not universal. Porter (2003) notes that in the Canadian case, fissures in the male breadwinner model were evident as early as the 1950s, when women began to enter the labour force in increasing numbers, and began claiming what then were called Unemployment Insurance benefits. By the 1980s, the male breadwinner norm was not an empirical reality in Canada because it took almost double the number of hours to earn what a typical man earned in the 1970s (York 1992). Meanwhile, public policies and labour market structures persist in assuming a full-time female caregiver. The gender order that supported Fordism was a critical element in its reproduction and stabilization. The crisis in Fordism in conjunction with broader structural economic changes destabilized the mode of regulation and remains a central factor in constituting and legitimizing the neo-liberal regime.[10]

Neo-liberalism and the Adult-Worker Model

The state-mediated entente between capital and labour in Fordist-Keynesianism rested on a relatively stable and institutionalized gender and class order (Land 1980; Cameron 2006). As neo-liberal policies were adopted by governments from across the political spectrum, a significantly less stable order began emerging in its stead. The labour market is 'flexible' and no longer supports a social wage, social policy is concerned increasingly with employability, and an adult-worker rather than a male breadwinner model has come to dominate in policy prescriptions (Daly and Lewis 2000; Young 2001). In Canada, although most women continue to live in nuclear families, family structures have changed significantly. More women are living alone, in common-law relationships and as female lone parents, and they are having fewer children (Statistics Canada 2000b). The state is increasingly a geo-economic rather than a political actor (Young 2001), and aligns itself less with social welfare than with facilitating business interests (Carroll and Shaw 2001; Clarke 2004). Increasingly, neo-liberal states such as Canada have pursued targeted welfare state models and decreased labour and capital regulations, thereby shifting the costs of social reproduction away from states and onto families, making this work more invisible.[11]

The turn to neo-liberalism was imposed on or adopted by governments globally, beginning in the 1980s and escalating through the 1990s. The fall of the Berlin Wall in the late 1980s eased the Marshall Plan compulsion to invest in social infrastructure and redistribution, elevating the unfettered free market model as the development model of choice. The globalization of production, economic slowdown, and government budget deficits all fuelled the dismantling of Fordist-Keynesianism (Teeple 1995; Fudge and Cossman 2002). The neo-liberal economic approach, often termed the 'Washington Consensus,' involves a mix of specific macro-economic instruments and policies.[12] Principally, it holds that fiscal and current accounts should be balanced, that exchange and interest rates should be market-determined, and that policy barriers to the international movement of goods (i.e., principally tariff and non-tariff barriers) be eliminated (Bakker 1997). Markets, not states, should be the principal managers of the economy. Neo-liberalism extends the characteristic boundaries of macro-economics into such areas as the privatization of public assets, deregulation of labour and other markets, the elimination of national industrial strategies, and an emphasis on accountability and good governance.

In general, neo-liberal policies focus on supply-side economics. The neo-liberal view holds that the best way to meet people's needs is to increase the *efficiency* of economies by reducing the role of the state (including privatizing public goods and decreasing social spending), to reduce government regulation of industry and the market, and to increase the role of the market (Mosley 2004).[13] A focus on exports, that is, shifting to the production of goods that are internationally tradeable, is a significant feature of neo-liberal restructuring (Elson 1994). This neo-liberal approach led to economic policies and institutional changes that shaped radically different international development and national welfare state systems from the ones that had dominated from the Second World War to the 1980s. International lending and aid policies became inseparable from the expanded neo-liberal economic model. The policy orientations of the International Monetary Fund (IMF) and World Bank structural adjustment and stabilization policies were applied to developing and some OECD countries in the 1980s and 1990s. Canada's transition to neo-liberalism escalated in the 1990s.

In economic and social policy, the neo-liberal approach thus stands in sharp contrast to Keynesian welfare statism. Where Fordist-Keynesianism endorsed some degree of collective responsibility for social risk and encouraged solidarity between groups and generations, neo-liberalism encourages individual responsibility without solidarity (Ferge 1997; Bakker 2001; Bakker and Gill 2004). Where Fordist-Keynesianism presumed that state policy instruments could, and indeed should, counter social inequalities, neo-liberalism fosters the 'unchecked thriving of inequalities in the name of individual freedom and choice' (Ferge 1997:22) and accepts to varying degrees unemployment, poverty, and marginalization. Where Fordist-Keynesianism opted for economic equilibrium as a compromise with public supports covering for market inadequacies, neo-liberalism favours economic growth and competition, higher productivity, and economic efficiency (Brodie 1996; Ferge 1997). The power of capital compared to the Fordist-Keynesian period is intensified (see Amin 1994). In short, the neo-liberal project 'is about the withdrawal from social commitments and hence ... about the rejection of the importance of an integrated society or even of society: the *individualization of the social*' (Ferge 1997:23).

The replacement of the standard employment relationship with 'flexibility' and just-in-time production eroded the aim of the full-employment characteristic of Keynesian management, thus severing a key component of the Fordist-Keynesian compromise (Vosko 2000). Labour market attachments are less secure and lacking in some key state-administered social protections and regulations (Peck 2001).

Moreover, the passing of a relatively normative standard employment relationship has been accompanied by a change in expectations: workers often do not expect that their children will have a better standard of living than they have had, while citizens no longer expect governments to provide a social wage. Social citizenship is increasingly associated exclusively with labour market participation and an absence of claims-making on state services or redistribution (Brodie 1996, 1997). Neo-liberal ideology is rooted in an individualization rather than a collectivization of social life, making decreased citizenship expectations central to neo-liberal regimes (see Gill 1995).

Neo-liberalism generally leads to reduced standards of living for those already economically and socially vulnerable. The deregulation of markets and labour regulations exerts downward pressure on wages. In developing nations with little state regulation, the market in neo-liberal economic policies determines the price of labour power. Under these conditions, wages generally are gender and race ascribed, and gender and race intensive. Moreover, the failure to invest in human capital (health, education, and so on) produces a less skilled and able population which is more economically insecure, and whose labour market and household conditions are precarious. Elson (1995b) refers to underselling labour power in this context as a *distress* sale. The terms and conditions of female employment are generally weakened under these types of sales. Additionally, women's time commitments are intensified, both in terms of the extent to which they engage in paid labour and the extent to which they use their unpaid labour to make up for a loss of household income. Members, usually women, often reduce their consumption, borrow money or food, or attempt to substitute store-bought items with home-made goods, which requires more labour input. In other cases, women are forced to engage in paid work or intensify their labour market activities, often in the informal sector.

Although the transition is not complete or even, the 1990s in Canada was marked by a significant shift towards neo-liberal-styled macro-economic policies at the federal and at most provincial levels. This shift signals a change in the way in which the state sees itself in relation to capital. It aims to pursue more traditionally liberal avenues in fiscal and economic policy by decreasing taxation and regulation on industry, increasing the amount and extent of continental and international trade, deregulating the labour market, and decreasing social spending. These liberal avenues produce stark conflicts between standards of living and capital accumulation. One feature of the shift to neo-liberalism is a change in the nature of paid work, both for men and for women. Another is a decline in the standards of living for both working people and poor people. As Vosko (2000:29) notes, state policies 'shape the daily and intergenerational reproduction of people – social spending, together with the design of social policies, has the capacity to exacerbate or alleviate precariousness in households and in the labour market.'

The transformation of Canada's welfare state rests both on its 'path dependency' as a liberal welfare state (see Esping-Andersen 1990, 1999) and on its gendered policy legacies (O'Connor, Orloff, and Shaver 1999).[14] Social policy has been a terrain of dramatic change as the state attempts to move towards a more residual model of social service provision. Canada's historically mixed welfare state path, which combined American-style market liberalism and tenets of European-style conservatism and social democracy (Peck 2001; Noel 1995), came to focus more on market and family provision of social goods. The terms of debate surrounding the provision of social services have shifted as well. There was previously some degree of support at the federal and provincial levels for certain non-targeted programs. Aside from the fields of health care and primary/secondary education, social policy has increasingly been framed in terms of employability as opposed to reducing income inequalities. Indeed, women's greater independence from men has not equalled greater economic equality (Fudge and Cossman 2002). The goal of full employment has been dropped, and socialized services, not merely transfers, have been increasingly subjected to market criteria as a determinant of their usefulness (Fudge and Vosko 2001). The male breadwinner model has been replaced in practice, though not always in ideology, with an adult-worker model (Daly and Lewis 2000), without a mediated arrangement for social reproduction.

The restructuring of Canada's welfare state along neo-liberal, workfarist lines has failed to grasp the implications of women's caring and labour market patterns. In contrast to Britain, where a 'one-and-one-half earner' model predominates (Lewis 2001), trends for Canadian families have not followed this pattern neatly. In 1999, for example, 67.9 per cent of all employed mothers whose youngest child was under age three were employed full time (30 hours or more a week). For all mothers with children aged 16 and under, 71.4 per cent were working full time. Although most Canadian women worked at one full-time paid job, non-standard work arrangements escalated for women throughout the 1990s. In 1999, 41 per cent of Canadian women (versus 29 per cent of men) were part-time workers, temporary employees, self-employed persons without paid help, and multiple job holders (Statistics Canada 2000a). Women in Canada have high labour force participation rates while public provision of child and elder care are quite low. For example, in 1996, there were about 300,000 licensed day-care spaces available to children under four years of age, but 900,000 families with at least one preschool-aged child in which either both parents or a lone parent was employed (Statistics Canada 2000a:101). The vast majority of daycare spaces are not state-subsidized. Moreover, despite the increased participation of women in the labour force over the last quarter-century, women's share of unpaid work has remained relatively stable, at about two-thirds of the total (Statistics Canada 2000a:97). The neo-liberal practice of relying on the private market and on 'family' in social policy produces serious conflicts for work/life balance. Just as Fordist-Keynesianism rested on settlements between men and women, along with capital and labour, the 'silver era' (Taylor-Gooby 2004) of the neo-liberal welfare state requires new mediations. The tensions between paid work and responsibility for unpaid care work suggest an escalating crisis in social reproduction. To stabilize the neo-liberal regime, states must re-regulate the labour market, gender relations, and social policies.

Women's relationship to the Fordist-Keynesian welfare state regime was a complex one. The institutions associated with this regime viewed women largely as pre-commodified, that is, their labour power was not (yet) directly for sale. Fordist-Keynesianism did not offer substantive labour protections and supports for employed women. It proffered de-commodification (access to income and supports based on citizenship rather than a wage) on the basis of a spousal or dependent relationship (O'Connor 1992; Orloff 1993; O'Connor, Orloff, and Shaver 1999). The Canadian Fordist-Keynesian welfare state actively curtailed the formation of autonomous *sustainable* households with female heads, as it constructed women both as secondary earners and as largely ineligible for de-commodified social supports.[15] In the neo-liberal era, these tensions remain, but women have been commodified along with men, and, further, both genders have little access to de-commodification because the welfare state has eroded. Labour market legislation and public policies of the federal and most provincial states in Canada continue to reflect a standard employment norm, thus leaving increasing numbers of workers unprotected (Fudge 1997, 2001). The neo-liberal regime thus reflects a convergence of men's and many women's labour market experiences, marked by a decrease in security and social wages (see Armstrong 1996; Cohen 1994; Vosko 2002). This suggests an ambivalence and a deflection of responsibility on the part of both federal and provincial states as to how to properly mediate changing social and labour market relations.

The rise of neo-liberalism is marked by several interrelated trends: the power of capital on an international scale is increasing; the welfare state is being retrenched; paid work norms and structures are significantly altered towards more non-standard forms; gender relations and familial forms have and are shifting; and a politics and practice of neo-liberalism is being embraced by governments from across the political spectrum. The neo-liberal regime of accumulation has elements of continuity and discontinuity with Fordist-Keynesianism.[16] On one hand, the employment and welfare state models associated with Fordist-Keynesianism have changed significantly, while in contrast, social policy continues to reflect some Fordist-Keynesian assumptions about the structure of the labour market and the family/household.

The neo-liberal regime has resulted in significant changes in the labour-capital accord, as well as shifts in the ways that states and families mediate this accord. The shift in the regime of accumulation, and its attendant effects on the postwar labour capital accord, has produced a new gender paradigm. Economic and social policies tend increasingly to assume that individuals are gender-neutral, while the work that women in particular do in taking up the slack for cuts in social services and labour market insecurity is explicitly gendered. The processes involved in neo-liberal restructuring, including re-privatization, familialization, and commodification, increase the paid and unpaid work of families/households while undermining the conditions that could support that work. The neo-liberal settlement, with its economic emphasis on globalizing economies, increasing production for export, decreasing social spending, increasing 'efficiency' (including making waged labour more precarious), and letting the proverbial market decide, has reconfigured the relations among gender, class, and race/ethnicity. The terrain of gender orders and regimes, then, offers a path for theoretical exploration of the interrelation between capitalist modes of production, state forms, familial forms, and social reproduction. In a sense, gender orders/regimes summarize the organization of social reproduction in a given period. While Fraser (1997) argues that a crisis in the gender order – in the relations between men and women, and, ultimately, in the responsibility for and accomplishment of the work of social reproduction – is what predicated the collapse of the Fordist model, a closer examination of the parameters of the shift away from the Fordist model is required in order to sketch out the workings and contradictions within the new regime of accumulation, its mode of regulation, and its gender order.

Towards a New Gender Order?

The rise of neo-liberalism has been associated with the idea that gender is simultaneously eroded and intensified in the current period (Haraway 1991; Armstrong 1997; Fudge and Cossman 2002). The concept of erosion and intensification highlights both a literal and metaphorical contradiction in global economic restructuring (Brodie 1997:237). Bakker (1997:7) explains: 'The present shift in the global order is, however, revealing the contradictory effects of what is a dual process of both gender erosion and intensification. In other words, gender appears to be less important in understanding the global political economy and, at the same time, more of a determining factor in its transformation.'

The relevance of gender for understanding shifts in the welfare state appears to be less salient than class- or race-based inequalities. Some women benefit from the processes of neo-liberal economic restructuring, as they are able to hire (usually) women of colour to underwrite the work of social reproduction, both in their homes and in paid care work, such as home-based care (Arat-Koc 2002, 2006; Vosko 2002). In addition, as labour markets restructure, men appear to be moving into jobs traditionally held by women. In the case of women entering jobs previously dominated by men, the status and rewards for such employment are tending to decline. These two shifts – the so-called feminization of the labour force,[17] and the decreasing status of jobs once women enter them – suggest 'a convergence of male and female labour-market experiences within what are increasingly polarized [class-based] labour markets' (Bakker 1997:8).

The intensification of gender has been noted in particular in the privatization, familialization, and commodification processes occurring in Ontario, which are elaborated on in the next chapter. The process of neo-liberal economic restructuring has meant that in terms of paid work, many women and increasing numbers of men are concentrated in the service sector and/or female-dominated sectors, which tend to be low-paid, precarious, and often part-time. The intensification of gender also speaks to policy outcomes that explicitly or implicitly intensify the work of social reproduction borne by households while at the same time intensifying the kinds of labour market demands placed on women. The shift towards individualism and employability models of social policy suggest that a process of *de-familialization* and *re-familialization* is taking place: women are seen as autonomous workers, as are men, and social policy does not consider externalities like responsibility for social reproduction while the practices and decisions in social policy transfer the work of social reproduction onto women (see Ellingsaeter 1998). Immigrant women of colour with few citizenship rights are filling the roles of caregivers in many private homes, accomplishing social reproduction for wealthier working women in neo-liberal regimes.

In feminist political economy, welfare state theory, and political science, the terms *gender orders* and *gender regimes* have been developed to identify the gender arrangements that emerge in response to particular models of capital accumulation (see Walby 2004). The two terms are often used interchangeably to refer to the ways in which the work of social reproduction, by and large, is organized so that accumulation can continue and amass. Walby (1997:5–7) suggests that in order to grasp different patterns of gender relations, concepts capturing different levels of abstraction of varying forms of gender systems are needed. She refers to six structures of patriarchy that conceptualize a system of oppressive social structures, which function at different levels of analysis. She suggests that these different forms of patriarchy can be termed different forms of gender regimes. Connell (1990:523) defines gender regimes similarly. 'The gender regime,' he says, is 'defined as the historically produced state of play in gender relations within an institution, which can be analyzed by taking a structural inventory.' He argues that each state 'has a definable gender regime that is the precipitate of social struggles and is linked to – though not a simple reflection of – the wider gender order in the society.' (523). Fraser (1997) employs the term *gender order*, which she situates at the macro level of an economy. She asks what kind of gender order will replace the family wage model, suggesting that the gender order operates at the level of the mode of production. Based on this understanding of the difference between regimes and orders, the concept of gender order refers broadly to aggregate gender arrangements at the broadest level of the economy; that is, at the macro-economic and ideal typical level.

Specifying gender regimes, and hence a broader gender order, is aided by household-based research that considers the ways in which gender is a central organizing feature of the relationships among states, markets, and families/households. Elson (1998) makes a strong case for a reconstitution of political economy in general, which centrally includes domestic structures in the triad of the economic, the political, and the domestic. She claims that there is a general failure to 'recognise the role of economic restructuring in disabling the domestic sector and undermining its ability to make provision for both its needs and the needs of the other sectors' (206). The modes of operation of the sectors of the domestic, the political, and the economic as well as the three circuits which connect the sectors and channel the flows between them (the market, the tax-and-benefit circuit and the communications network) are built, according to Elson, on the prevailing gender order (195–197). If, as noted welfare state scholar Esping-Andersen (1999:6) has suggested, the 'household economy is alpha and omega to any resolution of main post-industrial dilemmas,' then the so-called domestic economy, in which social assets are produced, must be a starting point for establishing the kind of gender order generally and institutional regime specifically in a particular period of capital accumulation.

Assessing the impact of neo-liberal restructuring at the household level, a project that this book undertakes, requires an approach that considers gender as an interactive category at all levels of analysis. Such an approach reveals the extent to which a new gender order is stabilizing, or failing to stabilize, social relations in the neo-liberal period. Social reproduction is the starting point for understanding the ways in which standards of living are in conflict with the pursuit of profit. The concept of gender orders can serve as an expression of the macro-organization of social reproduction in relation to state provision and shifting labour market regulation. The shift from a Fordist-Keynesian welfare state to a neo-liberal state in Canada in the 1990s appears to have placed significant demands on women's paid and unpaid work, while constructing women as earners and carers, without the institutional supports that might have underwritten such roles in a previous era. The case of Ontario's restructuring experiment, because it was so vast and far-reaching, serves as a means to examine the parameters of a neo-liberal gender order as they play out in public policy and people's lives. If the gender order of neo-liberalism necessitates that women's labour stretches elastically in response to decreasing socialized supports and a declining social wage, is it a gender order that can be stabilized or sustained over the long term? What are the long-term consequences? An examination of the state-market-household relationship in Ontario between 1995–2000 begins to answer this question.

3 Legislative and Regulatory Changes in Ontario, 1995–2000

Between 1995 and 2000, the Ontario government emphasized a preference for limited government intervention and regulation in the economy and implemented a neo-liberal economic strategy that transformed the relations between the state and citizens. The resulting changes offer an important example of the enactment of neo-liberal policies in an advanced welfare state. This chapter sketches how the provincial government actively altered the state-market-family/household nexus in Ontario by centralizing power but decentralizing administration, reducing democratic process and consultation, shrinking social spending, curbing labour rights, and casting suspicion on 'special interests,' notably the poor. A review of labour market, social, regulatory, legislative, and budgetary policy shifts reveals how the state circumscribed the conditions of social reproduction to the detriment of vulnerable groups in a period of significant economic restructuring.

The chapter first specifies the broad processes involved in 'neoliberalization' (Graefe 2004), which took hold in Ontario during this period of restructuring. Second, it documents these processes at work via a review of the major changes in the areas of governance, education, health care, income support, and labour regulations. Finally, it asks how this redesign affected members of households, and women in particular, as they put together a living and provided care.

Neo-liberal Reorientations

The Ontario Conservative government's neo-liberal model of economic and social policies incorporated several interrelated processes: *privatization, familialization, decentralization* and *commodification* (Brodie

1997; Bakker 1997; Fudge and Cossman 2002), all of which bear on the gender regime. It simultaneously involved increasing suspicion, and often, a *criminalization* of the poor, particularly of single mothers receiving social assistance, accusing them of widespread cheating and welfare fraud (Evans and Wekerle 1997; Little 1998; Mosher 2000).[1] The creation of government snitch lines that urged people to identify cheaters fuelled the hostile climate towards social assistance recipients (see Hermer and Mosher 2002; Mosher 2000; Little 1998). The Harris Conservatives actively encouraged the private market, the family/household, and, to some extent, the third (or voluntary) sector, to take up work previously provided via the welfare state while simultaneously elevating the individual, preferably the individual-worker (Evans and Wekerle 1997; Brodie 1996). Government policies presupposed that market criteria were the best tools by which to measure the delivery of services.

Under *privatization*, goods owned or delivered publicly were shifted to the private market or to the unpaid work of (usually) women in households, and to some extent to volunteers.[2] This process closely paralleled *familialization*, or policies and practices that increase individuals' reliance on the family/household (Esping-Andersen 1999). Familialization has profound gender connotations. Brodie (1997:236) expresses familialization's ideological process succinctly: 'it is up to families to look after their own and it is up to the state to make sure that they do.' Both privatization and familialization shifted costs to the family/household. In the case of familialization, the assumption was that the work should be forced back to where it 'belonged,' in the family/household unit. Both privatization and familialization relied and built upon an existing gender division of labour, taking place in a context where most households consisted of dual earners with female carers. Thus a tension between *de-familialization* and *re-familialization* existed: women were viewed as autonomous workers; social policy did not consider externalities such as responsibility for social reproduction, but social policy practices transfered the work of social reproduction onto women. The processes of privatization and familialization increased pressures to provide care for household and extra-household members.[3] For example, in the case of health care reform, services were removed from hospital-based care, but attendant public supports for providing home and continuing care were usually insufficient.[4] Purchasing home care services in the private market was an option only for those with adequate disposable incomes. Women in particular were called upon to make up for this gap with their unpaid caring labour when people were sent home 'quicker and sicker' (Bezanson and Noce 1999; Aronson and Neysmith 2001). These demands were difficult to meet, as they required both technical skill and job-time flexibility.

Shifting responsibility downward is also a hallmark of *decentralization*. The process of decentralization involved shifting responsibility for the delivery and often the funding of services from one level of government to another, usually from the province to the municipalities. Decentralization tended to increase inequalities among regions because municipalities did not have either the tax base or the human resources to take up the services that were downloaded to them.

The process of *commodification* is widely noted in welfare state and economic literature, yet its gender dimensions are not well understood. This process is intimately tied to the others. Brodie (1997:236) asserts that the process of commodification rests on 'the unverifiable claim that services initially created in the public sector are better delivered and maintained through market mechanisms and the price system.' In advanced (if retrenching) welfare states, the term requires further explanation, as this definition seems to be part of – if not synonymous with – privatization.

The process of commodification is a referent for the commodity 'labour power.' In welfare state literature, the process of de-commodification refers to the 'degree to which welfare states weaken[ed] the cash nexus by granting entitlements independent of market participation' (Esping-Andersen 1999:43). It was associated with the highest form of welfare state development whereby the state socialized some of the responsibility for the work of social reproduction (e.g., state-subsidized day cares) as well as the risks of labour market insecurity (e.g., unemployment insurance). The process of commodification shifts goods and services back to governance by the market mechanism, while individualizing risk based on labour market attachment, hence re-commodifying them. Yet the work of social reproduction, even at the height of the welfare state, was never adequately borne by states. The family/household, and women's labour within it, remained the main source of welfare for most households. Many women in these households were in fact pre-commodified.

Decommodified entitlements are increasingly unavailable to citizens (Orloff 1993). Feminist scholars assert that many women need access to commodification in the form of access to paid work and market income, and hence a reconfiguration of social reproduction and labour market responsibilities (O'Connor, Orloff, and Shaver 1999). Yet without the prospect of de-commodification offered by state-assumed collective risk bearing, commodification will usually mean labour market insecurity for women workers. This includes insecurity over the means of social reproduction as well as refamilialization of many goods and services. One of the contradictions of this emergent welfare and gender regime is an extensive racialization of gendered work as more women hire nannies and domestics, many of whom are immigrant women and women of colour (Silvera 1989; Glenn 1992; Arat-Koc 2006). While hiring nannies or domestics is not a new phenomenon for wealthy households, the increase in middle-class households hiring immigrant women and women of colour is relatively new.

A final aspect of neo-liberal restructuring, which is less a process than an ideological claim affecting both the labour market and families, is the concept of criminalization. Criminalization refers to the process by which a group comes to be perceived as, or is actively constructed as, deviant (see Mosher 2000). In the case of Ontario, this process bore with severity on the poor. The neo-liberal state is intent on individualizing social responsibility, particularly for incomes from wages (Brodie 1997; Evans and Wekerle 1997; Fraser and Gordon 1994). It insists that structural problems such as poverty are individual problems (e.g., moral or character flaws), and suggests individual rather than collective responses. In Ontario, this generated debates about the acceptability of non-participation in the labour market, with a particular focus on women's roles in caring for children (Mosher 2000). Criminalization became virulent in Ontario around the provision of social assistance, and the provincial government characterized lone mothers who received social assistance as undeserving, rife with moral failings (and likely addictions which required mandatory drug testing), and as drains on the public purse. Being unemployed, single, female, and a parent became rhetorically synonymous with stealing from a hardworking, taxpaying Canadian public.

This focus on single mothers is part of another incarnation of familialization, because dependence on a male wage is seen to be the ideal income source for women; marriage and the family, *not* social assistance, are the alternative to the market (Chunn and Gavigan 2004:233). This is why, as Segal (1999:206) points out, 'single mothers can be demonized if they *don't* work, even while married women with young children can be demonized if they *do*.'[5] The dispute is not about how the work of social reproduction should be met by family/ households, but that the state should not de-commodify mothers to perform these tasks. Yet at the same time there remains a tremendous ambivalence about female participation in the labour market, especially for those with young children. Particular social groups *are* seen as having a legitimate claim for non-participation, at least for certain periods: those with very young children, the elderly, the very ill, and those with severe disabilities (Peck 1996:28). The introduction of work for welfare in Ontario attempted to balance the state's ideological demand for the labour force participation of women with children with its refusal to underwrite the cost of the work of social reproduction.

In Ontario, the state mediated its version of a neo-liberal welfare state by reorganizing and reorienting its relationship with the private market sector and the family/household. As the state attempted to shift costs across these two sectors, it became involved in the process of creating a new gender regime, drawing on the insecurity and lack of stability in the existing structure. We turn now to an examination of the specific kinds of changes that took place in Ontario between 1995 and 2000 to elucidate the changing relationship among the state, market, and family in relation to social regulation and gender regimes.

Implementing the Neo-liberal Project in Ontario, 1995–2000

Cutting Spending, Centralizing Power, and Devolving Responsibility

One of the most notable elements of the Conservative agenda was its stated commitment to decrease the size and scope of government itself.[6] The Conservative government presented itself as 'anti-government,' reflecting the common neo-liberalist view that governments over-regulate businesses and individuals. It borrowed heavily from other models of sub-national and national state restructuring, such as the Thatcher government in Britain (1979 to 1990), the Reagan administration in the United States (1981 to 1989), the Klein government in Alberta (1992 to the present), and experiments in workfare-driven social policy in Wisconsin and New Jersey in the 1990s. In the field of social policy, the Conservatives sought to increase user fees for social services, decrease stabilizers such as rent control, increase private sector involvement in the public sector, contract out services, and transfer administration to the private sector.[7]

Between 1995 and the early 2000s, the Ontario Conservatives enacted legislation that reduced the size of some parts of the government itself (cutting jobs and agencies), downloaded many of the costs and delivery of key social policies (like social assistance and child care) to municipalities, pursued the wholesale privatization of government agencies, and significantly reduced their involvement in regulating industry. During this period of intense downsizing the provincial government also pursued significant decreases in the rates of personal income tax. Ministries and agencies were asked, in 1996, to submit 'business plans' with the initial goal of 10,600 public sector layoffs. In order to redesign the delivery of services by key ministries, the government also set up arm's-length appointed commissions to make recommendations (and deflect decision-making responsibility) on restructuring. These included the Health Services Restructuring Commission (health care), the Education Improvement Commission (education) and the Who Does What Commission (municipal restructuring). The aim of this kind of restructuring, according to the Conservatives' Common Sense Revolution campaign document, was that every program, service, and dollar spent by the Ontario government would face the axe if it could not be justified under the 'business plan' system. Premier Harris himself claimed that he intended to 'run the government more like a business' (*Toronto Star* 1996).

Within its *first* year in office, the provincial government cut $5.5 billion in funding, including cuts to almost every ministry and agency,[8] and cut funding to not-for-profit agencies. It declared a moratorium on non-profit housing. Social assistance policies were immediately reformed to reduce rates, alter the terms of eligibility, lengthen waiting periods, and make youth social assistance harder to get. The government introduced a welfare fraud hotline to cut back on the numbers receiving assistance and to increase public surveillance of the poor. In order to meet its targets, the provincial government enacted a series of legislative changes that gave authority to ministers, third agencies, and the management board secretariat to restructure or eliminate agencies, ministries, and government bodies. For example, the minister of health was given authority in 1996 under the Savings and Restructuring Act to eliminate hospital boards, take over hospitals, shut them down or merge them, and decide what services should be provided (Bezanson and Valentine 1998).

The Conservatives moved quickly to facilitate the implementation of their policies. They used omnibus legislation to effect major legislative changes with as little public discussion and citizen engagement as possible. The provincial government enacted a series of Red Tape Reduction Acts, along with eight bills governing various ministries entitled Government Process Simplification Acts. Nine Red Tape Reduction Acts were initially tabled in the Thirty-sixth Parliament (September 1995–September 1999). Three major omnibus bills, all fulsomely entitled An Act to Reduce Red Tape, to Promote Good Government through Better Management of Ministries and Agencies and to Improve Customer Service by Amending or Repealing Certain Acts and by Enacting New Acts, or the Red Tape Reduction Acts, for short, were ultimately proposed and passed in 1998, 1999, and 2000. These acts constituted a massive series of regulatory changes and amendments in areas ranging from the Sheep and Wool Marketing Act to the Marriage Act, to the Ministry of Health Appeal and Review Boards Act.[9] In total, eight new acts were enacted through these large pieces of red tape omnibus legislation.[10]

These acts had such a broad scope that provisions were enacted without permitting discussions about how municipalities would pay for the services downloaded to them. For example, one bill entrenched municipal responsibility for ambulances, with little legislative debate or attention. In each of the three omnibus bills, time allocation was imposed by the government, limiting the amount of time allowed for debate and public consultation on legislation. The first bill (Bill 25), was passed after the standing committee on the Administration of Justice heard submissions over the course of eight days; one day was given for Bill 11 and three for Bill 119. Each of these omnibus bills was lengthy and cross-cutting in scope. While couched as housekeeping legislation, the Red Tape Reduction Acts, along with their counterparts, the Government Process Simplification Acts (S.O. 1997, c. 36; S.O. 1997, c. 39), in fact served as measures to limit debate on a range of regulatory and statutory measures, eliminated or redesigned regulatory regimes and governing bodies for a broad range of agencies, corporations, and ministries, and reinforced the idea that government and its regulatory agents should at best be minimal and focus on 'customer service.'[11] The legislation also made provisions that further regulatory changes would, in many cases, *not* be subject to parliamentary debate. The government, under the auspices of decreasing 'red tape,' decreased its role in the monitoring, setting, and revising of regulations, and opened the door for the partial or wholesale privatization of government goods and services.

The passing of the Red Tape Reduction Acts was one example of attempts on the part of the provincial government to restructure and downsize diverse areas of provincial legislation within one bill. The most notable omnibus bill passed by the Conservative government, which paved the way for massive reorganization of municipal responsibilities, was the 1996 Savings and Restructuring Act.

The Savings and Restructuring Act was a legislative package that affected 44 separate statutes, created three new acts, and repealed two others. At over 2,000 pages in length, the bill covered a great deal more than housekeeping. This legislation laid the foundation for subsequent bills aimed at reducing the size and scope of provincial government involvement in social provision and regulation, and included provisions to levy user fees and privatize public goods. The legal foundations for what came to be known as the Megacity Bill (Bill 103, City of Toronto Act 1997, c. 2; and Bill 148, City of Toronto Act (2), S.O. 1997, c. 2), which merged eight municipalities in the Toronto area and changed funding structures for municipalities, were rooted in this legislation. The Savings and Restructuring Act covered areas such as health care, pay equity, municipal affairs, public employee contracts, environmental laws, and freedom of information laws (Bezanson and Valentine 1998:3). It afforded enormous power to the minister of municipal affairs and housing, including the capacity to abolish local governments and to force mergers and amalgamations of local municipalities.

The Savings and Restructuring Act was notable both for its significant scope and range, and for the manner in which the legislation was passed. One of the hallmarks of the Conservative government was the way it ignored conventional consultative practices, in this case contravening accepted legislative processes. No provision was made for public consultation on the Savings and Restructuring Act, and the government only consented to consultation after the opposition staged a sit-in in the legislature to protest the departure from established democratic and parliamentary practice.

A pivotal strategy in creating a minimal welfare state in Ontario (while at the same time centralizing power) was to cut funding to all but certain core services strongly supported by the public.[12] Another was to move to local or community-based delivery of services and goods, based on the claim that it would be more responsive and democratic (Ontario Legislative Assembly, 18 October 2001). Yet the process of change and the funding structures for administering the municipal arrangement or community delivery further compromised the delivery of services and shifted responsibility for service and program shortfalls away from the province. The shift from hospital-based care (governed under the Canada Health Act) to community-based care delivered through the newly created Community Care Access Centres (CCACs) had the effect of reducing levels of service for needs like home care and long-term care when waiting lists for services were already extensive.[13] In keeping with more fundamentalist conservative outlooks on the economy and moral values, the Ontario government espoused a minimal state and relied on a discourse of family, friends, neighbourhood, community, and church to manage the effects of reduced social spending and support (Regimbald 1997; see also Noce 2004).

The shift in responsibility for the delivery and funding of certain public services was most clearly visible in the massive overhaul of municipalities across Ontario. In January 1997, during what came to be known as 'Mega-Week' (13–20 January), the provincial government announced major changes to the municipal structure of Toronto, amalgamating it with surrounding municipalities.[14] Simultaneously, changes were introduced affecting the numbers of school boards and their power in the province, cutting the number of elected trustees and increasing the role of school councils made up predominantly of parent volunteers. Announcements were also made about the devolution of responsibility and funding for social assistance, housing, long-term care, and public transit. New property tax assessment guidelines were also introduced (S.O. 1997, c. 43).[15] The initial proposals for the offloading of costs onto municipalities would have shifted over $6.5 billion in new costs to municipalities (Ontario Federation of Labour 1999:6). In exchange, the province proposed taking over residential property taxes for the financing of public education.

Provincial transfers to municipal governments were cut severely in 1995, and many municipal governments increased local taxes as a result. A new property tax assessment structure increased property taxes (a variant of market value assessment was introduced in Bill 106, the Fair Municipal Finance Act). Public outcry over the new provincial-municipal arrangement was enormous, and the initial proposal was revised, with the province taking over education financing while cost-sharing some of the programs initially planned to be delivered at the municipal level.

As programs and services were downloaded to municipalities, political and financial responsibility shifted from the province to the local level. In 1996, the provincial government enacted the Family Responsibility and Support Arrears Act (S.O. 1996, c. 31), which also served to shift financial responsibility away from the province and onto individuals. This act created the Family Responsibility Office, charged with seeking out 'deadbeat dads' (those owing child support and alimony payments). The act also served to transfer the financial responsibility to support children and poor women away from social assistance and onto individual men. This ignored issues of poverty and economic insecurity among men. Furthermore, in many cases, women did not wish to name their ex-spouses for fear of reprisals. This new legislation enforced the idea that financial support should be made available through the nuclear family and that the state should have as small a role as possible in underwriting a family's costs or the work of caring for children.

The Ontario government also opened the door for the privatization of public goods. It created the Ministry of Privatization, which became an office within the Superbuild initiative, whose focus was on public-private partnerships. One of its largest initiatives was the dismantling of Ontario Hydro, with the aim of subjecting energy prices and delivery to a competitive market. In 1998, the provincial government enacted an energy deregulation bill (S.O. 1998, c. 15) allowing for the sale of Ontario Hydro to private companies. Public outcry in the early 2000s over the subsequent massive increases in electricity rates forced the government to maintain majority ownership of the utility and reintroduce a freeze on hydro rates.[16]

One of the provincial government's stated aims was to consider whether non-governmental agents (especially those in the private sector) could deliver goods and services 'more efficiently.' All areas of government were scrutinized to consider whether private sector involvement was appropriate. The most obvious instance of privatization – with dramatically negative outcomes – was the privatization of water testing plants at the municipal level. In 2000, a crisis erupted in the town of Walkerton when the municipal water system became infected with e-coli bacteria. Seven people died and over 2000 more fell ill (some developing long-term disabilities) as a result of the contaminated water. A public inquiry revealed that the privatization had led to reduced water testing as well as a serious lack of training of the individuals charged with water safety. In June 2001, Premier Mike Harris was called to testify at the Walkerton Inquiry. He was questioned in detail by the commission about the speed with which the decision to privatize laboratory testing was taken. Initially, according to Paul Cav-alluzzo (the commission's counsel, primarily responsible for examin-ing the causes of the Walkerton tragedy), the option of privatizing laboratories was slated to be studied and then undertaken over a two-to three-year period (Walkerton Inquiry 2001:3). As a result of a press-ing imperative forced on the Ministry of the Environment to cut its operating and budgetary costs almost in half, privatization was imple-mented within a matter of two *months*, without the regulatory require-ments that provincial testing facilities had been subject to (Walkerton Inquiry 2001: 12–19). According to provincial government documents (both public and ministry specific documents and memos).[17] presented in evidence, the result was that the facilities were not provincially accredited, reporting practices for irregularities were not in place, and microbiologists who could interpret water findings were not on staff (Walkerton Inquiry 2001: 51–53). Reporting requirements to the Minis-try of the Environment and to the local medical officer of health were not mandatory by regulation.[18]

One of the aims of the inquiry was to assess whether the province's privatization initiative contributed to the deaths of the seven Walker-ton residents. The commission focused extensively on the role of cost-cutting measures and private sector measures of efficiency in its assessment of the decision to privatize water treatment. The commis-sioner's counsel attempted to establish that no criteria were put in place to ensure quality of testing and accuracy of reporting, and that cost reduction was the primary motivation for shifting responsibility for water safety onto the private sector (*CBC* Newsworld Live 2001; Walkerton Inquiry 2001:50–61).[19] In keeping with the ideas laid out in the Red Tape Reduction Acts and the Red Tape Commission, privati-zation was viewed as a cost-saving measure and the involvement of the private sector in the monitoring and assessing of public utilities was considered efficient, in terms of regulatory and actual costs.[20] More broadly, evidence submitted at the commission revealed that no plans were developed to manage the health and environmental risks (identified as early as 1996 by the Ministry of the Environment and the environmental commissioner) that resulted from staffing and budget-ary cutbacks and a lack of regulatory controls (Walkerton Inquiry 2001: 13–27). New systems of water regulation have since been put in place (Safe Drinking Water Act, 2002; Sustainable Water and Sewage Systems Act, 2002; Nutrient Management Act, 2002), but a tragic fore-seeable collapse of public infrastructure and surveillance and the resultant political crisis was the impetus for re-regulation and state intervention.

The government's focus on efficiency, cost savings, and decreased regulation of industry was complemented by a commitment to tax cuts and balanced budgets (see Philipps 2000). This focus on tax cuts and balanced budgets is itself a form of privatization in that the role of markets is elevated over the role of governments in allocating resources, hence allowing the market to decide who has access to income and wealth. Tax cuts have played a vital role in winning popular support for neo-liberal policies.

The Conservatives implemented their fiscal interest in economic bottom lines, prioritizing free market activity over the delivery and regulation of public goods, by passing legislation that penalized governments for running deficits. The Balanced Budget Act (1999) and the Taxpayer Protection Act (1999) entrenched a minimalist state by leaving no provision for Keynesian style spending in economic slowdowns.[21] The state, then, through regulatory, budgetary, and legislative means, actively entrenched a welfare state that minimized spending on social infrastructure. Instead, privatization and efficiency measures translated into decreased income security, decreased health and safety protections, and decreased access to public services.

Reorganizing Education and Health Care

Two of the largest social policy and program areas, education and health care, were key targets for the Conservative government. The government subjected education to dramatic restructuring, and introduced new policies that allowed for direct privatization. In June 2001, the provincial government introduced legislation that provided tax credits for parents with children in private schools (Responsible Choices for Growth and Accountability Act), despite the underfunding of primary and secondary schools in the province, and the increased fees and costs associated with post-secondary education.[22] The government emphasized that religious schools in particular needed this credit, yet applied it broadly to all private schools. This move undermined the public system in several ways. First, the tax breaks reduced funding available to the already underfunded public system. Second, while private schools can select which students to admit, public schools must accept any applicant. The more competent, able students register in private schools, the greater the proportion of special needs students in the public system. This distortion of the population in the public system further strains its resources. Third, the parents most likely to get involved as volunteers and as education activists are those with resources who are therefore in the best position to choose private over public education. When significant numbers of such parents no longer have any interest in the well-being of the public system, there is less support available for public education overall. Emphasizing that the tax credit for private school education was about the budget and not about education, the bill was passed as part of the 2001 budget bill, with little consultation and an imposed time allocation.

Beginning in 1995, the provincial government significantly cut funding to all levels of education.[23] It introduced a series of reforms to restructure and eliminate school boards while increasing the role of school and parent councils; introduced standardized testing in schools; decreased funding and support for adult education; decreased 'non-classroom' spending; changed labour relations with educators; and privatized out-of-classroom expenses such as curriculum development, early childhood education, and school custodial services (O'Connell and Valentine 1998).[24] The government also changed the regulations governing Ontario student loans and decreased transfers to post-secondary education, resulting in an increase in tuition fees (Ontario Ministry of Education and Training 1998:1). In most professional faculties, tuition has been largely deregulated and annual fees escalated markedly. In dentistry, fees increased 316 per cent between 1993 and 2003. Medicine saw a 248 per cent increase and law a 168 per cent increase over the same period (Kwong et al. 2002; Statistics Canada 2004).

Again, many of the changes in legislation governing education in the province were done in a rushed and rigid fashion. Time allocation was imposed and public hearings and consultations were kept to a minimum. In contradistinction to trends in downloading and decentralization, the government centralized funding control over public education, while contracting out elements of the institutional apparatus of the system. It centralized decision-making power in the education sector through the enactment of an appointed, quasi-independent commission, the Education Improvement Commission, which reported directly to the minister of education. Many of this commission's recommendations were later incorporated into legislation enacted by the provincial government (Fewer School Boards Act, 1997). The centralization of control gave enormous powers to the minister of education to dramatically overhaul the education system and bypass dissent at the board level, while reorganizing its content towards labour market and business goals.

Massive labour disruptions in education became common in Ontario following the 1996 reductions in education funding. Public school teachers staged a work stoppage in 1997 to protest educational funding and institutional changes. Teachers and education workers went on strike in several school boards, and many high school teachers refused to offer extra-curricular activities, arguing that their workloads increased significantly as a result of the government's policy changes. Families and parents were increasingly relied upon to make up for funding shortfalls in the public education sector through fundraising, and parents were called upon to increase their involvement in school councils, at a time when many of them simultaneously were seeing demands increase in other areas, such as in their paid work lives.

While quality, centre-based early childhood education and care is increasingly recognized as crucial to work-life balance and to elevating cognitive and social development among children (OECD 2001; OECD 2004; Government of Canada 2004b), Ontario under the Progressive Conservatives rigidly adhered to a custodial care model characterized by increased privatization, decentralization, familialization, and, to some extent, commodification in child care. The Conservatives reshaped child care and early childhood education by cancelling capital funding for new centres, eliminating pay equity for childcare workers,[25] making municipalities responsible for a portion of fee subsidies and their administration, eliminating many childcare centres located in schools, and encouraging informal, unregulated child care (Tyyksa 2001).

Although the federal government has announced intentions to develop a national daycare strategy (Government of Canada 2004b), child care and early childhood education remain within provincial/ territorial jurisdiction. Child care in Ontario is a user-pay service (Childcare Resource and Research Unit 2001), with some low-income parents or guardians eligible for a subsidy from a combination of provincial and municipal resources delivered at the municipal level. Instead of formal child care, as recommended by the 1999 *Early Years Study*, commissioned by the provincial government (McCain and Mustard 1999), the province used new money it had received from the federal/provincial Early Childhood Development Initiative in 2001 to launch Early Years Centres (information clearing houses for parents) and a Early Years Challenge Fund (programming for specific circum-stances such as teen parent workshops). None of the $266 million Ontario received in 2001 and 2002 went to child care. Between 1995 and 2001, the provincial government decreased funding to child-care services by $160 million (Canadian Centre for Policy Alternatives 2003). Sixty-one per cent of mothers in Canada with children under three participated in the labour force in 1999 (Statistics Canada 2000a). In Ontario in the same year, there were only enough regulated child-care spaces to meet the needs of 12 per cent of the province's children (Childcare Resource and Research Unit 2001; OECD Directorate for Education 2004). Despite this evidence, the emphasis in childcare pol-icy and early childhood education in Ontario was on educating parents and caregivers and allowing for greater 'choice in childcare' (Vosko 2006).

Health care was subject to restructuring similar to that experienced in the education sector. An arm's-length appointed commission, the Health Services Restructuring Commission, was established early on in the Harris government's tenure with a mandate to restructure hospi-tals in the province (Savings and Restructuring Act, 1996). The result of this commission was the recommendation that 45 hospital sites in the province close, and dozens more amalgamate (Bezanson and Noce 1999). According to the commission, $1.1 billion was to be cut out of hospital budgets between 1995 and 2003 (Health Services Restructur-ing Commission 1998; Bezanson and Noce 1999). The closing and merging of specialized hospitals (such as Toronto's Wellesley Hospital providing gay-positive care, and Toronto's Women's College Hospital, focusing on women's health care) saw targeted care services disappear for particular populations. The cuts in funding to hospitals meant that staff and services were reduced, resulting in longer waiting lists for needed care. Hospitals began trying to recoup some of their costs through the privatization of services, increasing fees, or fundraising (Bezanson and Noce 1999).

Few of the changes to health care in Ontario were made through leg-islative initiatives. As in the education sector, major changes were made by providing increased power to the minister (in this case, the minister of health) to make decisions about the delivery and funding of health care services, and removing decision-making powers from hospital or community-based boards. One of the main thrusts of health care reform was to move services out of hospitals and into community-based care (a form of decentralization) through the creation of local Community

Care Access Centres.[26] These centres coordinate services such as long-term care placement, home care, and community-based care such as Meals On Wheels. Although funding for long-term care increased by 10 per cent between 1995 and 1998, hospitals lost at least $575 million, putting increased pressure on the long-term care sector. Despite warnings from the Health Services Restructuring Committee that resources should remain in place in hospitals until the long-term care sector was equipped to manage new demands, the pattern of rapid change with little public consultation persisted (Bezanson and Noce 1999).

The privatization trend also accelerated in the out-of-hospital sector, particularly in home care. For-profit providers bid against not-for-profit providers for home care contracts (Picard 1999). Because for-profit providers were able to undercut the costs of their staffing and servicing through a combination of taylorization of the work process and lower wages, the not-for-profit sector lost contracts and saw wages pushed downward. New fees for services both in and out of hospital placed additional demands and costs on patients.

As the health care sector restructured and moved resources out of hospitals and into homes, families were increasingly called upon to make up for shortfalls in services. The direct underfunding of health care services was predicated on the assumption that either the private market sector or individuals would be able to make up in care what was no longer being provided publicly. Few of the legislative changes that implemented health care restructuring were ever subject to debate either in Parliament or with the public.

Blaming the Poor

The Conservatives' approach to social assistance reform was punitive.[27] One of the government's first acts in 1995 was to cut social assistance rates by 21.6 per cent. Subsequently, it overhauled the entire program of social assistance. In 1997, the provincial government introduced two new programs, the Ontario Works Act and the Ontario Disability Support Act, which replaced the previous social assistance programs of General Welfare, Family Benefits, and Vocational Rehabilitation Services.[28] In creating these two acts, groups of social assistance recipients, many of whom were single mothers raising young children, were moved from the marginally more generous Family Benefits program to the one-size-fits-all Ontario Works program. This legislative reorganization placed single mothers receiving social assistance in the same category as single, childless, employable men, and subjected most (except those with very young children) to mandatory labour market training and participation programs (popularly known as workfare). Only those with long-term disabilities were exempt from the workfare and training components of the new legislation. One of the aims of the new Ontario Works program was to find 'the ... shortest route to employment' (Ministry of Community and Social Services 1999), and more generally, to decrease the number of people claiming social assistance in the province.

The overhaul of social assistance was coupled with a diminution of tenant rights in landlord-tenant disputes. While rental rates and landlord responsibilities do not only affect social assistance recipients, changes to these areas disproportionately affect those who are poor. In 1997, the provincial government introduced the Tenant Protection Act. This new legislation removed rent control from vacant units and from new buildings. It also made it easier to evict tenants. It significantly affected those of low income – particularly following the cuts to social assistance rates – and was compounded by the province's withdrawal from non-profit and co-operative housing (see S.O. 2000, c. 27). No new social housing was built in Ontario between 1995 and 2000, and, in 1999, the Ontario Housing Corporation announced plans to sell off 5,800 units of social housing (Bezanson and McMurray 2000).

Eligibility requirements for social assistance in the province were, through regulation, made more restrictive, while benefit levels and additional supports for Ontario Works decreased. New policy initiatives prohibited students from receiving Ontario Works (O. Reg. 364/01; O. Reg. 134/98), reinstated 'spouse in the house' rules (wherein a woman living with a man is assumed to be supported by him, and therefore ineligible) (O. Reg. 409/95),[29] and proposed fingerprinting, drug testing, and literacy testing for social assistance recipients (Government of Ontario 2001). As part of the redesign of the welfare state in Ontario towards a minimal provision of public goods, the government fostered discourses about dependency and fraud to criminalize those receiving social assistance. These discourses capitalized on negative stereotypes of single mothers and immigrant populations as villains draining the welfare state of resources (see Little 1998). Welfare fraud hotlines were set up to permit anonymous callers to report on those receiving social assistance whom they perceived to be cheating. They were part of an intended initiative to divide 'honest taxpayers' from 'welfare scammers.'

The case of *Rogers v. Greater Sudbury (City) Administrator of Ontario Works* (2001) provides a tragic example of both the punitive nature of social assistance reform as well as neo-liberal ambivalence about how the costs of social reproduction can and should be met. Rogers pled guilty in April of 2001 to welfare fraud after failing to declare $49,000 in student loans. She was given six months of house arrest and her social assistance benefits were cut off for three months. Under the Harris government, the province banned those convicted of welfare fraud from ever receiving social assistance again – for life. Rogers filed a motion for interim relief while waiting for a determination of her constitutional challenge to the regulations. In May 2001, the judge granted an interlocutory order against the attorney general of Ontario. The effect of the order was to declare that Rogers was exempted from the application of the regulations on an interim basis, and to require that her benefits be reinstated retroactively. Rogers had no other access to income, few supports, and was pregnant. She was still confined to house arrest. During a heat wave in August of 2001, Rogers died in her apartment. A supplementary endorsement by the presiding judge detailing the amounts payable to Rogers was only released in August 2001, after she had died. The Rogers case reveals that financial considerations – in this case, a focus of fraud – superseded any other considerations under Harris.[30]

Attacks on social assistance fit well with a renewed emphasis on labour market flexibility and decreased labour regulations and bargaining power. Creating a pool of cheap workers – couched in a language of giving 'a hand up, not a hand out' (Progressive Conservative Party of Ontario 1994) – is one of the ultimate aims of the redesign of welfare delivery. While new policy emphasized the imperative that single mothers receiving social assistance should work, the state was not prepared to underwrite the costs of social reproduction associated with facilitating labour market participation. Subsidized child care, for example, was only marginally expanded when the workfare and training components of Ontario Works were implemented, and did not meet demand. Underwriting this cost proved to be expensive for the state, and hence its emphasis on labour market participation as the necessary alternative to social assistance receipt, was disrupted by the increased cost to the state of shifting social assistance recipients into the labour market. Discussions of social assistance reform, in campaign documents, in legislation and regulation, and in press releases from the Ministry of Community and Social Services, focused on dependency (Progressive Conservative Party of Ontario 1994; Ministry of Community and Social Services 2000). Welfare dependency, similar to substance abuse, was framed as an individual shortcoming that is both blameworthy and avoidable; only children were able to claim a socially condoned dependence (Fraser and Gordon 1994). The new thinking de-gendered single mothers, and recast them as employable. It then re-gendered them as welfare dependents needing to take personal responsibility for their children at risk of losing them (Brodie 1995:19).

The Ontario government's ambivalence about whether the workfare component of social assistance was social policy or labour market policy[31] was crystallized in a piece of legislation passed in 1998 (Bill 22) called An Act to Prevent Unionization with respect to Community Participation under the Ontario Works Act (1998). The act amended the Ontario Works Act (1997) to provide that the Labour Relations Act (1995) would not apply with respect to involvement in a community participation activity (the workfare component of the Ontario Works Act). The act also provided that participants could not join a trade union, bargain collectively, or strike with respect to their community participation under Ontario Works. The one and one-half page piece of legislation was a punitive measure, since non-participation in Ontario Works community placement resulted in a withdrawal of social assistance benefits. The sanction, then, for collective organization would be a withdrawal of social assistance.

The Ontario Works Act, with its community placement component in particular, served as a commodifying process for many social assistance recipients. While the presence of social assistance in an advanced welfare state suggests a de-commodification of citizens via access to income through non-participation in the labour market, many women receiving social assistance in Ontario had not been commodified in the first place. The program moved them from non- or pre-commodification to commodification without the intervening attainment of non-stigmatized citizenship rights associated with advanced welfare state de-commodification. For women who gained access to income via a relationship with a male who had wages or social entitlements, the dissolution of a spousal relationship often meant social assistance was one of their very limited options for income support. The new legislation focused on placing recipients in any job, hence moving them into an insecure and precarious labour market – commodifying them – without providing the social citizenship rights assured and assumed by male citizens in the Fordist welfare state. The emphasis on commodification without the attendant stage of full de-commodification reflects the tension over social reproduction evident in state policy towards children and women. Underwriting the costs of social reproduction generally means de-commodifying aspects of this work through state funding, or commodifying this work by providing it through the private market. In either approach, the aim of de-commodification or commodification necessarily presumes that women will be commodified. However this plan does not address how the attendant costs of managing social reproduction and its costs will be met. Therefore, the provincial government's shifting of the work onto community, family, and friends proves unsustainable as a strategy for long-term social reproduction demands.

The legislative changes enacted through the Social Assistance Reform Act (1997)[32] were sweeping in scope and included making further changes to the program through regulatory realignments and therefore without legislative debate. Perhaps more than any other area of social program and labour market reform, social assistance is an area of contradiction for neo-liberal proponents. The work that goes into putting together and maintaining a standard of living is most clearly evident in this social program. It encompasses basic allowances for food, housing, and clothing; it accounts for increases and decreases in family size; and it collides with the realities of a labour market in which stratification based on gender, race, and class are key factors in determining household income. The realities of balancing the work of social reproduction and the state's interest in labour market participation as the only means to income are not resolvable. They remain in conflict.

Social assistance reform is also the area in which the gender divisions in social policy are most evident. The ongoing tension between women's roles in social reproduction and in paid work illustrates the contradiction between the ideology of individual responsibility and the state's interest in keeping its social investment costs low.

The Decline of Labour

Changes in the regulations and legislation governing social assistance were complemented by changes in labour market regulations and protections. Consistent with its aims to decrease regulations on business and industry, the provincial government sought to substantially

weaken labour market protections and the rights of workers to unionize. Legislative changes increased labour market flexibility. This flexibility, however, tended 'to remove protection primarily from the
weakest groups in an economy rather than exposing all groups to competition' (Fudge 2001:5).

Among the provincial government's first acts was the introduction
of two bills: one (the Labour Relations and Employment Statute
Amendment Act, 1995) substantially weakened labour unions, and the
other (the Job Quotas Repeal Act, 1995) eliminated Ontario's Employment Equity program. The Labour Relations and Employment Statute
Amendment Act made it legal to hire replacement workers in a strike
and established mandatory union certification voting, thus allowing
employers to instigate petitions for a union de-certification vote. Suc-
cessor rights were eliminated for Crown employees and for contract
service sector workers. For Crown employees, it meant that if a Crown
corporation was sold or privatized, workers lost collective agreements
and bargaining rights. Contract service workers lost their wage security and were faced with the possibility that wages could drop to the
minimum level with a new contractual agreement.

The government also cut the Ministry of Labour's budget by 46 per
cent, laying off workers, including employment standards inspectors
(Bezanson and Valentine 1998:15). In 1995, the government introduced
the Workers Compensation and Occupational Health and Safety
Amendment Act, which disbanded the Workplace Health and Safety
Agency and replaced it with the Workers' Compensation Board (part
of which was privatized), removing requirements for worker participation and for inquests into on-the-job deaths. The minimum wage in
Ontario was frozen in 1995 and was not adjusted until 2004. The Savings and Restructuring Act (1996) eliminated or changed more than 40
pieces of social legislation, including discontinuing the use of the
proxy method for developing pay equity plans for women in the lowest paid jobs. The Employment Standards Improvement Act (1996)
(which was a Red Tape Commission proposal) introduced amendments that permitted longer working hours while reducing overtime
pay and severance pay. This act was followed by the Workplace Safety
and Insurance Act (1997) and the Public Sector Labour Relations Transition Act (1997), which reduced workers' compensation benefits and
established a dispute resolution commission to oversee the changes in
public sector negotiation rights.

In 1998, another two bills – the Prevention of Unionization Act, 1998

(Ontario Works) and the Economic Development and Workplace Democracy Act (1998) – were introduced. The first barred workfare participants from attempting to unionize. The second eliminated protections for employees who faced employer intimidation during a union drive, and gave employers the power to dispute union estimates for the number of persons in a proposed bargaining unit (Ontario Federation of Labour 1999:15).

In 2000, the provincial government further restructured the legislative parameters of employment standards in its Employment Standards Act (2000). The government claimed that the legislation needed to be updated to ensure flexible work arrangements that respond to production and delivery systems, while allowing workers to balance work and family responsibilities (Ontario Legislative Assembly 2000, 23 November). This legislation changed the provisions regulating work time (overtime, maximum hours of work, rest periods, public holidays, and vacations) and proposed a new provision for family leave (S.O. 2000, c. 41). The legislation extended the maximum work week to 60 hours from 48. It also granted employers the power to ask employees to work up to 180 hours over a three-week period (averaging maximum hours). According to the Ontario Federation of Labour (2000:4), an employer 'would only be required to pay overtime if the employee has worked over 132 hours in 3 weeks (overtime will be averaged over 3 weeks). This means that an employee could work 30 hours one week, 32 hours the next and 70 hours in the third week and not be entitled to overtime in the third week for the hours worked above 44 in that week. The weekly rest provision would be 24 hours of rest in every 7 days or 48 consecutive hours in every 14 days.' Unpredictability in work times poses an enormous challenge for those individuals managing child care and/or elder care responsibilities.

The legislation gave 10 days of unpaid, job-protected leave a year to deal with family crisis, personal or family crisis, and bereavement situation (S.O. 2000, c. 41). This leave provision excluded many workers. Under section 50(1), a worker whose employer employs 50 or more employees is able to take 10 days off without pay due to personal illness or family crisis.[33] Fudge (2001:11) underscored that the 10-day unpaid family leave time reflected 'the government's implicit assumption that women's unpaid labour would continue to mediate the tension' between paid work and unpaid work. While leave times are necessary to compel employers to bear some of the responsibility for social reproduction, the provision itself was weak and reflected the

Conservatives' commitment to a deregulated and flexible labour market in which families, and usually women within them, bore the primary responsibility for social care and support.

The significant series of changes enacted in the areas of unionization, employment protections, and protections for historically disadvantaged workers were couched in terms of efficiency and removing red tape. Coupled with reductions in the provision of social services such as health care and education, and attendant protections such as tenant protection legislation, access to income and to standards of living for most workers were substantially eroded in Ontario. The invitation to the private sector to take over both the delivery of services and entire publicly owned organizations disrupted services and made them inaccessible for many. Layoffs of workers in these sectors, as well as increasingly precarious standards and working conditions, were also a result of the partial or total privatization of services.

The interaction of these various changes was illustrated by the growing housing crisis throughout Ontario. At the same time as many workers were forced to get by on lower incomes and social assistance recipients faced a 21.6 per cent cut, the province withdrew from non-profit and co-op housing. Rents soared in most communities and affordable housing became increasingly difficult to find. The result was an increase in homelessness, especially for families with children (Hulchanski 2003). The Conservative government's claim that a deregulated housing market would encourage developers to build low-cost housing never materialized.

Escalating Tensions in Social Reproduction

The regulatory, legislative, and budgetary changes enacted by the Ontario government reflected both an embracing of a neo-liberal welfare state and a regulatory framework that prioritized business interests over public interests. The government attempted to mediate this overhaul by weakening the bargaining power and decision-making authority of key stakeholders in the running of the province, and further weakening those already marginalized in society: the poor, many women, youth, and people of colour. In order to stabilize and mediate the integration of Ontario into a neo-liberal market economy, it relied on regulatory mechanisms and a shifting of costs away from government.

The neo-liberal economy and welfare state that emerged in Ontario in this period rested on the invisible work of social reproduction done by women (and some men) in homes, as well as on men and women working for pay in an increasingly insecure labour market. While some women benefited from neo-liberal policies and were able to hire others to underwrite their social reproduction, those whose incomes prohibited this mediation of the demands of unpaid and paid work experienced a gender order that was less than stable.[34] Neo-liberal restructuring in Ontario resulted in an intensification, both of unpaid work as social services were reduced and restructured, and of paid work as it was made increasingly insecure for many. Women were called upon to make up for the regulatory and legislative supports no longer available and for the social supports that were shifted to the home, to the volunteer sector, or to the market.

The welfare state in Ontario in the mid- to late-1990s was subject to significant labour market and social policy as well as regulatory, legislative, and budgetary shifts. A review of these shifts demonstrates that the provincial state redrew its role in mediating labour market insecurity as well as vis-à-vis the role of families and communities in society, suggesting an alteration in the dominant gender regime. Households and families were pressured to absorb the tensions and stresses of redrawn relationships among states and markets. The implementation of a neo-liberal model in Ontario required an interventionist and centralizing state; the state's redesign of social and labour market policy weakened those with already minimal bargaining power and increasingly shifted the work of social reproduction onto the invisible labour done largely by women.

4 Putting Together a Living in Ontario in the late 1990s

The shift towards neo-liberalism and welfare state residualism in Ontario exacerbated a situation in which paid work was already often insecure and unprotected, and in which many workers and citizens were compelled to lower their wage and social welfare expectations. An analysis of the incomes of the members of the households in the three-year panel study shows how vulnerable people are if they cannot secure a well-paid job and if state income and other supports are made less generous and harder to access. Households, especially those with low incomes, were hard-pressed to pick up new burdens imposed on them as the state retreated and re-privatized and as employers, in a context of intensified neo-liberal globalization, sought greater flexibility in investment, wages, and working conditions.

In a period of economic expansion and growth, over 40 per cent of the members of 41 households who were interviewed for this study reported that their incomes and support from market and state sources had dropped over the course of the 1990s. Over 30 per cent said that their incomes had remained the same. The experiences of the households interviewed for this study challenge the idea that the market should be viewed as the main, or even the most appropriate, means for securing a living, particularly when the care of young children is a factor. What happens to household access to income and to income security when economies restructure along neo-liberal lines? To address this question, this chapter takes up the household case study in the context of the themes developed so far. First, I provide an overview of household incomes, demonstrating that the majority relied on a combination of paid employment and a variety of income supplements, including state and private transfer payments. Second, I analyse household members' labour market participation patterns. Third, I detail improvements and deteriorations in household income positions over the second half of the 1990s. Fourth, I show that market income pressures were compounded by reduced inputs into social reproduction from government and other sources and a tougher social policy context. This chapter, then, focuses on access to income, while the next chapter details access to welfare state supports and services.[1]

Overview of Household Incomes 1997–2000[2]

Almost all adult household participants worked for pay at some point between 1997 and 2000. While job types, working conditions, pay, and security varied widely, most households gained a significant proportion of their income through the wages or salary of at least one household member. However, few of the participants were able to rely *solely* on wages or salaries to meet their needs. Many households relied on the provincial, and to a lesser extent the federal, state to offset wage insecurity and inadequacy, especially when access to income from paid employment was insecure or when health, age, ability, or unpaid care demands prevented them from maintaining a steady paid job. Most lower-income households relied on market income combined with income sources and supports from transfers (like social assistance) and tax credits (such as the Canada Child Tax Benefit).

Some people relied on indirect social spending initiatives (usually targeted, based on income) such as subsidized child care or subsidized housing. Others alleviated income shortages or augmented limited incomes by drawing on investments, other assets or remittances, and loans or gifts from family or friends. For example, people who owned cars could use them as collateral to borrow money. Others were able to move into their parents' homes when they could not afford housing. As Table 4.1 shows, there were a total of 20 different income sources under the four main categories: wages/salaries, federal transfers, provincial transfers, and private transfers.

Over 90 per cent of adult participants worked for pay during the course of the study, and 68 per cent had employment as their *main* source of income in 1999.[3] This is slightly below national data, which indicate that 80 per cent of family income in Canada came from earnings in 2000 (Statistics Canada 2003:7). In 1997, women in Canada received 18 per cent of their total income from government transfer

Table 4.1. Household Income Sources

Income Source	Variations
Wages/Salaries	Salaried employment Hourly employment Self-employment Cash work
Federal transfers	Employment Insurance Canada Child Tax Benefit Canada Pension Plan Old Age Security Scholarships
Provincial transfers	Ontario Works Ontario Disability Support Program Workers' Compensation Aid for Children with Severe Disabilities Ontario Student Assistance Program Scholarships/grants
Private transfers	Child support Rental income Registered Retirement Savings Plan (RRSP) Family Private pensions

payments, while men received about 10 per cent of their total income from government (Statistics Canada 2000a:140).

The details of household income in Figure 4.1 and in Table 4.2 show that 27 per cent of households depended on income from market sources alone; 15 per cent got by on income from market and private transfers; and 59 per cent depended on a combination of market, government, and private sources.

These data illustrate the impact of child-care responsibilities on income level and income source. They show the ways that income configuration is influenced by gender, marital status, and health or ability. The data suggest that those with *male* market income and/or *male* cash income (usually 'under the table' jobs) fared considerably better than those without, and those with *dual* incomes fared best. Those reliant

Figure 4.1: Household Income Sources, 1999

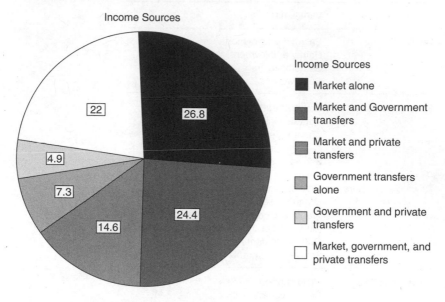

Income Sources

Income Sources
- ■ Market alone
- ■ Market and Government transfers
- ▣ Market and private transfers
- ▢ Government transfers alone
- ▢ Government and private transfers
- □ Market, government, and private transfers

on income from government in combination with either little income from market sources or income from *female* wages/salaries fared the worst; these households overwhelmingly were made up of single mothers.

Gender composition and the presence of young children are notable in the income from market sources category. Five of the 11 households that relied exclusively on income from market sources were male-headed, and the rest consisted of households characterized by semi-professional to professional, multiple adult-earners. Ninety-one per cent of the households in this category were in the middle- and high-income categories. All adult household members (male and female) worked for wages/salaries, and the majority (82 per cent) had post-secondary education or training. Of the two two-parent, opposite-sex households in this category, one had a very high income and was therefore able to pay for high-quality child care and the other was a primary caregiver for her own as well as her partner's older teenage children. Four of 11 households (36 per cent) had active child-care responsibilities; among these four, only two households had very young children.

For the 10 households with incomes from both market and govern-ment sources, eight had children and received some income from the Canada Child Tax Benefit (CTB). Seven of the eight households with children were composed of two-parent households, with income from a male household member. Among two-parent households, six of seven were middle-income. Of the remaining two all-male households in the market and government sources category, one includes a man with HIV/AIDS, and the other a man who had been homeless and found housing shortly before the study began.

The six households with income from wages and private transfers have one member who worked in a well- paid profession or semi-pro-fessional job at some point over the course of the study; three were composed of couples and three of single women. No children were present, and five of six were middle class.

Of the three households that relied exclusively on government trans-fers for their incomes, two were female-headed. The single mother had very young children and was a recent refugee, and the other was living with a severe disability. The third household consisted of a teenage heterosexual couple with two babies. All three households were very poor.

The two households with incomes from both government and pri-vate sources were again female-headed households, with income from social assistance and/or Child Tax Benefit and child support. Both had young children and both were very poor.

Six of the nine households with mixed-income sources were female-headed households where the women combined paid work with a variety of arrangements in order to make a living. Sixty-six per cent of households in this category had low incomes.

For households whose incomes were low, it was a constant strug-gle not only to get by, but to manage various income sources. The number of women in the last three income-source categories in Table 4.2 is high and status as a single mother played a determining role in income source and income level. A key element that lifted medium- and low-income female-headed households into higher-income cate-gories was a relationship with a wage-earning man. For example, in 1999 Angie was in the category 'income from market alone' because she moved in with a high-middle income-earning man. She moved from low-middle income to high-income over the course of the inter-views. Women who have partners who share costs and responsibili-ties are often able to manage, although they are always just a layoff or

Table 4.2. Detailed Household Income Sources, 1999[4]

Income source[5]	No. of households (out of 41)	Household structure	Male market or cash income (including private pensions)	Female market or cash income (including private pensions)	Children present	Income level
Income from market alone	11*	2 lone father households 3 single men 4 opposite-sex couple households 1 housemate household 1 mixed-generation household	9 of 11 (1 does not contain a male member)	6 of 11 (5 do not contain female members)	4 of 11 contain children	1 high-income 9 middle-income 1 low-income
Income from market and government transfers	10	1 lone mother 7 opposite-sex couple households 1 same-sex couple (HIV/AIDS) 1 single male	9 of 10 (1 does not contain a male member)	7 of 10 (2 does not contain a female members)	8 of 10 contain children	6 middle-income 4 low-income
Income from market and private transfers	6	1 same-sex couple 2 opposite-sex 3 single females**	3 of 6 (2 do not contain a male member)	5 of 6 (1 does not contain a female member)	None present	5 middle-income

Table 4.2 (concluded)

Income source[5]	No. of households (out of 41)	Household structure	Male market or cash income (including private pensions)	Female market or cash income (including private pensions)	Children present	Income level
Income from government transfers alone	3	1 lone mother 1 opposite-sex couple 1 single woman with severe disability	None	None	2 of 3	All low-income
Income from government, and private transfers	2	2 lone mother households	None	None	2 of 2	Both low-income
Income from market, government, and private transfers	9	5 lone mother households 1 opposite-sex couple household 1 single female household 1 retired opposite-sex couple 1 three-generation household	3 of 9	9 of 9	7 of 9	3 medium-income 6 low-income

*Included in this calculation is one participant whose main income was from wages/salaries, but who also relied on undeclared cash gifts from family periodically.

**One woman receives an indirect male wage from child support payments for her co-resident adult child.

a breakup away from need. Most women on their own with children have to rely on other sources of support. This situation is inevitable as long as the main burden of social reproduction remains a private individual responsibility.

The gender composition of the households was not the only characteristic affecting income status: in 1999, five of the 17 low-income households (29 per cent) were composed of people of colour or First Nations, while only four of 23 (17 per cent) people of colour or First Nations were in the middle-income category.

Better or Worse? Household Income Fluctuations in a Restructuring Ontario

As Table 4.3 indicates, incomes improved for 11 households between 1995 and 1999. It shows that for some household members, such as Sara and Anand, their incomes improved because they have skills that are in demand in the labour force and they are working very hard. For others, such as Angie and Barbara, their incomes rose because of a new relationship with a male partner. Some, such as Patrick and Rosa, moved from social assistance into low-income jobs. Carl's income improved because he found full-time work and he separated from his partner, Kate. Kate's income dropped dramatically.

Table 4.4 shows those households for whom income levels remained relatively constant between 1995 and 1999, but fluctuation occurred between these time periods, indicating that uniformity in income level did not necessarily mean income security. It is notable that with the exception of Antonio and Natalia, all of the households are in the middle-income category and none relied on government income transfers as a main source of income.

Table 4.5 shows that income levels dropped for 17 households between 1995 and 1999. These changes reflect job losses, reductions in work hours, relationship dissolutions, health crises, and caregiving responsibilities. Twelve of the 17 are low-income, and of these, 11 are female-headed. This table clearly demonstrates the impacts of cuts in funding to the public and para-public sectors. The economic boom in which the project of neo-liberal restructuring took place in Ontario did not distribute benefits evenly across the population. Household income data suggest that those who fared well or managed to stay the same were already well positioned, with education, private pensions, and/or multiple incomes on which to rely.

Table 4.3. Who Was Better Off 1995–1999?

Household	Income level	What changed?
Sara and Anand	Moved higher in high-income range	He got a promotion and a raise, she found a permanent job and grandparents provide free child care.
Angie	Moved higher in medium-income range	Worked extra hours, began relationship with Travis who has a well-paid job and a house.
Barbara	Moved higher in medium-income range	Began relationship with Adam, who has a well-paid job and a house.
Carl	Moved higher in medium-income range	Found full-time work. He and his partner separated.
Janet and Christopher	Hers was low, his medium: both are now medium	Moved in together. He works more than full-time hours, she cleans more houses.
Monica and Randy	Moved from low into medium-income range	Moved into her mother's home. She started paid in-home child-care business, he began receiving workers' compensation benefits and training and is able to do some work.
Jessie and Mark	Moved from low into medium-income range	She left social assistance for full-time job and consulting, he started and lost small business.
Richard and Henry	Moved up a bit in low-income range	Started receiving dietary supplement under Ontario Disability Support Program; family gives Richard money.
Patrick	Moved up a bit in low-income range	Found low-paid part-time retail job and left social assistance.
James	Moved up in low income range	Was homeless, now receiving full social assistance; augments this by selling crafts and doing cleaning; has more stable housing.
Rosa	Moved up a bit in low-income range	Left social assistance for low-paid clerical jobs, began receiving child support and receives Canada Child Tax Benefit.

Source: Adapted from Bezanson and McMurray (2000).

Table 4.4. Who Did the Same 1995–1999?

Household	Income level	What was life like?
Gary and one teenager	Medium	Self-employment fluctuated and earnings went down while his wife was dying because he periodically took time off.
Christine, Dwight, and one teenager	Medium	Her in-home child care business fluctuated, his job remained low-paying and his small business generated no income.
Frank and Michael	Medium	Both changed contract jobs and one returned to school, got a large grant, bought a house.
Rosie and Bob	Medium	He started receiving Old Age Security and Canada Canada Pension Plan benefits, she gained and lost part-time job.
Cheryl, Paul, and two children	Medium	He had steady job, she worked briefly at a few short-term jobs.
Josie, married daughter and husband, and four children	Medium	Her job became permanent full-time job; she adopted grandchildren, family members moved in and out.
Lisa, Ray, and two children	Medium	Ray downsized and then placed in a similar job
Jerry and one child	Medium	He was in university, then had a child and got married; now has permanent job, and is living rent-free in his parents' home.
Denzel	Medium	He was in university, then received welfare, found and lost two jobs, received Employment Insurance benefits, and is now working full time but has large Ontario Student Assistance Program debt.
Aida, Xavier, and one adult daughter	Medium	She works more hours, his business earns less, son's medication is very expensive, they are paying Employment Insurance overpayment and back taxes.
Melanie, Heather, and Ron	Medium	All three moved in together, Melanie's hours were cut due to provincial funding cuts, Ron got a full-time job, Heather's full-time job ended due to cuts to arts funding; she worked at intermittent contracts but was ineligible for Employment Insurance.
Victoria and adult child	Medium	She was downsized and then placed in a similar job.
Natalia, Antonio, and two children	Low	Moved from social assistance augmented by his cash employment to college to low-paid work for both. They have large Ontario Student Assistance Program debt.

Source: Adapted from Bezanson and McMurray (2000).

Table 4.5. Who Fell Behind 1995–1999?

Household	Income level	Why were they worse off?
Pamela, Bert, and one adult child	Still medium, but lower	She retired from a position about to be eliminated because of provincial funding cuts, he chose to retire, helping son with university tuition.
Maria and Leo	Still medium, but lower	She took early retirement from teaching because of incentives in provincial education to reduce staff, his work is now seasonal.
Liz	Still medium, but lower	Was working half-time after taking early retirement because of incentives in provincial funding to reduce staff; now earning a bit less working nearly full time.
Denise, Rick, one adult child, and two teenagers	Still medium, but lower	Her full-time hours were cut back, now patches together part-time or temporary jobs. He no longer is eligible for overtime.
Sabrina and Elizabeth	Still medium, but lower	Sabrina was laid off due to provincial funding cuts, drew Employment Insurance benefits, received welfare, patched together jobs, and now combines several into full-time work. Elizabeth has received steady raises.
Julie	Fell from medium to low	Moved from permanent job to government job that was then eliminated; now working part-time.
Michelle and two children	Was low, now lower	Has been working a variety of contract and part-time jobs, no longer has supplementary health benefits; social assistance says she owes $70, 000 in overpayments.
Jackie and three children	Was low, now lower	Family is larger; she is working part-time.
Ashley	Was low, now lower	Laid off, patched together income from Employment Insurance benefits, and part-time jobs, moved to small town and collected social assistance, now receiving assistance from the Employment Insurance self-employment program.
Amy and three children	Was low, now lower	Separated, went from income from husband's job and welfare top-up to social assistance, to Ontario Student Assistance Program-supported college. Province disallowed students from receiving Ontario Works. Has large student debt and no supplementary health benefits.
Anne and four children	Was low, now lower	Separated and lost part-time job as a result, began receiving social assistance, and is now working part-time.

Table 4.5. (concluded)

Household	Income level	Why were they worse off?
Veronica and two children	Was low, now lower	Separated, moved, lost part-time job, now combines social assistance and new part-time job
Jenny and four children	Was low, now lower	Social assistance rates were cut.
Teresa	Was low, now lower	Her social assistance for persons with disabilities took small cut, rent went up, Vocational Rehabilitation Services eliminated.
Sadan and five children	Was low, now lower	Social assistance rates were cut, was shifted to General Welfare Assistance because husband returned home briefly.
Kate and two children	Was low, now lower	Social assistance rates were cut, started some cash employment, cut off social assistance, partner left.
Samantha, Nathan, and two children	Was low, now lower	Both were in school and living at home with parents, now live together with children and receive social assistance.

Source: Adapted from Bezanson and McMurray (2000).

Income from Labour Market Participation

The demands of paid employment dominate household plans and decision-making. People in the study valued secure jobs with good pay and benefits such as extended health and dental care and manageable schedules. But of the 64 adults interviewed in 1999, only 16 said that they felt their employment had been secure between 1995 and 1999.[6] But most of the paid workers did not see their jobs as secure, anticipating cuts in public spending in the broader public sector, layoffs in their industry, and a forced change to part-time, a contract job, or reliance on temporary help placement.

Table 4.6 shows participants' employment status in 1997 and in 1999. While 25 per cent more individuals were working for wages in 1999–2000 than in 1997, almost 35 per cent were working in non-standard jobs or multiple jobs. Almost half of all participants changed jobs between 1997 and 1999.

Only 6 of the 19 adults (31.5 per cent) employed full time in 1997 were women, and 8 of 24 adults (33 per cent) employed full time in

Table 4.6. Participant Employment Status

Employment Status	Number of individuals 1997	Number of individuals 1999[a]
Full time [b]	19	24
Part-time [c]	11	9
Self Employed		
Part-time	0	2
Full-time	5	4
Retired	2	5[d]
Multiple jobs [e]	2	6
Not in labour market	23	14
Total	62	64[e]

a. Richard acquired a housemate, Henry, in 1999 who was employed in part-time work. Frazer, the father of Josie's youngest grandchild, moved in with the extended family in 1999 and worked full time.
b. The category 'full-time workers' included workers who were seasonal and who had self-employed income in addition to full-time work.
c. Part-time workers often combined income with Employment Insurance benefits and social assistance.
d. Of five retired workers, two were working part-time to supplement their incomes. In 1997, neither was working for pay.
e. Reasons for not being in the labour market included: long-term illness, full-time school attendance, Employment Insurance receipt, maternity leave, and seeking paid work

1999 were women. In 1999 in Canada, 41 per cent of women aged 15 to 64 had a non-standard employment arrangement (part-time, temporary, self-employed without paid help, or multiple jobs) compared to 29 per cent of men (Statistics Canada 2000a:103). The study found similar patterns: 32 per cent of women and 20 per cent of men in the study had non-standard employment arrangements in 1999. Consistent with national trends, most non-standard work for women participants was in part-time employment, while men were equally represented in part-time and self-employed work arrangements.

For some people, full-time jobs were insecure or short-term. Full-time workers were increasingly subject to seasonal layoffs or cuts in overtime. Leo, a worker in the manufacturing sector, had his hours cut to four days a week. He was also laid off for four months every year.

He could claim Employment Insurance benefits each time he was laid off but he was penalized for repeated use of the program. He had been on several job retraining programs, but none turned into sustained work for him. As a result, his household income had dropped steadily since 1995.

Those who worked in the broader public sector (education, social services, and health care) were deeply affected by changes in provincial spending and planning as layoffs and privatization undermined previously secure jobs. Melanie, an ESL teacher, took a large pay cut in the mid–1990s when school board budgets were reduced. She was later laid off for part of the year, which decreased her income even further. Her work intensified as many of her colleagues left, and she was forced to pick up their work and manage the effects of fewer resources for students. The same story of the effects of spending cuts is told by Josie about jobs in the health care sector: wages were cut and the quality of work deteriorated, while patients received less care. Front-line social service workers like Elizabeth, Frank, Carl, and Ray confronted increased workloads and fewer resources as a result of the cuts both to social service budgets and to social programs used by clients. Sabrina went from being a full-time social service worker to being laid off in the first round of cuts in the mid–1990s and then patching together two and sometimes three part-time jobs.

Job changes affected many households between 1995 and 1999. Of 57 household members who worked for pay during this period, almost half (26) changed jobs two or more times and 12 changed jobs once over this period. For a few, the job changes were positive, while for most, the changes were negative or uncertain, especially after more than one job change. Nineteen people stayed in the same jobs. Most of these worked full time with medium incomes: five characterized staying in the same job as positive, eight said it was negative, three thought their jobs were the same, and three were uncertain. Job changes reflect voluntary and involuntary forces, such as downsizing or leaving work for school. They also underline discontinuity and often insecurity, even when total income remains relatively constant.

Multiple jobs were another feature of the labour market in the 1990s. National data suggests that 6 per cent of women and 4 per cent of men were likely to have more than one job in 1999 (Statistics Canada 2000b). In this study, all multiple job-holders were women. Aida, for example, fled political persecution in her home country in the early 1980s and came to Canada as a refugee. A mother of three, she worked in the social service sector with various cultural/linguistic groups. Her hours were never full time, and were cut consistently every year following the 1995 restructuring, while her hourly wage remained constant. Despite the loss of hours and wages, her workload was unchanged. She supplemented her income by working several hours a week for a local board of education, until those hours were also cut.

Self-employment, which was actively supported by the Conservative government, provided little security for most. Two women ran home day-care businesses that generated modest income; one ran a growing home-cleaning business; and one was trying, through a self-employment grant funded by the Employment Insurance program, to get a small business off the ground. Most self-employed men were contractors. Gary, Randy, and Xavier worked in various areas of construction, which tended to be seasonal. James, who was homeless when we first met in 1997, was trying to make and sell crafts for a living. None of these workers had job security and all were vulnerable to illness or seasonality. Temporary employment proved equally precarious for many participants. Denzel and Denise both worked in the temporary help industry, and, while their earnings were relatively reliable, this did not lead to secure employment. Both spun from one short-term, low-paying contract to another, with few protections.

Conservative government labour market policies had a direct effect on the kinds of jobs and job opportunities available. In the years immediately following the 1995 election, the Conservatives decreased labour standards, eroded workplace protections through changes to the Workers' Compensation Act, eliminated employment equity, reduced unionization rights, and curtailed pay equity measures (see Chapter 3). The Employment Standards Act was revised and the minimum wage was frozen.[7] The government also reduced key training initiatives, such as the Ontario Training and Adjustment Board. Most notably, it introduced massive reforms to the province's social assistance program and linked it closely to insecure, part-time, or temporary employment.

Reductions in provincial spending also affected those working in the public, broader public, or not-for-profit sectors, who suffered job losses or reductions in hours and income. Budget cuts in areas such as social housing, health, education, the arts, municipalities, legal aid, the environment, transportation, and social assistance led to reductions both in service and personnel. These sectors often provided women workers with relatively good, well-paid, often unionized positions with security and mobility. The erosion of such jobs not only reduced women's opportunities in the labour force but undermined the efforts of those trying to access a diminishing social service system.

Income from the labour market, then, became insecure for many households. As a coping strategy, household members looked to other income sources, a process that demands considerable work. Yet due to changes in government spending, access to other sources of income became increasingly unstable and unpredictable. One of the effects of such increasing insecurity is that employees became more vulnerable. For example, Anne, a single mother of four boys with high health care needs, noted that she jumped every time the phone rang at her new part-time retail job because she feared it was a call to pick up a sick child or come to the hospital. She felt that she would lose her job if she had to leave work for one of her children's illnesses.

Income from Government

The most significant sources of government income for participants of this study came from three programs: Employment Insurance (EI), social assistance, and the Canada Child Tax Benefit (CTB). After 1995, both EI and social assistance became more restrictive, more difficult to access, and, generally, provided lower-income transfers. For women with children, in particular, many of whom had low incomes, government resources significantly offset severe poverty. According to Statistics Canada (1999, cat. no. 75–202), for the 20 per cent of families with the lowest incomes, government transfers contributed over half (54.3 per cent) of all income received in 1998.

The impact of government transfers grew after 1989, despite cutbacks federally and provincially, in part because of an increase in the number of people over 65 years of age receiving transfers. After-tax income increased in 1998 for most family types, except elderly families. This was in part due to changes in federal and provincial taxation rates, which resulted in the top two income quintiles experiencing significant gains in average income. As a result of these changes in transfers and taxes, the disparity in after-tax income increased during the 1990s (Statistics Canada 1999). For households in the bottom quintile, there was an average 5.2 per cent drop in after-tax income.

Employment Insurance[8]

In 1996, the federal government replaced the former Unemployment Insurance Act and the National Training Act with the Employment

Insurance Act, which provides for two types of benefits: income and employment benefits. The first, income benefits, pays temporary income support for claimants while they look for work. Employment benefits include a package of measures such as wage subsidies, self-employment assistance, job creation partnerships, and skills loans/ grants (Torjman 2000; HRDC 1998; 2000; Bezanson and McMurray 2000). Overall, eligibility, benefit levels, and duration of benefits were decreased and the numbers of people eligible to claim EI benefits declined sharply in the 1990s.[9] In addition, in 1997, the federal Liberal government added a repeat user clause in its administration of Employment Insurance benefits, rescinded in 2000.

At least one member of 13 households (32 per cent) had received Employment Insurance benefits sometime during the last 10 years: four received EI before the policy changes in 1996, nine after.[10] Four of 13 received EI for maternity leave. The changes to EI policies regarding eligibility and benefits not only affected those who claimed after 1996, but shut out many workers who were laid off and required EI assistance.

The policy changes at both the federal and provincial levels created a group of workers who could be barred from accessing any level of government assistance. If an individual did not qualify for EI from the federal government, new provincial criteria regarding assets and income levels could bar potential claimants from getting social assistance.

To illustrate, Ashley was receiving EI at the time of the last interview, in 1999. In 1998, she had returned to the rural community where she had bought a small, run-down house many years before. She was part of the self-employment program that permitted her to earn income from her small business while receiving EI and start-up supports. Ashley received social assistance for several months while waiting for her EI benefits to begin. Despite extensive experience with community-based organizations and several contract administrative positions, she was not confident that her entrepreneurial venture would succeed. She saw the EI program as a short-term solution. She said, 'Every day I think about when the EI runs out, and what have I got to put in place of that?' The danger for Ashley was that if her self-employed business failed, she would not be eligible for EI.

Leo's experience with EI reveals the trends affecting workers with seemingly standard employment relationships. Leo lived in the Greater Toronto Area with his wife, Maria, a retired teacher. He had worked in the manufacturing sector for most of his adult life. In 1989, his annual earnings were almost $35,000. In 1990, he began to be laid off and recalled, on a more or less systematic basis, and, by 1998, his annual wages from his manufacturing job were only $15,000. During layoff periods, Leo claimed Employment Insurance benefits, which in 1998 added about $4,000 to his annual income. He also retrained for work in other fields; however, his new skills led only to short-term, low-wage jobs.[11] 'I would like a stable, full-time job like I used to have,' he said. 'I trained with EI in computers ... and I came back to textile work after I got laid off from a computer job.' The repeat user clause meant for Leo that 1 per cent of his Employment Insurance pay was cut each year.

For others, like Michelle (who worked on short-term contracts as a receptionist) and Jessie and Mark (who lived in a northern Ontario community with high levels of unemployment), EI served as an effective short-term income support when they were laid off or between jobs.

Data on the effects of changes to the EI system suggest that women's ability to access the EI program was reduced as a result of the program's restructuring (see Porter 2003). Because women tended to be concentrated in part-time jobs, predominantly in the service sector, many could not meet the number of ensured hours needed to qualify for the program.

This is true of several women in the study. Veronica, Sabrina, Aida, and Heather explored EI as an option when faced with unemployment and underemployment in the 1990s; none qualified the first time they applied. Though part-time workers paid into the program, under the reformed EI system many could not qualify for benefits. Veronica worked part-time as a school bus driver 10 months of the year. An advantage of her job was that she was able bring her disabled son with her on the bus. In 1998, she applied for EI for the summer. She was denied due to a lack of ensured hours. In 1999, she reapplied. At the time of the last interview, she was not sure whether she would receive EI. She said, 'It's hazy. You're supposed to have 907 or so hours, and I think I had somewhere in the neighbourhood of 890 ... It was really, really close, so they may give it to me this year.' The reforms to EI saw access to the program decrease at the very time when labour market attachments were tenuous or volatile for many people.

Social Assistance[12]

As detailed in Chapter 3, the Ontario government introduced two new social assistance programs in 1997 – Ontario Works and Disability Support – which replaced the previous General Welfare, Family Benefits and Vocational Rehabilitation Services. The restructuring of social assistance not only reduced transfers and supports, but signalled a revamping of the state's role in labour market regulation and social reproduction and a lowering of its standards on acceptable levels of income inequality. The realignment of social assistance affected many aspects of participants' lives. Those working in social services saw both layoffs and reductions in the kinds of services they could provide; those receiving Ontario Works (social assistance recipients not eligible for the Ontario Disability Support Program) saw an intensified focus on labour market participation, even for women with very young children, along with decreased support and increased regulation.

ONTARIO WORKS

The number of participants who had claimed Employment Insurance benefits in the 10 years prior to this study was substantial; the number of participants who had some relationship with social assistance over the same period was even more striking. While public perception often views social assistance as serving a small and marginal segment of the population, the experiences of participants suggested that many people access these programs, some for very short periods or as a 'top-up' to other sources of income. What is interesting is that many of the participants who were on social assistance for short periods now have middle incomes, and a great many are women.

A full 57 per cent of adults in the study (68 people) collected social assistance benefits *at some point* in the 10 years prior to this study. Of these, 17 started and stopped collecting benefits before cuts and changes to social assistance programs in 1995. Twelve adults stopped collecting benefits after the cuts. Eleven adults were receiving benefits at the end of the interview process in 2000 (see Appendix G for details).

Over 90 per cent of participants who stopped collecting social assistance before 1995 had received full benefits. What is significant about this group is that up until the cuts and changes in social assistance, the program allowed recipients to enrol in university and college. Those

Table 4.7. Ontario Social Assistance Allowance Calculations

Number of persons in household	Rates of social assistance benefits (reflects 21.6% cut in 1995)
1 single person	$520
Couple (the legislation recognizes same sex couples)	$901
Couple plus one child under 13	$1,020 ($100 for each additional child 0–12 for basic needs, small increase in shelter allowance)
Single parent plus one child under 13	$957

Source: Ontario Works Regulations, 1997 (with amendments); calculations of allowances for shelter and basic needs.

able to complete post-secondary degrees while receiving social assistance had later managed to acquire jobs that gave them incomes in the middle-income range. In fact, nine of the 11 participants had middle-level incomes by 1999. For women with children, in particular, access to university/college training was a significant factor in lifting their household out of poverty.

Among those households that received social assistance after the cuts and changes came into effect, most collected a mix of full benefits, top-ups (which adds to a low wage earned in the labour market), medical benefits, and child-care subsidies. Of the six who left for paid work, five found their paid work very insecure. Seven of the 11 households who received some benefits from social assistance after 1995 were headed by single parents – five single mothers and one single father.

Cuts to social assistance made it difficult for many participants to survive on income derived only from this source. (Table 4.7 illustrates the meagreness of income amounts for Ontario Works after the 1995 cuts.) Among those who stopped receiving benefits following the changes, six of 11 had low incomes, and five had middle incomes. The option that allowed social assistance recipients to pursue college and university training was eliminated. The push into a low-wage labour market meant that the move from social assistance to paid work did not increase overall household income substantially.

Among those who continued to receive social assistance through the cuts and changes were four single mothers, two participants with physical/health disabilities, and James, a man who had been homeless or incarcerated through most of the interviews. With the exception of

James, none had post-secondary training. Three of the four single mothers left abusive relationships and were raising large families on their own.

These data are consistent with data gathered by the Ministry of Community and Social Services in a survey of individuals who left social assistance (1998).[13] The survey indicated that 23 per cent left social assistance for work reasons; of that 23 per cent, 28 per cent were employed on a temporary or casual basis, while 23 per cent were employed part-time. The ministry data shows that the average weekly earnings among those who left social assistance for a paid job was $325. In 4 per cent of the cases, living arrangements changed, usually the result of a reconciliation with a spouse. While it is difficult to obtain data that details whether or not women returned to abusive partners, the cuts in provincial funding to shelters, second stage housing, and violence-specific services suggest that reconciliation was often financially motivated. Another 4 per cent entered educational programs (usually by accessing a student loan), while 3 per cent were found ineligible (Ministry of Community and Social Services Ontario 1998).

The changes to social assistance affected more than monthly income. Both eligibility and access to benefits (such as drug and dental care, child care, supplements for pregnant mothers, and discretionary items such as funeral expenses) were restricted by the changes. The strong employment emphasis of the new legislation also included penalties for non-participation in the training/employment streams: a recipient could be cut off social assistance for three to six months for failure to meet requirements. A number of participants received a 'top-up' to a low wage earned in the labour market or the medical benefits portion of social assistance if, after leaving social assistance, their income was insufficient to cover medical costs and they had no other coverage. But the provincial government's focus on determining social assistance 'overpayments' – dating back 10 years in the case of one participant – meant that leaving social assistance did not free people from the administrative arm of the program. Most people found their income from social assistance to be insufficient, increasingly insecure, punitive, and linked to the quickest route to employment.

ONTARIO DISABILITY SUPPORT[14]
The Ontario Disability Support Act (ODSP) (1997) was met with mixed reactions by activists in the disability community while Ontario Works

was harshly condemned by Anti-Poverty Groups (Ontarians with Disabilities Act Committee 1998; OSSN 2000). The introduction of separate legislation governing disability was welcomed because the categories under which people with disabilities were covered under the Family Benefits Act were not specific to those with disabilities. However, those who moved from the Family Benefits program to ODSP found it challenging to navigate the new system, especially if they had multiple disabilities. Moreover, the ODSP legislation fell short of providing the support needed to assist those with long-term disabilities to move into employment or training, and was subject to the same kinds of administrative scrutiny and eligibility restrictions found in Ontario Works.

Only two participants (Richard and Teresa) received ODSP (although others had received Family Benefits support under the previous legislation). These two relied on a variety of supports (income and in-kind), many from the health care sector. Richard was in his fifties and had advanced AIDS. He received part of his income from ODSP and part of it from the Canada Pension Disability program. He also relied on supports such as the drug plan and transportation subsidy. While he initially supported the shift from Family Benefits to ODSP, by 1999, he had become increasingly frustrated with the program, especially with the high turnover in administrators. When he did not receive his transportation tickets, which he needed to get to medical appointments, he ran up against administrative barriers. He said, 'It's [ODSP] gotten much worse, much, much worse. Basically you don't have a case worker any more, you've got a team of people. I found the best thing to do was go [to them]. Now they just give you any old worker. And they don't know you and they don't know your case unless they look it up on the computer. It makes me feel insecure and it makes me feel that everybody knows my business now.' Richard found the new requirements for continued eligibility demeaning, because he knew that his condition was permanent. As he explained: 'I have to go every six months and fill a form out still, and take it around to different doctors and have the form done and submit it, like I'm going to get better. Within six months I'm going to be fine and cured and everything, according to ODSP.'

Although the benefits were higher with ODSP than with Ontario Works, both participants who received ODSP said it was not enough to cover their expenses. Once their rent was paid, neither had enough money to buy supplements and food. Both regularly used food banks.

Following the 1995 restructuring, then, most people's income from social assistance not only decreased, failing to cover costs, but it became increasingly insecure.

Canada Child Tax Benefit[15]

The Canada Child Tax Benefit (CTB) is a federal policy (introduced in 1993) that had a significant impact on many Ontario residents. Geared to low- and middle-income families/households, the CTB is the one program in which transfers increased between 1997 and 2000 (Battle 2001). The CTB became an almost universal, non-intrusive income transfer. The CTB is usually sent to a female adult household member, and is sometimes the only money a woman receives 'in her own name' (McKeen 2004). The structure of the CTB is rather complex: it is two-tiered, targeting the highest level of benefits to the lowest income earners.

The base benefits to the CTB increased in the late 1990s, and in the 2000 federal budget, the benefit program was indexed to inflation, guaranteeing a constant income transfer to low- and middle-income households. A stumbling block, however, was that the National Child Benefit Supplement (NCBS), which is part of the CTB, was administered in part through provincial child benefit programs, and those receiving social assistance saw the difference 'clawed back' from their incomes.

Provincial governments were directed to reinvest savings resulting from federal transfers to low-income households to other programs and services for low-income families/households with children. Ontario put these funds into the Ontario Child Care Supplement for Working Families, which was directed at working poor and modest-income families/households with children under seven. In Ontario, municipalities administered the NCBS reinvestment, and costs were shared between the province and the municipality. Municipalities had some discretion over how they spent their portion of the NCBS. Social assistance recipients were not eligible for this program (Battle and Mendelson 2001; Government of Ontario 2001).

For most middle- and low-income participants with children who were not receiving social assistance, transfers from the CTB/NCBS made a significant difference in household income. Twenty of the 23 households with children under 18 received various amounts in transfers from the CTB/NCBS. Of the 20, six received social assistance, seven were low-income households, and the remaining seven were middle-income households. For households with low incomes, young children, and labour market attachments like Antonio's, the CTB/NCBS was the money used for the children's winter clothing, school-related activities, transportation, and birthday/Christmas gifts. For households receiving social assistance, however, the increase in the rate of CTB/NCBS, which was clawed back by the province, was mainly an administrative hassle, which made predicting monthly household incomes difficult.

Anne and Jenny were both single mothers receiving social assistance. Jenny explained: 'I'm just waiting to get my daughter's baby bonus. I'll have this one nice chunk [of money], but I know welfare's going to deduct it so it'll just be an overpayment from all my cheques. I had to even phone my worker and say, "Look, you have a guideline you go by, you know how much I'm going to receive. Can you please start deducting that from my cheque now?" And she said we can't do that until you receive your money which means they're going to just do it all in one lump so it's going to be like $50 off each cheque for so many months.'

Anne's experience was similar: 'They just deduct whatever that bonus was, they just took it right off us. It went up again $15 per child and they deducted that too. It's just paperwork for them. Like why bother giving it to us, you're just taking it anyway, it's going from this hand to this hand and you guys got to do all the paperwork.' Although social assistance recipients had difficulties with the administration of the CTB/NCBS and had no access to the program into which the moneys were reinvested, the program made a significant difference in offsetting low incomes in working households.

Income from Other Sources

Participants also had access to income from a variety of other sources. Two households received money from a provincial program called Aid to Children with Severe Disabilities, along with some health-directed money called the Assistive Devices Program, which paid for some travel to and from medical appointments, medical equipment, and child care. Amounts for this program depended on a child's health care needs. One household received the Old Age Supplement along with the Canada Pension. Two households received some income from Workers' Compensation.

Another area of government transfers, which affected households with taxable incomes, were income tax cuts. Beginning in 1995, the provincial government cut its share of income taxes to 38.5 per cent of the federal tax. In its 2000 budget, the federal government raised taxable income thresholds, increased personal credits, and reduced the middle tax rate from 26 to 23 per cent over three years. Both the federal and provincial governments re-indexed their income tax systems (Bezanson and McMurray 2000:27). However, for most low-income households, provincial cuts in income taxes did not made a significant difference in their overall household income. Many participants were unsure whether they had benefited from income tax cuts or not, because changes in other aspects of their lives (such as job changes, pay changes, changes in CPP and EI contributions, increases in property taxes) obscured the impact (27). Sara and Anand, a high-income professional couple who live in Toronto, explained the impact of tax cuts on their household: 'We're seeing more [money from tax cuts] now, but on the other hand, our property tax went up by a couple of thousand [dollars] ... We could move to the States and cut our tax load quite a bit and probably double our incomes, but we've lived in the States and we choose to live here because of what governments provide: basic services and a social safety net.'

Child support payments were another source of income for many women. Nine women not receiving social assistance received child support, and one woman on social assistance received child support (which was deducted from her monthly social assistance payment). In most of these cases, getting regular and adequate child support payments was a struggle, often involving mediators or agents from the newly created Family Responsibility Office. Child support payments were often irregular or paid late, making it hard to plan budgets. Moreover, the Conservative government's policies emphasized that the state had little or no role to play in provisioning for families with children. It emphasized that *biological* fathers, and thus hetero-patriarchal family forms, were the only legitimate sources of financial support for children. The government's definition of support was narrow, and included only a financial transaction and not the building or sustaining of affective relations or parental involvement.

Informal financial support from family or friends was a final source of income for some household participants. In two cases, Richard (who has advanced AIDS) and Julie (a woman with a physical disability), family financial assistance was relatively constant. In both cases, however, participants felt that their relationships were affected by their inability to offer reciprocity (see Chapter 6 for more discussion of this point).

Putting It All Together

For many household participants, income from all sources became more precarious as the provincial government moved towards a more liberalized economy and a more restrictive welfare state. Many participants had to combine income sources to make ends meet, and juggling the demands and eligibility restrictions of multiple programs made it hard to plan even small budgets. Many women in participant households remained far below the poverty line, despite increases in programs such as the Canada Child Tax Benefit. The erosion of the supports – such as education, training, and health care – that can assist households in moving out of poverty means that low-income spells are lasting longer among participant households. Interpreting how participant households combine income sources and assessing their relative security is made more complex by the fact that resources are not pooled equally in all households. For some household members, this means a denial of access to opportunities and options, and thus a decline in their human capital formation. For many women, the quickest route out of poverty remains a relationship with a man who has wages. For policy-makers, these experiences signal that a reliance on labour market measures as a single solution to poverty entirely miss the mark; social policy must provide transfers and supports that address constraints and care needs across the life course.

Insecurity in access to the means of subsistence affects and is affected by the ways in which the work of social reproduction done in families is able to absorb the shocks of changes in income or adjustments in social spending. The next chapter considers the ways in which changes in social policies in Ontario affect the work of social reproduction in households – which always acts in tandem with the work to secure living standards – in order to illustrate how households are managing in the 'new' Ontario.

5 Interactive Effects of Social Policy Change on Households

To build a good society, to build a good country, and to make life better, everybody has to share in certain things. As a citizen you have the right to certain protections and assistance from all of society. If you're desperately down on your luck and you lose your job, you're entitled to unemployment insurance and if worse comes to worse, you're entitled to welfare. Now we are called customers. You're called a customer now when you go for social services. Citizens have rights. Customers are there to be manipulated. They're there to be cajoled. You don't respect a customer. You pretend to. You sort of nod and say, `Oh yes, yes, yes, you're always right,' but you have no respect for that person because you want them to buy what you're selling. And then they're gone and it's on to the next. A citizen is someone with rights and responsibilities and is a participant. Well, we all have to realize that some day it'll be our turn in a hospital bed. Some day it'll be our turn with children in kindergarten. Some day, in the next horrific recession, it might be our turn to be 'down on our luck.'

– Sabrina, a participant in the study

As participants tried to manage their incomes in an increasingly insecure labour market and social transfer environment, they had to contend with the erosion of the complementary supports of the welfare state. This chapter explores the new demands placed on household participants by investigating the interactions between insecure incomes, new or rising costs, and decreased access to social services. It shows that the need for social services, when cut, eliminated, or simply not provided, does not disappear but its provision is often shifted onto the work of women in households, who may or may not have the time and energy to cope with all the work. The extent to which households can take up these tasks depends on their income, their ability to navigate complex social service structures, and their own social support networks.

This chapter demonstrates some of what happens to the work of social reproduction as welfare states restructure along neo-liberal lines. What work is shifted and to where? How do social policies interact with one another? Who is called upon to pick up the slack? In each major policy area, the processes of familialization, privatization, decentralization, commodification, and, to varying extents, criminalization are evident.

The speed and scope of policy changes were dizzying in the second half of the 1990s, and household experiences reflected these circumstances. Participants in households identified five interconnected social policy areas – health care, education and child care, social assistance, housing, and transportation – where changes had a significant impact on their lives. In each of the policy areas, social service redesign and social spending reductions meant an increase in unpaid work and/or a re-prioritizing of household finances to meet new expenses. However, participants did not experience the policy changes as discrete categories: the joint effect of the interacting policy changes meant participants were constantly scrambling to adjust to substantial new time and money demands in response to the reconfigurations.

Health Care

Restructuring Access and Costs

Health care is the policy area in which changes to spending visibly shifted the costs of care either to the family/household or to the private sector. Private sector involvement in health care was supported by a provincial discourse about a lack of federal transfers to provinces for the funding of health care as well as a philosophy of private sector management.[1] Ontario did not follow a wholesale privatization program in the field of health care; rather, it shifted public costs towards the private sector by contracting out various services, courting private financing, and re-familializing care work.[2] The privatization of health care, then, can be understood in a dual sense: the private sector in the marketplace took up some of the costs associated with the delivery of health services while the private sector of the home, and specifically women's work within it, took up the slack for reduced spending and supports for the ill or infirm.

The primary ways that members of households experienced this dual process of privatization was through increased unpaid work, higher hospital expenses, greater costs for out-of-hospital care (such as home care and drugs), increased waiting periods associated with medical testing, and reduced quality for in-hospital services, such as food services, which were contracted out. Participants also noted that they were frequently asked to make financial donations to hospitals.

The restructuring of health care in the province between 1995 and 2000 involved cuts to hospital budgets, the closure of some hospitals, fewer nurses, longer waiting lists for specialist care, restructuring of community-based-care budgets,[3] under-regulated nursing home facilities, unregulated retirement homes, the delisting of services covered by the Ontario Health Insurance Plan, and an increased population with little or no access to drug, dental, or vision insurance. These changes meant that the task of providing care and support to an ill person increasingly became an individual or family/household task.[4]

Providing care involves not only the actual work of feeding, changing, bathing, or spending time with the ill person, but requires navigating and advocating for the ill person through an often under-resourced health care system. From getting on a waiting list for long-term care to getting a referral to a specialist, skill at navigating the health care system is an important factor in getting access to better care. Access to care is not an equal opportunity game: those with experience working in the social service field, those with a good doctor who will advocate on their behalf, or those with confidence fare far better.

Because it was almost exclusively women who managed their own, their children's, and sometimes their spouse's and their parents' health care needs, it was generally women who advocated and navigated the health care system. They took children to appointments, often missing work and/or pay as a result. Women also were responsible for administering medications, and, increasingly, using technical machinery at home to do so. For example, Anne, a participant mother of four, noted that she had to keep track of 13 different medications, along with administering asthma medication through a machine. In addition to managing her kids' health care needs at home, she had to spend the night in hospital with them if one was sick because there were insufficient staffing levels to adequately care for a child overnight.[5]

Moving care out of hospitals has financial consequences for patients, as well as for caregiving. The Canada Health Act covers costs and services performed and delivered in hospital settings; there are no similar provisions for care delivered outside a hospital setting. For example, drugs are covered while a patient is in hospital; when at home, drugs must be paid for by the individual. In many cases, people do not have drug plans and the cost of prescriptions can be high.

Of 124 participants, including children, 32 (26 per cent) had no private health insurance coverage. In some cases, one member of a household had medical coverage benefits that did not extend to other members. Forty-one per cent had some form of medical coverage through employment, 4 per cent had coverage from multiple sources, and 5 per cent had coverage associated with First Nations status (Bezanson and Noce 1999:28). Another 24 per cent had some coverage through the Ontario Drug Program (usually associated with social assistance or Old Age Pensions), but it was limited. Some low-income households without coverage did not take the prescribed dosages of their prescriptions in order to save on drug costs, others shared medication, while others did not fill prescriptions at all. For participants receiving social assistance, the two-dollar co-payment for prescription drugs introduced in 1995 was prohibitive, especially if the household had high health care needs. For example, Anne often resorted to writing post-dated cheques for two dollars to cover the costs of her children's medication.

The Elderly

The aging of Ontario's population put an added strain on already stretched health care resources. It increased 'kinscription' (Stack and Burton 1993), that is, demands on adult children, particularly daughters, to provide care, in this case for older persons. In many cases, new or increased demands on women to care for elderly parents came at the same time as they were managing and caring for their own children. The stories of Cheryl, Paul, and Victoria (detailed below) graphically illustrate the struggles of adult children to access and provide care for their elderly parents while managing their own families, careers, and health care needs.

CHERYL AND PAUL[6]
Cheryl and Paul had a higher-middle income and both were university educated. Paul held a senior teaching and administrative position at a high school. They lived in a medium-sized south-western Ontario city

with their two sons, Michael and Jason, in a home that they owned. In early 1997, Cheryl described their household as 'a pretty close-knit, happy, traditional family.' Cheryl stayed at home when her children were young. As the children got older, she periodically took short-term contracts in a number of fields, and at the time of the last interview, she was considering returning to school. The children, by then both teen-agers, attended a local high school.

Although the changes to education were a central worry for Cheryl and Paul throughout the four rounds of interviews, the health of their parents took precedence over most other concerns. When we first met, Cheryl and Paul's parents, who lived nearby, were relatively healthy and self-sufficient. In 1998, Cheryl's mother was hospitalized and then sent home. She received some home care support. Then Paul's father had a stroke and was diagnosed with Alzheimer's disease. Both Cheryl and Paul were shocked by the deterioration of the health care system, and the difficulties in getting quality care. Paul recounts his father's experience at a hospital in the Greater Toronto Area:

> My dad had a stroke, and he went to the hospital. He was there in emer-gency for five hours before they saw him. When finally somebody did see him, she said he had better stay overnight. There was no bed for him, so he spent the night in emergency. I went to see him, I guess it would have been about 18 hours after he had been at the hospital, and he was still in emergency. They finally got a bed for him up in the maternity ward and that's where he ended up staying for a couple of days.

Paul's parents decided to move closer to Paul's siblings in another part of the province. Paul was upset that they were so far away, but Cheryl felt relieved, saying that she could not have handled their care. Her own mother's health had rapidly deteriorated, while her father also needed support.

Cheryl's mother was in hospital for several months, waiting for a bed in a nursing home. Cheryl had to fight to get her mother into care, and then to get her rehabilitation services and better-quality care. Cheryl said:

> I can't tell if I'm being fair or not. She's my mother. But I go there and she's not dressed properly and they've lost her clothes ... I'm trying to be reasonable, but sometimes I just don't know what to think. I went to visit her one night, and she had to go to the bathroom, and they just put her to

bed. I said, 'It's seven o'clock at night, and I'm visiting. I know it's conve-
nient for you to put her to bed now, because she's been to the bathroom,
but couldn't you wait?' And they say to me that she likes to go to bed
now, and I think, oh yeah, I just bet. This is what your mother wants, they
say. And then I went there at four o'clock, and she had to go to the bathroom, so they put her to bed. I said, 'Well, you know, she only had her
dinner at ten to four, it seems a little early to me. I understand that she's
tired at night, but what the hell is going on here lady? What are you talking about, putting her to bed; this is the summer and it's four o'clock. This
is supposed to be such a great place? They did a real PR job on me, saying,
'I know it's upsetting for you.' Well, you know, the reason it's upsetting
for me is how she is being treated.

Until her mother's death in 1999, Cheryl visited her mother almost
every day and also provided some care for her father, having dinner
with him and visiting several times a week. Her father was distraught
when he learned that Cheryl was considering taking part-time work.
He worried that she would not be available to care for him or his wife.

Paul noted that since the health care services did not provide adequate care for the elderly and/or sick, the assumption was that a family member would be able to provide the needed care: 'Everyone is so
dispersed. We all have two jobs. It is not like an extended family the
way that it might have been a hundred years ago with everyone living
in the same village, looking after each other. That does not happen
now.' Cheryl described her stress and fatigue levels as extremely high.
'Last week I told Paul that I'd had enough,' she explained. 'I said I
just can't take care of you, my mother and my father, the cat, and the
kids.'

Cheryl's story illustrated a problem common to many in Ontario.
Even for those who were relatively well off, services were hard to get
and the care levels simply were not adequate in nursing homes and
homes for the aged. In response to the growing waiting lists for long-
term residential care, provincial money was targeted to increase the
availability of places in nursing homes and homes for the aged. However, decreased standards of care, the closing of hospitals and hospital
beds, and the pay rates and working conditions for employees meant
that the funding was inadequate to deal with the needs of elderly
Ontarians and those with special needs.

Cheryl and Paul had the resources to purchase care services for
Cheryl's mother, and Cheryl had time to devote to caregiving. They

also had the knowledge and confidence to challenge the health care system and demand services. Despite these advantages, insufficient funding for areas such as home care, long-term care, and emergency hospital care meant that adequate care could not be counted on. And for Cheryl, as for many women, the burden of caring fell disproportionately on her shoulders.

After her mother's death, Cheryl contended not only with her personal loss, but also encountered barriers to re-entering the labour market. While she had experience and training in social work and home care, she had been out of the full-time workforce for a number of years as she cared for her parents and raised her children. Paul's experience as a public sector employee was so demanding that she feared working conditions in those sectors would be unbearable. She took a part-time job at a retail store and considered returning to university, but did not want to start at the bottom in a new position in the labour market. Cheryl's mother had left her some money when she died, so she was able to take potential working conditions and experiences into account as she attempted to re-establish a relationship with the full-time labour market.

Cheryl and Paul's story reveals the pressures placed on people, particularly women, caring for aging and infirm parents while navigating an increasingly insecure health care system. There was little respite for Cheryl from the day-to-day demands in her own household as she took on more and more responsibility for her parents. She was forced to be active, persistent, and assertive to ensure her mother would get the care she required. Even when her mother was in the nursing home, the ratio of staff to residents was low, meaning that Cheryl had to supplement the care they provided just to ensure her mother's basic needs were met.

The line between providing care based on love and care based on the inadequacy of public services is blurry: there is no clear demarcation of where love ends and professional care begins. Cheryl, Paul, and Cheryl's parents' class location and education significantly contributed to their ability to obtain a higher level of care for Cheryl's mother. Nonetheless, the assumption is that there is someone able to take over the managing of care for the elderly or the sick, and more often than not this responsibility is picked up by women.

VICTORIA

The experiences of Victoria, who was managing the care of a frail elderly parent as well as her own chronic health care needs, also demonstrates the importance of access to some financial resources and knowledge of the health care system. Victoria was a 49-year-old divorced mother of two daughters living in eastern Ontario. Her eldest daughter lived with her biological father in another Ontario city, while her youngest daughter, Erin, had grown up with Victoria. Victoria held a graduate degree, and worked as a full-time professional social worker in an urban hospital. She had a stable income, owned her house and car, made regular RRSP contributions, and had sufficient spending money.

In 1996, Victoria lost her job as a direct result of shifts in provincial health care policies, hospital funding cutbacks, and hospital restructuring. At the same time, Victoria, her youngest daughter, and her parents all experienced significant and ongoing health problems. From the time of her first interview in 1997, Victoria was balancing the demands of her job (especially patient care), increased job insecurity, her own chronic health condition, her daughter's precarious health problems, and the demands of her aging parents. Compounding the stresses in Victoria's personal life were her concerns about the impact of provincial government policy changes on education, social assistance, and municipal affairs. As a frontline employee in the health and social work fields, Victoria witnessed the direct and often negative impacts of social program cutbacks on her clients. All of these elements affected Victoria's ability to cope on a daily basis. She said, 'Sometimes when I come home from visiting my mom, I get teary-eyed because I just think that she has to be okay. I can't juggle one more thing. Who is taking care of me? There is nobody taking care of me. I don't know how I do it. I just do it because I have no choice.'

In 1996, the Ontario government imposed a 6 per cent cut on hospitals across the province. Each hospital had to independently determine how to absorb the decrease. The hospital where Victoria worked decided to close her specialized unit because of high operational costs and a lack of external research funding. When Victoria's job was terminated, she felt powerless: 'The people on the front lines are not a part of the decision-making process. Decisions are presented as a fait accompli.' At the time of the layoffs there was no union in place and despite 10 years' seniority at the hospital, Victoria had no job security. In time, Victoria managed to find a new job at the same hospital, but her professional community was fractured and she lost contact with many of her colleagues.

Not long after Victoria had secured her new position, the Ontario government appointed the Health Services Restructuring Commission, whose mandate included responsibility for hospital closures. Less than a year after finding a new job, Victoria was again at risk.

In the late 1990s, a union local was formed at her hospital, increasing her sense of job security and giving her access to extended medical and dental coverage. In the same year, after an almost decade long battle, Victoria and a number of her colleagues successfully negotiated a pay equity settlement with the hospital. The compromise settlement provided her with a lump sum payment and an hourly raise of $1.75. Although she had more confidence and felt a greater sense of security because of the job protection offered by her union, the health restructuring process was a significant threat.

Throughout the period of Victoria's job instability her own health was poor. In 1997 and 1998, she underwent what she described as 'significant health crises' which required hospitalization and blood transfusions. Victoria's recovery was slow and her health status remained tenuous at the time of her last interview. Her newly acquired health insurance was vital to her financial stability. In 1998, for example, she spent $8,000 on prescription drugs.

Victoria also applied for and received a provincial Assistive Devices Program (ADP) grant for medical supplies. While she retained the grant throughout our study, she found it increasingly difficult to qualify for support under the program when the provincial government introduced new regulatory frameworks and narrowed eligibility requirements. The only doctor with the specialized knowledge required to appropriately treat Victoria's serious stomach condition was located in the Greater Toronto Area. Thus, during her recovery, Victoria had to make frequent trips to the city from eastern Ontario. She was unable to drive the long distance alone. She did not have a support network of family and friends upon whom she could rely and there was no provincial mechanism in place to assist her with transportation. This caused Victoria great stress and anxiety. She said,

'I was really frightened. I had to get to [the GTA] 10 days after I was released from the hospital. I thought, 'Well, how am I going to get there?' At first when I was at the hospital in [eastern Ontario] they talked about transferring me by ambulance, but once you leave the hospital you aren't their responsibility. They just get rid of you. The ambulance would have given me a bit more assurance, but I thought, 'Well, I'll have to go on the bus.' I was worried that I might have to do the [maintenance medical] procedure on the bus, and start to bleed. I had a lot of anxiety, but I did it. I just didn't eat anything before I left, and hoped for the best.

Compounding Victoria's ability to cope with her health status and the insecurity of her job was the failing health of her parents. They received home care services from May 1997 to November 1997. As noted in Chapter 3, the provision of home care in Ontario changed substantially after 1995. Without the formal protection of the Canada Health Act, the availability of, access to, and quality of home care varied considerably across the province. Those who could afford it were forced to buy home care services from the private sector. In 1997, Victoria described home care as 'marvellous.' By 1998, however, as the province restructured home care, the situation was very different. Her father's health deteriorated and her mother was no longer able to manage, even with home care support. Victoria described the problem of her mother caring for her father and the inadequacy of home care coverage:

> The home care case manager said, 'Yes, I'm hearing loud and clear from the treatment team that he needs more services, and we just cut your hours by 33 per cent because of budget cuts. We know it's terrible and so you should go to the private sector and pay.' So we did that, and we had 24-hour nursing care for him because about a week after the care conference, he got shingles, he couldn't feed himself, and he became incontinent, bowel and bladder both. We needed something. My mother – this little old lady with her diabetes who is exhausted – had been up for 26 hours because my father was calling out. A hospital-in-a-home is a great concept, but it doesn't work. My mother had been doing laundry, because my father wouldn't wear a diaper. They had gone through all the sheets, all the towels, all the long underwear, everything that they could use. The nurse was doing the care, supposedly freeing up my mother to be resting. That's a great concept. But my mom was doing all the laundry. Finally, we all agreed that this wasn't working, so the nurse came with us to the hospital and told them that my father was no longer a home care case. He was hospitalized, and we waited for a bed in a facility. He never went home again.

Victoria's parents were able to afford private home care services and user fees. Her father incurred a daily fee in the hospital for two months while waiting for a bed at a home care facility. Victoria said,

Anyone who is not receiving active treatment, someone who is waiting for some kind of residential placement, is what the hospital titles an 'alternate level of care.' My father was in acute care for 10 days. He had dementia, couldn't walk, feed himself, was incontinent. Then he improved in those areas, so he was no longer acute. Then he got his nursing home papers and he was just waiting for an available bed. While he was waiting to get into a facility, the hospital charged us $42.16 a day, which is the portion of the cost not covered by OHIP [Ontario Health Insurance Plan]. From my experience working in a hospital, I know that it's a way for the hospital to recoup costs, and it puts pressure on families to accept the first available bed at any facility. My dad was in the hospital for two months waiting for a bed, so it was really expensive. Luckily, they had saved, and my mom was able to pay those costs.

When Victoria was asked to describe how her father's situation would be different if the family had not had the necessary financial resources, she said, 'Oh gosh, well I know exactly what it would be like for him because I work with people at the hospital in that situation every day. He would end up in a facility at a ward rate, which is peanuts. My mother would not end up at a nursing home, but a regular home supported by supplementary aid, or special care through the municipal government. It's not adequate either. She would get a living allowance of $112 a month. That's what happens to people who have no money, and can't self-manage.'

After more than 30 years of marriage, Victoria's parents were separated from each other. This was a difficult situation for them, and for Victoria. The compounding stress associated with her insecure job, unstable health, and elderly parents began to take its toll. One day in 1998, Victoria sat in the hospital emergency waiting room with her mother from 7 PM until 1 AM. Her mother had the flu and was dehydrated. Victoria found herself getting frustrated and angry at her mother. She said, 'I had to tell myself to calm down. My mother is 87 years old, she is frightened, and I can't be that testy. But, I notice it in my work as well. I am usually a person with infinite patience, but I'm not that person anymore. So, I guess that's the difference. I'm not patient anymore. I get angry now. I guess I'm not coping.'

Over the three years of interviews, Victoria had to navigate increased job insecurity, her unstable health, and the significant needs of her elderly parents and her daughter. In each case, changes to provincial government policies in health care, home care, long-term care, and hospital funding significantly affected her quality of life. Although she was financially stable throughout this period and did not require outside financial assistance, she was nevertheless anxious about her professional and personal future.

For Victoria, as for Cheryl, the work of managing the care of elder parents fell largely on her shoulders. The level of home care service was not adequate for her parents' needs, and the fall-back position, both because of her field of work and her gender, was for Victoria to take on more of her parents' care. Victoria was uniquely positioned among participants of this study to speak to the many sides of health care restructuring and its consequences for households in Ontario. Her experience of budget cuts, decreases in staffing levels, attacks on social programs assisting those with acute illnesses, and her struggle to find good and consistent care for herself and her family demonstrate that on all sides, workers and patients bore the costs of public spending that didn't keep up with increased costs and population changes.

One of the determining factors in the adequacy of care levels received by both Victoria's and Cheryl's parents was an ability to pay for additional hospital services and for home care. This option is not available to low-income households. In Victoria's case, as in Cheryl's, the inadequacy of public services was shifted onto the work of women in households. In both cases, the work required to make up for these shortfalls harmed their relationships with the person receiving care, affected their abilities to manage their own paid and unpaid work lives, and stretched their coping capacities to the maximum.

Home Care

The attempt to shift care out of hospital-based services into community-based services has an obvious benefit: many people would prefer to recuperate in their own homes. However, the community-based care needed to absorb such a shift was not supported by the provincial government. The shift away from hospital-based care resulted in individuals – often women – taking up the slack for this reorganization.

The intensification of unpaid work by women in relation to health care is paralleled by the intensification and erosion of the paid work of women done in this sector. For nurses and home care workers (who are predominantly women), changes to funding and organization resulted in overwork, part-time, or on-call work. It also meant an intensification of tasks and an erosion of resources and time.

For example, Josie worked as a nursing assistant in a long-term care facility. As the number of staff per patient decreased, the amount of work expected of her increased. She and her colleagues bore the brunt of family members' anger over the decreased level of care, while at the same time, nurses and nursing assistants simply did not have the time that they needed to care for patients. She explained:

> Quite often, I'll have 25 residents to care for. I put them to bed far too fast. Quite often, I can't give them a bath. If they argue and say that they don't want a bath tonight, I used to be able to sit there, chat with them, and talk them into having a bath. Now, I don't have the time to do that. You don't want your bath? That's too bad. Bye. I have to go on to somebody else. That's what it boils down to. Residents fall and break their hips because we don't have time to go and check on them, to find them. We found a resident the other night on the floor. She had no injury, but her knees were already bruised by the time we found her. She said she had been there on her knees for about four hours.

Keeping home care was often as hard as getting it in the first place. As Victoria's experience with her father demonstrates, maintaining the level of care required is challenging. Frank and Michael, a gay couple in Toronto, faced similar challenges. They fought to maintain home care services when Frank was released from hospital after major surgery. Both said that the assumption was that if someone in the home could provide care, there was justification to reduce publicly funded home care as the services were desperately needed by others. Limiting eligibility for services is one strategy for keeping costs low, but health suffers and the cost is transferred to caregivers. Caregivers, in most cases, do not have the skills or training to administer drugs or monitor progress, adding an additional level of stress to already strained personal relationships.

Jenny and Liz's stories are examples of individuals who slipped through the cracks of health care policies which assume the presence of a caregiver in the home. Jenny was a single mother living in southeastern Ontario. She had outpatient surgery for varicose veins in her legs that left her in enormous pain and discomfort. When she was discharged from hospital, she was not informed about home care services, and had no one at home who could help her on a full-time basis. The hospital's assumption was that there would be someone to care for her while she recuperated, and no provision was made to ensure that she could manage on her own. For the first two days, her legs were numb or tingling. She could not walk and therefore could not get to the washroom. She had three children to care for. Jenny finally asked a friend to help her for a few days. When she developed an infection as a result of surgery, she became concerned that it was because she had not dressed her own bandages properly. She had enormous difficulty arranging child care in order to have her legs checked, and when she returned to the hospital, was told that she could have had some home care. The person with whom she spoke wondered why no one had arranged it for her.

In another case, Liz was released from hospital from a day procedure. She was embarrassed when the hospital asked whether there would be someone to help her once she was discharged, because she had no one. They released her anyway. She was still feeling the effects of the anaesthetic, and could not afford a taxi. She almost fainted on the streetcar on the way home.

Effects of Health Care Changes

The government justified its restructuring of the health care sector by arguing that it was increasing efficiency, eliminating unnecessary costs, and reducing fraud. However, the restructuring depended on providing patients with less care, imposing on them either the costs of paying for services (which were increasingly delisted from coverage), or the challenges of mobilizing their personal networks of family and friends to provide voluntary care. These dynamics privilege those with money who can purchase additional services or support and those with the knowledge and skills to advocate for better and quicker services. Thus, class emerges as a central determinant in who will have access to quality care. Gender is also critical: women make up approximately 80 per cent of users of health care and workers in the system, and women are also typically the people who provide unpaid caregiving in the home (Armstrong and Armstrong 2004).

Education and Child Care

The shifting of costs in the education and child-care sectors among the state-market-family/household were less obvious than they were in the health care sector, yet the result was a similar increase in time and resource demand on households. Household experiences reveal that new costs emerged in these sectors as well, and the demands placed on households, and, in particular, on women, were significant. It is important to note that because education, training, and child care are intertwined with labour market and social assistance policies, policies related to education and child care affected participants' ability to take up opportunities or increase their skill levels vis-à-vis the labour market.

Almost all participants had some relationship with the formal education sector. Of the 124 people participating in 1998, 57 per cent had a connection to education. Of the 66 adults, four were employed as teachers in primary, secondary, or post-secondary schools; two were employed in other related capacities (as a school bus driver and a crossing guard); eight were pursuing post-secondary education or training; and 26 had children enrolled in a public, secondary, or post-secondary school. Of the 58 children 18 years of age and under, 27 were in primary school, 16 were in high school. The rest were too young for formal public education, and their parents relied on a host of arrangements to provide child care for them.

Primary, secondary, and post-secondary education were radically reorganized beginning in 1995. As with health care, an overriding concern of the people interviewed was about quality and accessibility. Participants who were employed in the education sector spoke about the intensification of their work as well as cuts in supports. Paul, a high school teacher, Melanie, an ESL teacher, Frank and Michael, college instructors, and Anand, a post-secondary instructor, all noted that their workloads had increased while their job morale had decreased as a result of funding changes.

Primary and Secondary Education

Participants with children in primary or secondary school highlighted a number of problems related to changes in education, including new school board structures, new or increased costs, and increased demands on their time. Parents (and the children who were old enough to participate in interviews) noted that supports for students with special needs – in particular those related to health care – were declining, forcing them to struggle for services on two fronts, both of which were being restructured.

The Fewer School Boards Act (1997) and the Education Quality Improvement Act (1997) ostensibly increased parental involvement in schools, making school councils a requirement at each institution. Simultaneously, the government curtailed the power of school boards, cut the pay rates of elected school trustees, and merged school boards to cover huge geographical areas. The government presented the restructuring as a way for parents to be more involved in their children's education.

Many participants, especially those with non-standard labour market relationships, noted that they wanted to be more involved but lacked the time to attend parent council meetings. Others noted that the councils mainly addressed fundraising issues and had little or no decision-making ability and no impact on policy. For example, Ray, who lived in northern Ontario, saw the parent councils as organizing vehicles for school fund-raising activities. In effect, the introduction of mandatory school councils, under the guise of giving parents more control in education, resulted in the paid work of trustees being transferred to the unpaid work of unelected people with the time and resources to serve on school councils (O'Connell and Valentine 1998; Dehli 1998). Dehli (1998) found that parent activists and council members were likely to be women who were not in the labour force.

As funding for education in Ontario decreased and was redirected, parents with children in the public education system were alarmed at the number of costs associated with their children's schooling. Participant parents estimated that they spent between $100 and $160 per child per year in extra costs for items such as materials, trips, outdoor education courses, agendas, student cards, locks, and photocopying charges. For low-income households, these costs were difficult to meet and caused anxiety when parents could not afford to have their children participate. Jenny, a single mother receiving social assistance, noted, 'They have popcorn orders for 25 cents a day and they have to bring it in the week before. While 25 cents isn't a whole lot of money, when you have zero, zero zero, it's just another thing! There's pizza day, hot dog day, popcorn day, book day, and they miss out on all of them and they don't understand.'

Parents were also involved in fundraising for basic school needs, such as textbooks. Many mentioned that schools located in wealthier areas were more able to underwrite some of the education costs for students, further entrenching inequalities between schools.

Participant parents noted that cuts to classroom funding, the implementation of standardized testing, and reduced preparation time for teachers resulted in a 'one-size-fits-all' model for education that was far less accommodating for children with special needs. A 1998 provincial survey done by People for Education showed that in the 642 elementary schools surveyed, 2,377 students were waiting to be tested and identified for special education.

Anne's experience as a single mother of four children with special needs illustrates the personal costs of the education restructuring. Anne worked part-time for pay and also received social assistance because her children's problems were so serious. In addition to severe asthma, three of her children had been or were in the process of being diagnosed with attention deficit disorder (ADD). One child had a bowel disorder, which interfered with his ability both to socialize with other children and to learn at school. Anne described the struggles she had with her seven-year-old son's school to get help to identify his learning disability, related to his attention deficit disorder. She watched as he fell behind while waiting months for tests to identify his learning disability. He ran away from school several times: 'I went through three weeks where Liam was leaving the school. It'd take me two hours to find him. He was taking off on his bike. He was terrified to go to school.' She was anguished about how to comfort her son, and railed against the school's inadequate ways of helping him: 'I was crying in the school. I looked awful. I was just like, "I'm done with this. You guys are making my son sit there in class, he's bawling his eyes out. I'm not allowed to go in there and get him."'

Liam paid a terrible price because he began to hate school and became increasingly unable to do the work.

> His reading is at an early Grade 1 level. This is Grade 2 that he's in right now. So he's behind a year in reading. Now they said that his math was above average for his age. Like he's very smart in math but it's going to go right down because now they're getting into problem solving where they have to read. And he can't read at all so he's going to start failing there now too.

Anne realized that Liam would only get the help he needed if she persevered:

> I've gone to that school about 10 times since September. They already know that he's a year behind in his reading. They've done some testing. That's why I thought, okay they're going to identify him. They're going to get these other resource teachers involved, which should have been done from day one. But I went in there on Friday and they said, no, we're going

to wait until December when the first report card comes out, see how bad he's flunking then, and then we'll let you know. I guess in some ways the school and the resources are there, but in some ways they're not. Like you have to kind of really push them, yourself as a parent ... I don't want him to fall behind. I would rather him get the help as soon as you see him slipping. And then of course they say, well there's only so many resource teachers and they're so many students, and da, da, da, da. And my child's just one of however many, and I understand that too.

Jackie also had to struggle to get the education system to deal with her daughter Kerry's health needs. Kerry had a degenerative bone condition that kept her from participating in gym classes and made walking to school and climbing stairs difficult. But Kerry was not considered 'disabled enough' to benefit from municipal or provincial government services and Jackie was not able to claim any exemption on her income tax for the high costs generated by Kerry's condition. Jackie could not get school bus service for Kerry because in response to provincial cuts to education, school boards were pushed to cut back on bussing and the local board claimed she lived close enough to walk. There were no in-between services for special needs. As a result, Jackie had to organize her day so that she could drop off and pick up Kerry. Jackie commented: 'The thing that is upsetting about having a kid with a special need is that the onus is always on the parent to prove that the child is disabled. It is such a disbelieving system. I think that because of cutbacks, the school board wants to justify every student, because they are always cutting back bussing. We're not asking for a bus because we think it's fun. Kerry needs it.'

Early Childhood Education and Care

The story in early childhood education and care over the late 1990s is one of a failure to fund, expand, and regulate the sector. Policy directions increasingly individualized costs for child care, and the province downloaded the administration of those available subsidies to municipalities. Child care for children under five years of age and education remain distinct in Canada. Against a growing body of global research on the importance of preschool education, Canada has in general relied on the market to provide *child minding* rather than early learning (OECD 2004). Centre-based child care is expensive: in 1998, *average* monthly costs for full-time child care in a licensed facility ranged from

$541 for preschoolers to $783 for infants (Childcare Resource and Research Unit 2001). While child care has never been well funded in Ontario, total spending by the provincial government declined 7.1 per cent between 1995 and 1999 (Childcare Resource and Research Unit 2001). The direction in child care in Ontario has been towards de-institutionalization, focusing on the provision of private child care in homes, which is under-regulated (Childcare Resource and Research Unit 2001).[7] With the reorganization of primary and secondary education, many schools that formerly provided on-site licensed child care lost their spaces.

Despite federal-level efforts to expand centre-based early learning and child care, the Conservatives actively moved away from licensed child care and pushed this work into the informal sector, encouraging more women to provide unregulated care in their homes and failing to direct provincial resources to child-care services. They drew on an atavistic discourse of cohesive and safe communities, summarized dramatically by then minister of women's issues Diane Cunningham: '[Ontarians] are perfectly happy to leave their kids with a neighbour ... a friend ... or a relative while they go off to work' (*Toronto Star* 1995). Michelle, a single mother of two young children, reacted in anger to this assertion: 'Harris says we should all get up and we should dump our kids on our next-door neighbours that don't have any formal qualifications. I don't want to do this. I don't know my neighbours. I'm a mother. My kids can't jump to my next-door neighbour. My next-door neighbours have friends drop in. They could rape my daughter. They could molest my son.'

In the mid-1990s in Canada, 20 per cent of all children in Canada aged six months to five years were in a centre-based daycare facility, 44 per cent were looked after in someone else's home by a non-relative, and 8 per cent were looked after in their own home by a relative. Fourteen per cent of children were looked after in their own home by a non-relative, and the same percentage were cared for by a relative in someone else's home (Statistics Canada 2005). For the participants in this study, as for Canadians generally, the organization of child-care provision was not uniform and depended on waiting lists, costs, and, often, access to subsidies.

Sara and Anand, a high-income professional couple, had hired a nanny to care for their children when they were preschool aged. When their children began school, Anand's mother moved into their neighbourhood and provided child care. The other parents in this study did not have these sorts of in-kind supports, nor were they able to hire full-time in-home child-care assistance. Many, like Veronica, performed juggling acts to make up for a lack of services. Her strategy for meeting her children's child-care requirements was to rely on friends when absolutely necessary and to bring her disabled son to work with her on her school bus route.

The absence of formal daycare spaces, the costs associated with them, and the waiting lists for subsidies meant that lower-income households struggled to obtain and maintain child-care arrangements. Natalia and Antonio, for example, both worked in the service sector. Their children were 12 and eight. They had no money for after-school care, so the children were either left alone or had to come to their place of employment. Antonio said, 'When the kids come home from school, they watch television. It is ruining their minds but it is the only babysitter we have ... it is really negative. The ideal would be for them to participate in some activities, but I don't have the money to cover this.'

Even centre-based care was not secure if parents received subsidies. Michelle, a contract worker who managed to access a small subsidy for centre-based day care, risked losing it if she was not working full time. The eligibility conditions of subsidy meant that continuity and stability for her children was dependent on her maintaining a steady job, which proved exceedingly difficult in a context of downsizing and restructuring. Likewise, Samantha, a teenage mother finishing high school, was able to get a subsidy while she was in school, but worried about losing the daycare position and reverting to the waiting list over the summer. For many of the people interviewed, the cost of licensed care without subsidy was unaffordable. Yet for those with small children, access to child care is essential in order to attain and maintain a job or an education.

Jerry, a single father who lived in an apartment in his parents' home, faced an ongoing struggle in securing quality and affordable child care. In order to get and maintain child care with a subsidy, he faced a legal struggle with the provincial government (subsidies were downloaded to municipalities in 1998). Jerry began a college program in January 1997, after having separated from his wife in December of 1996. He found a non-subsidized child-care space for his then-infant daughter at the college. He initially borrowed money from his family and used credit cards to make ends meet while he attended school. He applied for a child-care subsidy, but was denied on two grounds. First, his Ontario student loan was counted as income, despite the fact that this is a government-sponsored loan that must be repaid. Second, he and his wife had not formally separated, and, because she was not working due to mental health problems, the province argued that she should be providing care. After hiring a lawyer, he managed to get a partial subsidy and a partial repayment of his child-care costs. When he began working full time, the eligibility determination process resumed and he fought to maintain some subsidy. In the end, his parents paid a large portion of his daughter's child-care costs.

For those (mainly women) who work in child care, wages are extremely low, especially for women who provide care in their homes. Monica began a home daycare business as a way to combine the care of her own children and income generation, but her annual income never exceeded $8,000. Christine, a home child-care provider in a rural area in Ontario, spent three years in a pay equity court case against the Harris government following its legislation barring non-profit child-care workers from collecting pay equity. She finally gave up her case because the government appealed a decision in her favour, and she had run out of resources to pay legal fees. In 1999, following a court challenge, the government was forced to reverse its position and retroactively pay child-care workers (Childcare Resource and Research Unit 2001).

Child care is deeply intertwined with labour market, social assistance, and education policies. Ontario in the mid to late 1990s did not have an active early childhood education and care strategy. Households in this study spoke about it in relation to their own paid work needs, in terms of quality, and in terms of cost. Neo-liberal policies rest on the assumption that individual parents, which in practice are usually women, will care for their children and absorb the economic and social costs themselves. But as this study shows, there are real limits to what parents can absorb. Without either high incomes or social supports, individuals cannot manage both paid work and child care.

Post-secondary and Adult Education

At the level of post-secondary education, cuts in transfers to universities and colleges translated into higher tuition fees. The Ontario Student Loan Program (OSAP) was restructured to reduce eligibility, impose greater burdens on borrowers, and increase repayment schedules. The new costs and debt loads reduced the accessibility of post-

Table 5.1 Changes to the Ontario Student Assistance Program (OSAP), 1997 and 1998

- Students must report earnings over $600 per year (from $1,700 per year)
- Student and spouse's assets over $5,000 count in assessing financial need
- Students must take a 60 per cent full-time course load to qualify for assistance, limiting the ability of part-time students to receive financial support; students must pass 60 per cent of their courses to remain eligible for OSAP
- Eligibility criteria is restricted and a series of measures established to limit students who default on loans
- Parents are expected to contribute to the cost of their children's education before a student is eligible for a loan
- Students must pay a $10 fee to process OSAP applications

Source: Adapted from O'Connor and Valentine (1998).

secondary education for many, and increased demands on parents to find money to provide educational opportunities for their children.

Adults returning to college or university or attempting to complete high school requirements through adult education found that funding cuts made many programs inaccessible. Social assistance recipients had to forgo social assistance and take out student loans in order to attend college or university. In many cases the combined effect of changes to social assistance legislation and reduced supports for upgrading and education caused people to abandon plans to pursue further education.

For example, Jenny was a single parent with three young children who received Ontario Works, the new form of social assistance (which, among other things, placed single mothers in the same category as single employable men, and subjected most to mandatory labour market training and participation). In 1997, Jenny went back to school for adult upgrading. She faced enormous difficulties trying to coordinate placing her youngest child in day care (there were extensive waiting lists), managing transportation to and from school and the day care, and meeting the new costs and demands of both her children's and her own education.

I went back to school in the fall. You have to almost be psychic to know when you're going to be going to school and when you're going to need the day care. You've got to go on these lists, hopefully the two coincide with each other. I had to put my youngest on a waiting list and my second youngest too, because his kindergarten is on alternate days. I enrolled at the adult school. It was really hard to get things set up to get into school because I'm on a fixed income and I had to come up with a deposit for the day care, and my book deposit, and my first payment for day care. And I've got to scrape that out of what I have. So I eventually went to school in October. The biggest problem was getting from here to the day care. There isn't any assistance available for transportation, nothing.

Jenny also struggled to get appropriate care and supervision in school for her daughter, who had attention deficit disorder. The province-wide teachers' work stoppage in 1997 made these complications unmanageable, and Jenny withdrew from school.

Adult education programs, including English as a Second Language (ESL) programs, are predominantly utilized by women, people with disabilities, and immigrants. A 1996 survey by the Ontario Secondary School Teacher's Federation found that 63 per cent of adult students were female, 16 per cent had disabilities, and 53 per cent needed additional assistance with English as a second language. Almost half (48 per cent) received social assistance (Ontario Secondary School Teachers' Federation 1998). Funding for adult education was cut following the provincial restructuring; however, many potential adult education students in Ontario did not have the money to pay full tuition fees at colleges and universities.

Teresa was a disabled woman receiving Ontario's Disability Support benefits while attending college. The provincial government stopped funding college education for people with disabilities in 1998, forcing those receiving social assistance to take out student loans (O'Connell and Valentine 1998:19). Teresa's health was fragile and she was in and out of hospital; she did not believe that she could manage a full-time position when she finished her college program, making it impossible for her to repay a student loan. She withdrew from the program as a result.

Effects of Changes in Education

Participant parents were increasingly called upon to make up for funding reductions and institutional restructuring by augmenting their time commitments in their children's schools and spending more for basic supplies and services. They also had to navigate their way through a restructured education system to get services for children who do not fit into the standardized education model. For parents who had low incomes, demanding jobs, or children with special needs, meeting these expectations was strenuous. The restructuring intensified the unpaid work that parents, women in particular, were already contributing to the school system. In some cases, new costs or time demands could not be met, so children were not able to fully participate in school activities, thereby excluding them from a range of opportunities in the future. In early childhood education and care, high costs, few subsidies and supports, and little regulation constrained participants' labour market and education options. Parents patched together a host of babysitting arrangements, and few children had access to high-quality, programmed care or learning.

In post-secondary and adult education, increased costs associated with tuition and student loans, along with cuts in programs themselves, made education inaccessible for many students. In addition, restrictions on those receiving social assistance and waiting lists for programs such as child care and transportation subsidies made enrolling in the programs more challenging. The downloading of post-secondary educational costs onto people with disabilities themselves increased already steep barriers to educational and job advancement.

Social Assistance

Regulatory and legislative changes to social assistance, deep cuts to associated programs, funding levels and staffing, and changes to management procedures all combined to make it extremely difficult to get access to, let alone survive on, social assistance. These changes also made the jobs of social workers in those program areas more difficult because they were less able to meet the needs of their clients.

Participants who had received social assistance since 1995 experienced problems in several key areas. The introduction of a detailed and bureaucratic eligibility screening procedure called the Consolidated Verification System increased the paperwork and the range of personal information required in order to receive and maintain benefits. Social workers were available during very limited hours and staff turnover was high. Cuts were made to numerous supports, including dental care and the supplement for pregnant women, as well as to allowable assets. These changes increased recipients' struggles to maintain their standards of living. The workfare component of social assistance directed participants into training sessions that were ineffective or led them into very low-paying jobs. In addition, the anti-social-assistance political climate in Ontario deeply affected those receiving benefits.

Some participants identified with racist discourses, claiming that immigrants were defrauding social assistance and thus were creating a culture of suspicion for all those in receipt of benefits. Others were upset by the province's proposal to implement mandatory drug testing for recipients.

New regulations gravely affected family relations. For example, the reinstatement of the 'spouse in the house' rule (that a woman living with a man is assumed to be financially supported by him) drove Kate's family apart, and resulted in a fraud charge against her.

Kate and Carl had been living together with their children, and Kate was receiving social assistance. During most of the study, Carl was working part-time at low pay, while Kate worked sporadically at tele-marketing jobs. They hid their relationship from social assistance after the rates were cut because they were having a hard time getting by. They had to instruct their kids not to talk about their father, for fear that they would be found out. Kate agreed to let her eldest daughter, who had numerous medical needs, live with her biological father because she could not afford to take care of her. Kate assumed that social assistance discovered their relationship when Carl filed his taxes. She explained: 'The special investigation worker ... took me for an interview and they were questioning me. He looked like a cop and I was so scared. [They asked me] if I was the only one living in my house, how much I pay for rent, if I ever had a job within the time, if Carl was paying his child support, which he wasn't because he was living with us. It was degrading. I got in contact with a lawyer, and the lawyer said to just admit everything because I could get charged for serious fraud.'

Kate was shocked by the range of information they wanted about her: 'They wanted to have all the bills. They wanted to have all the rent receipts. They wanted to have my income tax. They wanted to have everything ... ID, bank books ... We thought that we were going to have cops come in here, searching for stuff. We went through everything. We were ... getting rid of all the letters he's ever written to me, all the pictures of us together. We sat here and cried.' The next week, Kate was informed that she was cut off social assistance, and that she owed them $1,200. 'It could have been more, with the fraud charge,' Kate said. 'So I'm grateful for the $1,200.' As a result of this stress, and her brother's death around the same time, Kate attempted suicide. She and Carl later separated. At the time of the last interview, Carl was paying some child support and Kate was trying to find work.

Jenny's experiences with changes to social assistance were less dramatic than Kate's, but revealed the level of scrutiny and distrust that recipients faced. Jenny said that her strategy for dealing with social assistance workers – when she could reach them – was to explain her story over and over again, keep a log of their names, the date, and the content of the conversation, and 'pretend you're dumb so they'll be more cooperative.' She said that she too had many social assistance workers because the turnover rate was high. She said that complaining or appealing led nowhere: 'You can only get hold of your worker for one hour a day, and half the time they don't want to hear it. If you have a complaint [they say] "You'll have to speak with my supervisor." They give you the supervisor's number, and she doesn't return your calls. So basically there's nothing you can do other than go down there and wait for six hours to speak to somebody that'll tell you, sorry there's nothing we can do. It's an attitude like, "You're welfare bums. We don't want to talk to you, we don't want to deal with you," so they make themselves unavailable.'

Jenny contrasts the difficulties of reaching a worker with the expectation that she always be available to them if they want to talk to her: 'Sometimes you really have to speak to a worker; it's an emergency. They're very rude ... you're treated like nothing. But then there are times when if your worker needs to get a hold of you, you're expected to sit by the phone for five hours. [They say], "It could be any time between this time and this time that I could call you." Just because I'm on welfare doesn't mean that I don't have a life. I should be sitting by the phone, waiting for you to call me, where if I try to call you, you don't get to me for two weeks?'

The level of paperwork required of recipients is staggering. When Jenny was pregnant, she was asked to fill out all of the forms for participation in the workfare component of Ontario Works, despite the fact that she would be unable to participate. When Family Benefits was replaced by Ontario Works, Jenny, like Anne, was told she had to come to the social assistance office to resubmit forms. 'I remember that specifically because I had to take all three children with me [as I could not get child care]. It's all information that they already had,' Jenny said.

Antonio and his family received social assistance when they arrived in Canada as refugees. When their rent was raised, but their social assistance rate remained the same, the family was forced to move into a tiny, vermin-infested apartment. Antonio found work in the retail sector, but his training was in community social work. Based on his personal experience and the experiences of his former clients, he viewed the 'new' social assistance as deeply punishing. He said, 'You need to have such courage in a system that treats you so badly. If you're there, it's because you really need it. There's no other alternative. What has changed [since 1995] is that people who continue receiving welfare are treated worse than ever. That's the difference in welfare. The people who are on it are treated as if they weren't human beings who deserve respect and consideration. The changes to welfare [especially workfare] are about cheaper labour, cheaper jobs.'

Angie had received social assistance in the 1990s. She saw the changes in legislation and regulation as an attempt to kick people off welfare, but she argued that welfare was essential to help some people get ahead. She argued that the government needed to give people more support, and time to adjust to the changes: 'You can't decide all of a sudden that someone has to be off assistance, and just expect them to be able to get out there. You have to put programs into place to help ease them into that. And child care is a really big issue, as well. I was on assistance. I decided to upgrade my skills, take this one-year program, go back to school. My ex-husband wasn't working. We needed to have income to pay the rent, all of that stuff. That's why I went on. Then there are people that have nowhere else to go. Like, perhaps they were working, they lost their jobs, EI ran out. Jobs aren't that easy to get.'

Angie pointed to the particular difficulties that women face when re-entering the labour market after caring full time for kids: 'I stayed at home with my children [for six years]. And to go out and get a job after six years of not being employed, you can't just do that; you have to upgrade your skills. So I think that there should be some training out there. I think that they should also offer counselling for the people, to help them to make decisions, and to look at what they're doing ... just to talk through that whole process of upgrading your skills or getting a job or dealing with the stresses of going back to work. [People] are just getting further and further into financial debt, and into emotional debt as well.'

Single men like Patrick and Denzel – who were employed in very low-wage jobs – said that the experience of receiving social assistance after the cuts and changes was arduous, both financially and emotionally. Patrick wanted to participate in the new Ontario Works training and placement programs. On several occasions, he requested training in his area of skill and expertise, but was instead instructed to attend a compulsory training session that was unhelpful. Although Patrick did find a part-time job in late 1998, he was disappointed that Ontario Works had not helped him find a better job: 'It [the training program] follows a very traditional, old-fashioned type of work model. That needs to be addressed, because getting people off welfare with Ontario Works and into jobs at the 7-Eleven is not long-term work. That doesn't sustain people.'

Denzel – who lived in a rooming house on $520 a month with few supports in 1997 – affirmed the need for a strong supportive social assistance program: 'Welfare is there so you don't fall flat on your ass, and the worst part is I don't think it's protecting people from that now. People are still falling flat on their ass. I know lots of poor people – outright, disgusting, nasty poverty. I always feel that I'm that close to being there. I remember living on $520 a month, and that was very difficult. Welfare is a safety net. I hope to God I never have to fall in that net again. People help out when they feel like it, at Christmas or Thanksgiving, but poverty is a 24-hour-a-day, seven-days-a-week, 365-days-a-year operation.'

Many social assistance recipients who participated in the study wanted help getting jobs, but they experienced workfare as punitive and unhelpful. Sadan begged her social worker to give her training so that she could find a job. The social worker told her that she should volunteer to meet the requirements of workfare. 'But I already volunteer!' she said. Rosa went through all the training programs offered by Ontario Works, but ultimately found a job without the assistance of the program.

The extent to which welfare recipients are policed was illustrated by Sabrina, who, several years after discontinuing her social assistance, said, 'I'm probably going to be a totally functioning, healthy person, but I feel that there is a scar there from having gone through that [social assistance] experience. And it is always looming now. I have yet to have a really good, secure job ... As soon as you say welfare I can visualize that welfare office and just never having enough money, never having enough to pay for food or for meds, let alone the finer things in life. I still ... have that fear every time I [deposit] a cheque at the bank. I'm thinking, "How am I going to justify that?" Then I think, "Oh no, I'm not on welfare anymore; no one is looking at my bank books."'

Sabrina found work in the social services field with clients who had serious medical needs. She pointed out that the changes in welfare and disability legislation were shifting the costs of caring for people – physically, emotionally, and financially – onto families: 'People I work with … I just don't know how they go on. There is so much pressure on families to provide such a high amount of support because the government is backing out. When families do get money or assistance, it amounts to grovelling. They are [emotionally] taxed to the hilt, and people are asking them to give more. They can't.'

Patrick, Kate, Teresa, and Anne were acutely aware of the perceptions of social assistance recipients being fostered in the province. Patrick explained that his sense of self was seriously undermined by others' views of social assistance recipients: 'There is a stigma attached. When you are on it you don't tell too many friends, because they'll be throwing comments and opinions about being a "welfare bum." [They think that the] welfare bum is the lazy sod that really doesn't want to work. [They think] that if any job is available, they should go out there and work. [They say] why should my tax dollars pay for this person who just lays about? Coupled with the fact that you're out of work, and your self-esteem is going to take a bit of shit-kicking, that's the last thing you want to hear.' Kate explained the effects of these preconceptions on social assistance recipients: 'After awhile you just don't have the self-esteem. You don't feel you're worth anything anymore, you don't feel that you can accomplish a job … People that have it made, they think that people who receive welfare are lowlifes, they think that they're all drug addicts, they think that people don't struggle. But if you have stress and struggle you understand, you have an understanding of why and how [it's hard].'

Teresa said that many people hate those who receive social assistance, and that the climate created by the Ontario government only intensified divisions: 'I think they hate us … I mean if they can see a person in a wheelchair that has a disability and they're okay with it, they understand and it's not a problem that they're on disability. There's not a lot of jobs out there for handicapped people, is the statement that I hear. But I don't look sick, so therefore I'm not and I should be working. But I don't look sick on the outside, it's my inside that's sick … It's not how I look, it's what is inside.'

Telling people that they are worthless is self-fulfilling, Barbara, a front-line social worker in northern Ontario, said. She saw the provincial government fostering a climate in which people have few options but to become the stereotypes that are perpetrated about them: 'Where I work, we're sitting the kids down together and we're telling them something, they believe it. They believe that they're strong and that they're powerful. They believe that they're artistic and they can create beauty if they have the tools, if they have the clay, and they have the paint. They believe it ... People believe what you tell them. If you tell them that people on welfare are pieces of crap and that they need to be stomped out, and they need to be forced to go to work, [they'll believe it].'

Housing and Transportation

Housing and transportation policies were areas subjected to consider-able redesign. The provincial government downloaded social housing to municipalities, and stopped investing in it in 1995. In 1997, it rewrote the Tenant Protection Act. Cuts in funding from federal and provincial levels of government to public transportation and trans-portation for people with disabilities meant that travelling for work, school, or to get basic necessities was made harder for some Ontarians. Because rents and access to transit vary by community size and loca-tion, there is great variation across the province in service provision.

Housing

Housing is the major expenditure for many households, and thus a determining factor in their ability to cope on small budgets. Support for affordable housing had previously helped participants manage on small incomes; the changes greatly increased their housing costs. For many households, particularly those with low incomes, housing costs escalated while incomes remained the same or dropped.

Average rents for a one-bedroom apartment in Toronto increased 16 per cent between 1993 and 1998 and 21 per cent between 1998 and 2003, for a 10-year increase of almost 41 per cent. For Ottawa and Hamilton, the 10-year change was an increase of almost 30 per cent (Canada Mortgage and Housing Corporation 2003). Many of those who owned homes faced substantial increases in property taxes as a result of the province's new property tax assessment system. For those on fixed incomes, increases or uncertainty about potential increases caused significant stress.

Patrick, a single man who worked part-time in retail, explained his experience of the deregulation of rent controls:

Table 5.2. Housing Costs and Household Income

Income status	Average monthly housing costs	Range of monthly housing costs	Average income spent on housing	Range of income spent on housing	Percentage of households who own homes
High income*	$5,000	$5,000	24%	24%	100%
Middle income	$892	$350–$1,750	22%	10%–51%	57%
Low income paying market cost	$725	$350–$1,100	52%	25%–88%	25%
Low income with housing subsidy	$325	$200–$383	26%	24%–30%	0%

Source: Adapted from Bezanson and McMurray (2000).
* I included the high-income household when comparing average income spent on housing, but not when comparing average housing costs.

There's some bachelors that are only $250 because elderly women ... live there for years and years and years so they [can't] put [rent] up as much. But with rent control off they will be allowed to put it up to market value. Within my own building where people have moved out, rent has gone up [by a lot each time someone moves] ... When I first moved in [to my bachelor] it was $430. I met a person in the laundry room [who had rented the exact same apartment as mine last year] ... They're paying now $480. So it's like, wow, the rent for that apartment [must now be] astronomical. And it's no different than mine.

Similarly, Sabrina recounted the struggles she faced in finding affordable housing at market rent for a disabled client in Toronto:

The removal of rent control and the fact that there is no social housing being built ... are huge issues for me and the people I support [in my paid work]. Like, Mike [a mentally and physically challenged client] is really stressed out because his living situation is really bad and we can't find a place for him to live. It is unreal ... Between March and now I can't believe how much the market has changed. A one-bedroom average apartment is $1,050. The guy is on [Ontario Disability Support] so it's not going to happen. Even if a landlord will give him an apartment ... his parents have to lie [and say they are not helping him in any way].

Amy's story about eight-year waiting lists for social housing revealed both the extent of the need for subsidized housing and the problems associated with relocating families within the Greater Toronto Area:

[I have had such as struggle with Subsidized Housing]. They had closed [my file] for what reason I don't know. I reopened it again, so now I'm on the file since 1991. They are [in 1999] serving people who applied in '92 and '93. But I applied in '91! Plus I have a disabled child, and it's not a lie or it's not a myth; it's not a theory, it's a fact. No, they told me that I'll hear from them. I'm calling them, and I'm not hearing from them. [So now] I'm going to go down there [to their offices], because what I really get to understand is, like, if you go down there and you swear and you carry on, they'll probably give it to you. I [have to] lower myself to disgrace ... for housing. [Now they tell me] they want to send me to [suburban] housing. I [can't move] outside the GTA! My school is downtown. My kids hospital is downtown. Everything is downtown for me. I don't drive [and my son is in a wheelchair].

Even when participants accessed social housing, there were problems with building conditions and safety. Samantha, a mother of two, lived in subsidized housing, but felt that it was substandard and unsafe. She wanted to move, but had no other housing options.

Services associated with counselling, housing, and income support for women who had left abusive partners were also scaled back. Between 1995 and 1998, first-stage emergency shelters for abused women saw their funding cut by 5 per cent, while counselling and advocacy programs in women's second-stage shelters were cut completely. Community counselling, crisis telephone services, and funding for ethno-specific services were also cut. Legal aid funding was reduced while training and education programs were cut (OAITH 1998). New monies were invested in the 1995–2000 period under the heading of domestic violence, but these funds went predominantly into the justice system and little was directed to community-based women's services or prevention projects (OAITH 1998). Funding for second-stage (secure) social housing for women and children (where they can be residents for one year) was downloaded to municipalities, along with social housing in general. Since no new money was forth-coming, housing capacities were stagnant while money for infrastruc-ture, security cameras, and support services had to be fundraised.

Cuts to social assistance, housing, and counselling supports made it more difficult for women to leave domestic violence. For three partici-pants, a lack of access to affordable housing and income insecurity led them to consider returning to abusive spouses. One permitted an abu-sive ex-spouse to return to her home, despite his having beaten her and her infant. The other two did not seek reconciliation.

Transportation

The availability of public transportation is important in accessing jobs and community services. Transportation is funded by a mix of federal, provincial, municipal, and fee-based sources. The federal government contributes a small amount to transport, equivalent nationally in 1999–2000 to 1.3 per cent of spending by local and provincial/territorial gov-ernments (Transport Canada 2000). In 1999–2000, provincial/territorial and local governments in Canada spent 4.1 per cent more ($16 billion) on transportation than they had the previous year. Ontario, however, reduced its spending by $1.2 billion, or 44 per cent, primarily as a re-sult of reduced transfers to local governments and transit authorities (Transport Canada 2000).

For those with disabilities, changes in the funding of and eligibility requirements for transportation services forced some participants either to absorb the costs of private transportation or to go without. Jackie, who lived in a medium-sized south-eastern Ontario town, was unable to get bussing to take her disabled daughter to school. She spent almost a year trying to coordinate her work and child-care schedules with picking up and dropping off her daughter at school. Teresa, living in the Greater Toronto Area, received help from Ontario Disability Support, but new eligibility requirements for accessing dis-ability-specific transportation meant that she was cut off. She was unable to climb stairs, so public transportation was not an option. As a result, Teresa's ability to leave her home decreased dramatically, and she had to pay for taxis to get to her numerous medical appointments.

Multiple and Compounding Effects of Policy Change

As the welfare state in Ontario restructured and social services moved towards increasingly minimal provision, participants juggled the mounting demands to take up costs and care work no longer provided through public funding. Participants experienced changes in several sectors at once, each making new or increased demands on them. While navigating changes in the health care sector, for example, household participants also had to find ways to respond to changes in the education or transportation sectors. As these costs – increased fees associated with education, increased unpaid time, increased health care-related work, increased costs of housing, transportation, and child care – are shifted onto households, women in particular take them up, in large measure because the gender division of labour within the home and in the workforce places the management of households and care onto them. The combination of increasingly insecure income sources and more inaccessible and ungenerous social support networks places disproportionate demands on those who are already stretched. The work of putting together a living – the work of social reproduction – is starkest when we consider the ways in which, in this context of restructuring, households manage or fail to manage their own and their members' care.

6 Coping Strategies of Low-Income Households

Despite a booming economy in the mid to late 1990s, the Ontario case study reveals that many household incomes and supports from market and state sources decreased with provincial government restructuring. This compromised the sustainability of household-based coping strategies along with household cohesion. It also undermined the capacity of women with children to form and maintain autonomous households, without having to enter into marriage or other relationships in order to survive.[1] The presumption in neo-liberal, state-level social policy is that the family/household will internalize and harmonize for its members the conflicts of income insecurity and insufficient welfare state supports. However, the family/household does not simply act as a shock absorber that stabilizes crises and manages insecurity. As this study shows, the role of the family/household (in particular, in the work of social reproduction) and its relation to markets and states is complex and conflictual, and the households' ability to stabilize with minimal support is not sustainable over the long term.

The experiences of household participants in managing complex social policy and labour market change underscore the fiction that community, friends, and family can be relied on to manage income insecurity and personal crises. The 'community' sector, largely made up of not-for-profit organizations, was the subject of considerable restructuring in the late 1990s (Shields and Evans 1998). Community can also refer to geographic location. Low-income and racialized communities tended to fare worse through restructuring, thus resources at the local level were also depleted (Noce 2004).

Close support networks of friends, sometimes referred to as fictive kin, can be enormous sources of affective and instrumental support

(Wellman 1999; Peters 1996; Finch and Mason 1993; Quershi and Walker 1989; Wellman and Hiscott 1983). They are, however, often unable or unwilling to absorb major financial or health requests (see Side 1999; Luxton 2006). In policies ranging from home care to child care and child support, the state in Ontario actively restructured and elevated relations of familial obligation in the late 1990s. Family members, who are assumed to be the first line of defence in managing crises and insecurity, are often in similar financial situations to persons in crisis or needing support. Moreover, a strong familial ideology in public policy – sometimes called kinscription (Stack and Burton 1993) or compulsory altruism (Evans 1996) – belies relations of obligation rather than relations of reciprocity. Thus, although welfare state residualism encourages reliance on immediate and extended kin and close friends, this case study shows that this often means that the most central and important relationships in people's lives are frayed or even destroyed.

As Picchio (1992:58) points out, the problems of reproduction are always more explicit in the experience of the poorest people/classes – and it is in studying them that the entire historical process of social reproduction becomes more transparent. In this chapter therefore, the lens of social reproduction is applied to the coping strategies of low-income participants, many of whom were single mothers and people with disabilities. In this study, the experiences of these low-income households reveal that the process of social reproduction involves a huge amount of labour, a complex division of labour, and enormous resources.

This chapter first considers the dynamics of gender divisions of labour and resource control within households. Second, it details the strategies participants used to cope with income and social service insecurity and to ensure the best possible standards of living for themselves and those they cared for. It is a tough look at how low-income households managed and failed to manage in a period of restructuring. Finally, it provides a detailed profile of one household employing various coping strategies in the face of multiple social policy changes.

Household Division of Labour and Resource Control

Much mainstream economic theory presupposes that the income that enters households is distributed equally among its members. But feminist theory on gender power imbalances, and empirical household-based data (Finch and Groves 1983; Finch 1989; Beneria and Feldman

1992; Finch and Mason 1993, 2000; Dore and Molyneux 2000; Chant and Craske 2003) suggest that the same stratification that exists in the labour market is replicated in households – and that households are sites of both cooperation and conflict (Sen 1993, 1999; Elson 1995b; Zipp, Prohaska, and Bemiller 2004). This study confirms these findings, demonstrating that a persisting gender division of labour and power imbalances plays itself out at the household level.

In almost all the 41 households in the study where a woman and a man lived together, gender determined the division of labour and influenced power dynamics. Women assumed most of the responsibility for managing basic needs, preparing foods, managing health care needs, arranging child and elder care, and carrying out household cleaning (although some children shared in the latter).[2]

Unpaid Work

Household participants were asked to detail the time they spent on unpaid work (following the questions established by Statistics Canada in the 1996 Census) in the final round of interviews in 1999–2000 in order to ascertain if and how their unpaid work had intensified following cuts in social spending and changes in taxation policy. In 1997, they were asked about who did what work in the household, and were prompted in 1999–2000 to assess if and how these divisions of labour had changed. The number of hours that household members reported were in most cases inconsistent with the stories they told: most did not consider increased time doing volunteer work at their child's school or navigating a family member through the health care system as part of their unpaid work.[3] Female household members especially habitually underestimated the amount of time they spent on unpaid work. Many noted that they could not easily separate the work of caring for children with their sense of love while doing it. While exact time-use was not adequately captured, the coping strategies and activities that household members engaged in to manage a changing social policy and economic climate indicate that what intensified was, for the most part, women's unpaid labour. As Chapter 5 demonstrated, the amount of time and effort participant households expended in managing changes and cuts in areas such as health care, education, social assistance, and child care, along with the efforts required to maintain services, suggest that unpaid work increased as funding cuts and policy changes took hold.

Members of 24 households responded with estimates of their unpaid work activities. Numbers varied widely, and in most cases did not reflect their descriptions of the amount of unpaid work they did. Some single mothers with young children, such as Jenny, Sadan, and Michelle, characterized their work as 'unrelenting,' 'unending,' and 'around the clock.' Amy, a single mother of two children, one of whom was physically disabled, reflected on the amount of time she *felt* she was putting into unpaid work. Her time estimate would be physically impossible given her paid work commitments and sleep needs: 'I think lots of hours, because every day I have to come home [and] cook, and I have to do the dishes or vacuum the place, or [clean] the washroom, or something. So, maybe I [work] 100 hours per week?' Jackie, a single mother of three who lived with her own mother, estimated that she spent about six hours a day on unpaid work, which is more in line with national Canadian data on households with children in which women spent about 34 hours a week on unpaid work (Statistics Canada 1999).

Other single mothers could not conceptualize their unpaid work as labour. Anne, for example, had trouble conceiving of the work that she did trying to access services and supports for her children as part of her unpaid workload, and included mainly cleaning and meal preparation in her estimates. Kate, a single mother of three children, claimed that she spent about five hours a week on unpaid work. Her own descriptions of a typical day gleaned from her four interviews revealed that she spent much more than that on cooking, assisting her children with their homework, cleaning up after them, and ensuring they were bathed and tucked in.[4]

In couple households, the gender division of labour was stark, and did not depend on whether or not members were in paid employment. Longitudinal time-use data from Statistics Canada (Statistics Canada 1999; Hamdad 2003) suggests that couple parents aged 25 to 44 who were employed full time increased their paid work activities by two hours a week between 1992 and 1998. Over the same period, unpaid hours increased minimally from 33.6 hours to 34.3 hours a week for women and from 22.4 to 23.1 hours a week for men.[5] Canadian women's average *share* of household work has remained almost unchanged since the 1960s despite dramatic increases in paid work (GPI Atlantic 2000). Fast et al. (2001) report the disturbing trend that parents allocated extra hours to unpaid work by cutting back on self-care, such as time spent eating, sleeping, washing, and dressing.

When Angie and her two sons moved in with her new partner and his child, the quantity of her unpaid work increased substantially. She explained that she 'does everything,' in addition to working full time: 'Sometimes I feel like I do everything. I do the housework. I do the cooking. I do the cleaning. I do all the household stuff. It's difficult to [estimate the amount of time]. I have a family of five, right? I do the laundry for everybody, I do all the ironing, I make all the lunches. The kids [help sometimes] but they come home from school when I come home. They need my help [with their homework which] has been taking up quite of bit of time in the evening.'

Canadian data on unpaid work shows that 6 per cent of people's time was devoted to community or persons outside of the household for 1998, and 94 per cent of unpaid work was performed for members within the household (Hamdad 2003). It shows that there has been a reduction in volunteer work time between 1992 and 1998 as Canadians experienced intensified time stress and a decrease in leisure time (Zukewich 1998). Between 1997 and 2000, the number of formal volunteers in Canada dropped from 31 per cent to 27 per cent of the adult population (Reed and Selbee 2001). In Ontario, rates dropped from 32 per cent to 26 per cent over this period. Many members of interviewed households, particularly those with young children and/or with precarious labour market relationships, echoed this trend, indicating that they had less time for formal volunteering. Changes in education and health care, however, have resulted for some in an involuntary conscription into formal unpaid work, whether in the form of fundraising for schools or providing care support to the ill.

Caring for elderly or ill parents, particularly when there are co-resident children, put high unpaid work demands on women in households. Janet and Christopher, a married couple with a blended family, spent most of their non-work hours on unpaid work in their own home, and at least five hours a week providing care to Christopher's parents. Janet is self-employed and Christopher works two part-time nursing jobs. This sandwich generation couple is time-crunched. As Janet explains: 'If I wasn't talking to you I'd be working [around the house]. I just go to [paid] work and then I come home and I work [unpaid] until I go to bed. And then I go to bed, and then I get up and I work. We would be better off to say how many hours a week do we do leisure stuff, like go and visit a friend and sit down. We do that maybe once a week for three hours maybe. I would say we probably do at least 40 hours a week on unpaid work. [I do about] 30 hours and Christopher about [10].'

Low-income Canadians spent considerably more time on housework than did high-income Canadians (see Table 6.1). This was also

Table 6.1. Time Spent on Housework for Canadians Aged 25 to 54, 1998

	High income	Low income
Time spent on:	Average minutes per day	Average minutes per day
Housework	30	50
Meal preparation	40	52
Shopping	48	51
Personal care, including sleeping	9.8	10.1
Leisure	277	317
watching TV	82	132*
Child care	68	82
playing with child	17	18
teaching child	4	9
reading to or talking with child	4	5

Source: Adapted from Williams (2002).
*Television was the primary source of leisure activity for low-income households in the Statistics Canada survey and in this study.

true for participant households. Most of the strategies that low-income participant households used to get by require an *increase* in unpaid work, usually work done by women.

Household estimates of the time participants spent on unpaid work were not a reliable source of information on work time, but the strategies that they used to cope with insecure incomes and social service support indicate that what was flexible in their time and money budgets was unpaid work. Further, the changes in actual policies such as health care and education reflected a strong familialization thrust which burdened women in households in particular with additional total work.

Control of Household Income

Managing the needs of the household in most cases did not mean controlling household finances. Nor did all members have equal access to household income or financial decision-making power. For example, although Olivia had worked as a bookkeeper before quitting to help Gary manage his painting company, Gary controlled household finances. He managed household bills and budget planning. Similarly, Natalia and Antonio had a traditional gender-based division of labour where Natalia managed the household and its needs but Antonio controlled resources. Antonio made most of the household's financial decisions, including bill paying and budgeting for food, and gave Natalia 'housekeeping' money. Until she began working with him in 1999, the only income she had in her own name was the Canada Child Tax Benefit, which she used to buy their children's winter clothing.

As Olivia battled against breast cancer, she also struggled with her wage-earning spouse's inability to manage the household finances so that many of her health-related costs could be met. 'If I was taking care of the budget, I would allocate money [to my own health care], but it's up to my husband ... I [asked] my dad for a bit of money a month ago, I was so concerned that Gary wasn't going to have the money. A lot of that went for my ... drugs.'

Women in heterosexual relationships who had incomes of their own exercised more control over household financial decisions. And more than the men, the women participants tended to direct their money towards their children or basic household needs.[6] For example, when Denise's hours were cut drastically, Rick stepped in to cover most of the household bills. He referred to Denise's income (which she used for her daughters' allowance and household food) as 'pin money' and gave her money for groceries when she asked for it. Denise was expected to perform all of the household labour for her children and for Rick and Rick's children. When she took on an additional part-time job, and had more income, her influence over the household finances increased. Rick still managed bills, but Denise was able to provide and pay for food, gifts, allowances, and 'treats,' which gave her a sense of greater control. The division of household labour, however, remained unchanged. When Denise was in a car accident and was then diagnosed with pre-cancerous cells in her cervix, she became seriously depressed. Only then did the division of labour in the household shift, but it was her daughters, not Rick, who took on more responsibility for household labour.

In households without heterosexual couples, the division of labour and resource control were usually more equally distributed. But this changed during times of crisis, such as the illness of one of the members. Frank and Michael, a gay couple living in the Toronto area who both had medium incomes, divided household tasks relatively evenly. However, when Frank was ill in hospital and later recovering at home, Michael took on the bulk of household tasks in addition to providing primary care to Frank and organizing and coordinating a 'care network' of friends and family. This primary caregiver and household-maintenance role was hard on their relationship, and Michael spoke of feeling frustrated with the amount of work, time, and energy it took to manage Frank's health as well as all the household needs.

When three generations were living together because at least one of the parties could not afford a separate place, household members tried hard to ensure reciprocity and good relations by providing housing and gifts of money, and doing child care or other domestic labour. For example, because Jackie lived with her three children in her mother's home, she felt obliged to assume almost all the household's unpaid work, including meals, laundry, house maintenance, cleaning, and shopping. She also directed as much of her income as possible to the household. She felt that she was never doing enough, which in turn made her resentful, but she could not share these feelings with her mother.

Ashley, her daughter Rosa, and Rosa's daughter, Mary, shared a home, but the strain of managing on a small budget and caring for a growing child damaged Ashley and Rosa's relationship. Ashley thought that Rosa was eating too much food; Rosa felt guilty that Ashley spent so much time looking after Mary. The expectations each had of the other in terms of division of labour within the household were not met, in large measure, because their resources did not permit them any margin for increased or unexpected expenses.

Extra-household responsibilities also affected household relations and financial decisions. Antonio sent money each month to his mother in Central America despite the fact that his wife, Natalia, who was not working for pay at the time, insisted they needed the money for food and clothes for their children.

Sabrina and Elizabeth had an unusual financial arrangement for housemates: each paid 25 per cent of her income towards household costs, although Elizabeth earned more than Sabrina. When Sabrina was laid off, Elizabeth assumed greater responsibility for household costs. Sabrina did not think she had to do more household labour in order to 'make up' for this shortfall in income. Elizabeth suggested that Sabrina's layoff and inability to continue providing financial support to her parents had left her stressed enough that she should not have to worry about unpaid work or maintaining her previous share of household costs.

These examples show that the income that enters households is not shared equally among household members. The presumption in economic theory, particularly the new household economics strand (cf. Becker 1985), that households have a joint utility function which sees resources distributed equitably and in which cooperation and consent reign, does not bear out in practice. Having their own incomes made it much easier for women to gain equal footing in household financial decision-making. Those with access to income or assets (such as home ownership) had more power in commanding household resources and shaping divisions of labour. In most cases, power divisions conformed to inequalities based on gender or age. And, in most cases, the more limited the resources, the more tensions were generated.

Coping Strategies

Most participant households, and low-income households in particular, had to combine a variety of income sources, most of which were stagnant or declining, in order to try to maintain their standards of living. As a result, the work of translating this income into goods and services that sustain household members, preparing them to participate in educational pursuits or the labour market, became much more difficult. This work – domestic labour – is centred on ensuring material resources such as food, clothing, or a clean and well-equipped house as well as on managing the complex interpersonal dynamics that are at the heart of caregiving. It is the one area in which individuals and households have some flexibility in managing their living standards. And in most households, it is women who perform the large part of the domestic labour that is fundamental to the endless effort to get by.

Participants in low-income households used a number of different strategies to manage decreased or stagnant incomes and a decline in social service support. Many combined a variety of strategies. The main strategies participants identified were the following:

- Develop and follow detailed budgets
- Increase labour market participation
- Do without basic goods

- Use food banks or request support from not-for-profit agencies or other services
- Increase time spent growing, shopping for, and preparing foods
- Sell household goods, crafts, and other handmade items
- Go into debt   ⦁
- Barter
- Borrow from or rely on gifts and in-kind support from family and friends
- Move to cheaper housing, or share housing

Budgets

Detailed budgeting required planning and creativity around inputs into social reproduction. It also gave participants a sense of control over their lives. Women in households did the bulk of food planning, shopping, and preparing and managing health care costs, as well as dealing with costs related to children.

Unpredictable increases in costs put enormous strain on low-income participants and on their relationships. Even meticulous budgeting and the use of all available cost-saving measures were not sufficient to enable most low-income participants to cover their costs. Teresa received $670 a month. She suffered from a severe allergy, and Epipen, an injection she carried in the event of an attack, was not covered under her drug plan: 'It angers me. I feel so helpless to be here like this. In regard to the other thing, I mean $50 for an Epipen that's life or death. Or even just [finding money for] dandruff shampoo. I've lived in fear of getting a letter in the mail, and I don't mind my bills, but it's the other things I'm like, oh no, here we go, social services sent me a letter [saying that they overpaid me and are going to deduct money], and it's like you live in fear waiting to see what's going to happen.' Even marginal fluctuations in costs, such as the introduction of a two-dollar user fee at her community recreation centre, made services inaccessible to Teresa.

Rosie and Bob, a retired couple on a fixed income, were affected by property taxes increases. Veronica lived in constant fear of one of her children becoming ill because she had no medical coverage for her kids and couldn't afford to fill prescriptions. Anne would try to save several dollars each month between January and July, when she would buy Christmas gifts during summer sales. Michelle, a single mother of two who works on contract, could not find the money in her carefully allotted budget to pay for her son to play hockey. This left her feeling as though she were denying him a childhood.

Labour Market Participation

Many people with low incomes attempted to increase their formal labour market participation. Liz, who is retired, took on a part-time retail job (from which she was subsequently laid off) so that she could cover 'the basics.' Jenny tried to earn back the amount that was cut from social assistance through a short-term telemarketing job, from which she was laid off. Veronica first worked cleaning houses to make extra income when she was receiving social assistance; later she got a part-time, seasonal job as a bus driver.

Jobs at the low end of the labour market were often precarious and difficult to coordinate with child care and familial responsibilities. Kate managed to coordinate child care with her partner by working nights in a telemarketing company, but her hours – and therefore her income – were unpredictable. Antonio and Natalia managed for two years with a combination of income from Antonio's OSAP loan and work cleaning offices at night. When he finished his training and had to repay his loan, Natalia joined Antonio at his retail job, both working almost full-time hours at slightly over minimum wage. The result of both of them juggling two almost full-time jobs was that their children were home alone for long stretches or had to sit behind the counter at the store with them.

'They are not having a childhood,' Antonio lamented.

Doing Without

Those who did without basic goods in the face of income shortfalls described going without food, making impossible decisions about whether to buy groceries or shoes, not filling prescriptions, sharing medication, going without a telephone or transportation, sharing winter boots, coats, and prescription glasses, and giving up social activities outside the home. They risked their health and endured social isolation or ridicule along with endless tension within their households.

In all of the eight low-income female-headed households, the most flexible item in the budget was food. Amy, a low-income single mother, noted that food was her negotiable expense: 'The rent first, then groceries, then the bills, but if one is going to be cut off, then that month it has to come before groceries.' Amy used food banks, going to three different locations each month while she was receiving social assistance.

The women described the dilemmas they faced every day, trying to feed themselves and their children. They often curbed their own consumption so that their children would have enough to eat.

In 1999, Jenny, a single mother receiving social assistance, described her situation: 'The last time I bought myself clothing would have been in 1995, and that would have been maternity clothing. I can't buy anything, because if I do I won't have enough money for bills or groceries. The kids always need stuff, and that's [my priority]. Sometimes I can find something [for them] in a second-hand store, which is really cool. There's a lot of things that you cannot do because of your financial situation. Like we can't go to church every Sunday. I would like to, but I'm thinking I don't have any clothes to wear there. My kids don't have any clothes. Like are we going to show up in our grungy clothes to church?' She also explained the effect of prioritizing her children's food needs over her own: 'I was at my doctor's. I've lost almost 70 pounds in the 10 months [since the baby was born]. You know why? It's because if I eat a regular amount of food a day, my kids wouldn't have any food. And I can't send them to school without lunch.'

One of the hardest things for the low-income women to manage was social isolation. Jenny said, 'I have had to give up a social life. I can't go out. I can't afford a sitter.' Jenny's closest friend recalled that one month Jenny did not have enough money to purchase menstrual pads and was reduced to wearing one of her daughter's diapers.

Teresa, who received help from Ontario Disability Support because of her physical disability and multiple health needs, recounted that she had often been faced with the choice of feeding herself or meeting other basic needs: 'Some of my medications they [social assistance] don't cover, and I have to pay for them myself, which they don't take into consideration ... Groceries [are hard] because I only have $40. I needed new shoes this month. My choice was, do I get new shoes or do I get groceries? So I got new shoes. I'm relying on the food bank this month because I had to get new shoes.' Teresa says that she often feels that she would be better off dead than living as she is: 'Many times, I shouldn't say this, but many times I wish that I was dead, because I can't handle the stress of all these things that are happening. And things happen all the time.'

Sadan, a single mother living in the Greater Toronto Area, who emigrated from eastern Africa, said she could make traditional food for her children, which met their dietary requirements. Her children, however, wanted North American foods, such as processed lunch foods and take-out hamburgers. She understood their wish to be part of their new culture but she could not afford fast food. Her difficulties in trying to accommodate her children's demands were compounded by her own medical problems. Her prescription medication had to be accompanied by juice or fruit in order to be effective, but Sadan could afford neither. She had no money for transportation of any kind, and no child care to allow her to walk to a food bank.

Ashley and Rosa, a mother and adult daughter who lived together in 1997–1998, agreed their priority was ensuring that Rosa's daughter, Mary, had what she needed. They describe their own struggle to meet basic needs. As Ashley says, 'we share. We have to share our boots now. Like if Rosa goes to school, she wears my brown boots during the day, and then I'm going to volunteer in the evening, I'll wear the boots. And those things came from the second-hand store ... I always have this feeling of anxiety, of some type of doom and gloom going to happen immediately.'

Rosa added, 'Every time somebody rings that doorbell, [I wonder] what next?'

Community-Based Support

Participants were resourceful in seeking out whatever sources of support were available. Anne used a community agency to get some baby formula and diapers, despite the fact that she disagreed with their anti-choice position on abortion. Jenny used a local agency when she was pregnant to get access to prenatal supplements and milk. However, through the 1990s, agencies that provided community-based services experienced financial cutbacks and staff reductions, which decreased their capacities to assist clients (Michalski 1999; Woolley 2001).

Food banks offset some shortfalls for low-income households but they posed a number of problems. Participants found that food banks were often inaccessible, the quality of food was sometimes poor, users were subject to scrutiny, and they could not accommodate special needs diets. For example, when Sadan moved to cheaper housing, the food banks were further away. As a result, she was cut off from the chance to offer her children the North American foods that would make them feel like 'normal' kids.

Richard, a low-income man with advanced AIDS, used food banks regularly. His drugs and supplements were not all covered by his drug plan, and he had special dietary needs that the food banks did not meet. As his health declined, getting around became increasingly difficult. In the last round of interviews, Richard was receiving Meals On Wheels for some of his meals, and his sister was driving from her home almost an hour away once a week to purchase his groceries.

Anne and Jenny, close friends at the time of the first interviews, found trips to food banks exercises in humiliation. Anne's income did not go far with four young children. She said that her situation was made even more difficult when the social assistance rates were cut in 1995:

> I receive my mother's allowance cheque,[7] and I'm broke immediately. My bills come to $900 a month and then I get groceries. My cheque's $1,128, so there's not a whole lot left, and that feeds five of us. I'm usually calling a food bank by the 10th of the month. Groceries don't last very long. And we buy bulk. Jenny and I are pretty good for splitting things and stuff like that. I've cut back. I used to be able to get certain medications on the drug card and now I can't. I have to pay for those medications. And my kids have chronic asthma so that's a constant expense for me. You live literally cheque to cheque, and once your money's gone there's no more money. And you have to do whatever you can. My baby is still on formula. He has to be on formula until he's a year old, the doctor has said to try to reduce the allergies from the milk that'll trigger the asthma. And that's $10 every three days for formula.

For Anne, food banks were not always reliable when she needed groceries and was short of money:

> So I went to the food bank last week. They said, 'We have no food.' I had nothing so I went to the Salvation Army [Food Bank]. And this is where this woman degrades people. She just makes you feel so awful. Jenny went with me to the food bank. The first thing this woman says is, 'Oh, didn't Jenny come with you the last time?' I [said], 'Well, actually we're neighbours and I have a car and I drove her down.' 'Oh, it's not just a joy ride?' she said. And I went, 'Oh we really enjoy driving down here to get a $15 food voucher to get a bag of milk and a thing of diapers for our kids, you know.' Like they really belittle you, and then she went, 'Well, where's all your money? It's only the 10th of the month.'

Jenny used food banks as last-resort community support throughout the course of the study, until after one trip her entire family became ill. The main food bank in her community was closed down for a day after she complained, and a sign was placed on the door, reading 'Eat at your own risk.' She said,

It's really bad because I won't even go to the city food bank any more, because every time we've been there we get sick. And I'm thinking, okay maybe it's stress or it could be the time of year, there could be bugs around. But since we've stayed away from that food bank, nobody has been sick. Like we'd all get the runs, stomach cramps, we'd be throwing up and I'm convinced it's the food. Like you know I'm not trying to knock it because it is a good thing, you know what I mean, and we do need it in this community, but the building that it's in is so filthy.

After Rosa and her mother separated, Rosa moved into a basement apartment in her sister's home. She described her experience with a 'good' food bank:

Well there's a food bank ... that [opens] at six o'clock. They have the best food. I mean you always have your officious types, but they were quite [nice]. Sometimes these companies donate, like, clothes, soap, Degree deodorant! I guess you consider them treats. You can only do it just once a month. You don't just walk in there. They have to take your income statement, and you give monthly expenses, and according to that they judge. And that's how much they give you, and that's how many times you can go. While you're there they give you [transportation] tokens to go back and forth. But you [have to get] there early. I got there early and I was still number 11, so I had to wait 40 minutes. It's funny, because I guess people don't want people to see them there, not that their neighbours would live in that area, but they come in there with their dark glasses on. I don't know them, but I see them in the neighbourhood, and I wouldn't think that they would be using the food bank, but they're using the food bank. I guess [they think that about me, too].

Growing, Buying, and Preparing Foods

Because they did not have enough money to purchase foods for household consumption, many participants managed by increasing the amount of time they spent growing, buying, and preparing foods. Jenny, for example, began to make bread as a way to offset costs, in part because flour was one of the things that was readily available at food banks. For a time, she was able to bake and store bread in Anne's freezer. After Anne moved, Jenny no longer had access to a freezer.

Liz, who was retired, employed several strategies to cut costs, including carefully budgeting for each shopping trip, buying day-old products, and relying on friends to drive her to discount grocery stores. She also planted a small vegetable garden. Janet and Christopher worked on Christopher's parents' family farm on a weekly basis, both to help Christopher's parents and to gain access to meat products and vegetables for their large household.

Selling Household Goods and Crafts

Jenny, Anne, Rosa, and Jessie sold various household items in order to get enough money to cover basic costs, like food. Jenny and Anne regularly pawned and then re-purchased household goods, such as televisions or Jenny's breadmaker in order to get through a month; buying back items usually meant purchasing them back at a higher price. Jenny sold her children's swing set one month in order to purchase needed items, such as diapers. Anne sold her children's movies to buy milk. Mark, an artist who lives in northern Ontario with his partner, Jessie, sold his tools in order to meet unexpected veterinary costs.[8]

Ashley, Jenny, Veronica, and Sadan all made and sold items informally to increase the amount of money they had for basic goods. Ashley bought fabric and made angels at Christmas in order to buy small gifts for her granddaughter. Jenny painted and sold cards. Veronica made curtains and pillow covers. Sadan tried to make and sell East African foods. These sources of income were, however, small, generally insecure, and often required capital outlays that were unaffordable.

Incurring Debts

High debt loads were common among low-income households. Many had student loans they were trying to pay off, or were considering defaulting on. Others owed taxes from previous years. Still others had credit card debts or owed money to family members. Many lived on overdraft at the bank. Some, like Antonio and Natalia, Leo and Maria, and Janet and Christopher, were financing some of their children's university or college educations on credit cards.[9]

Single mothers in particular were affected when the provincial government, in its cost-saving efforts, reopened old files and claimed that former social assistance recipients had been overpaid and owed the province money. Suddenly, these women faced new debts and most could not afford to challenge the charges. For Jackie in southeastern Ontario and Michelle in the Greater Toronto Area, letters from social assistance claiming overpayments added to their household stress. Jackie had received social assistance in the early 1990s, and was contacted by a collection agency claiming she owed several thousand dollars. Jackie was certain this was not the case. Much of her income had gone towards paying for legal fees in connection with her ex-spouse's failure to pay child support. Jackie hid from the collection agency – and reported no further incidents with them by the end of the study.

Michelle, on the other hand, was bulldozed by the letter she got from social assistance, saying she owed them $70,000. She had received assistance occasionally when she was between contract jobs and ineligible for Employment Insurance. She maintained a relationship with social assistance so that she could get some of her children's medical costs covered while she was working. Information about the disposal of Michelle's broken-down car was said to be missing from her file. Social assistance determined that she was retroactively ineligible.[10] Michelle explained:

> I thought it was a mistake! I have not received social assistance in quite some time. But Community and Social Services said to my MPP's secretary that it's not a mistake, it is correct. They were saying that is was too late to appeal it. They said that they're going to send it to the collection agency, which would seize all my income ... the child tax credit or any of my income tax. I'm just barely making $19,000 a year. In that 30-day period which they gave me to respond to the letter, I was calling the welfare office. I was calling my previous worker and there was no information given out to me. The last result I've got is that they're thinking of giving us a review to open the case, because there was so little information on why they claim that I owe them $70,000.

Antonio was juggling helping his daughter with her university tuition fees while trying to repay his own large student loan. In order to manage his debt load, he was forced to take a job outside his field of training. He said, 'This is the promise I got with this company: my boss will make the student loan payments for me. He will pay the monthly payments. I owe $200 a month, so this makes a big difference. That's why I stay. I cannot work in the field I trained in because I owe money for that training. But this is the only way I can manage because wages in other jobs are not enough to pay off the debt.'

The dissolution of a spousal relationship also significantly affected individual debt loads. Kate and Carl separated in 1999, and Carl claims that Kate's debts – for things like a microwave oven – were her own to manage, on a hugely reduced income.

Barter or Informal Exchange

Many low-income women bartered and shared costs to maximize their inputs into social reproduction. Veronica explained her strategies: 'We [my friends and I] do day care back and forth. If I have an excess of a staple and [my friend] has excess of that, we kind of swap. Almost everything my kids wear [comes from a friend].'

In the first round of interviews Anne explained the importance of her relationship with Jenny:

> Jenny and I do a whole lot of things to save [money]. Child care we both just switch [caring for the other's child] so that we don't have to pay. And then if we're stuck or if there's too many or if she's got all three of her kids and all four of mine, I'll have to pay somebody because that's just too many kids for her. The babysitting would be the one thing for definite that we split. A lot of times what we'll do is, we'll buy bulk and split. Like a bulk of toilet paper and we'll cut it in half, or a bulk of, you know, laundry detergent. A lot of the times we'll shop at each other's cupboards at the end of the month. Like, okay I really need this ... We're really good that way, if we're running out, and we're forever running out. Like diapers or formula and stuff like that.

Swapping child care and sharing costs was a good strategy for Anne and Jenny to manage their combined income insecurity. Tensions arose, however, when one was not able to reciprocate. When their relationship became frayed, in part because of the constant pressures of limited incomes, they both lost a central source of support in their lives. The same was true for Ashley and Rosa, and Amy and a close friend.

Christine, who worked as a home daycare provider, bartered in a more formal manner. She swapped child care for veterinarian bills as a way to offset unexpected costs related to her dogs. Jackie in southeastern Ontario made use of a local community exchange program to get services such as plumbers. Over time, she found that she did not have many of the skills or the time to reciprocate in the program.[11]

Josie, a grandmother raising her two grandchildren, said that accepting care forced her into relations of obligation with kin, which she sought to avoid: ' If I have a family member that is going to come and help, you can be guaranteed that you will have their kids to babysit after ... No thanks.'

Child care was one of the most common forms of assistance that extended kin, and sometimes friends, provided for one another. Statistics Canada found, in 1998, that 20 per cent of the hours devoted to informal caregiving benefited someone who did not reside in the household, with child care being the most common form of support. Canadians spent three times as many hours providing informal care to people in other households as they did on formal volunteer work (Cook-Reynolds and Zukewich 2004:15).

Bartering, whether formal or informal, places people in relations of obligation and reciprocity. For those with small incomes, little leisure time, and perceptions of themselves as low-skilled, it did not provide sustainable solutions to income and support shortfalls.

Borrowing, Relying on Gifts or In-Kind Support

Another – usually short-term – strategy participants used to meet their basic needs was to borrow money or rely on gifts or in-kind support from friends and family.[12] Although this strategy worked for some, especially if they had a family member who had assets, for most, members of their extended kin and social networks were in similar financial situations. Three-quarters of the members of 41 households said they were providers or receivers of support from non-cohabiting kin. The remaining household participants sought support from formal sources such as not-for-profits, government sources, and churches, or from spouses and friends.

Those who did borrow or accept gifts of money sometimes put their relationships at risk and often humiliated themselves when they could not reciprocate. Although most participants borrowed from kin, not friends, even kinship ties were vulnerable to the conflicts inherent in borrowing or unreciprocated gift-giving.[13] For example, Julie, a self-employed disabled woman living in the Greater Toronto Area, received a financial 'gift' from her parents every month. Julie noted that while she was grateful for the gifts, she stopped talking to her parents about her financial worries because she felt so indebted to them.

In-kind support, such as gifts, food, furniture, and clothing, made a big difference in how households managed their incomes. Janet and Christopher, a blended family of seven, relied heavily on food gifts, especially meat, from Christopher's parents' farm. They reciprocated by providing their own and their children's labour to the farm on weekends. Christine, a home daycare provider in a rural town, received frequent gifts for her son of clothes, furniture, and after-school activities money from her mother and her in-laws. 'We would not have three-quarters of the stuff we have without the relatives chipping in,' she said.

Relying on family members for financial, instrumental, or affective support, however, was not possible or desirable for some participants. Leo, a seasonal textile worker whose wife, Maria, was a full-time teacher, noted that he preferred to borrow from the bank rather than muddy familial relationships with financial matters.

Samantha, a teenage mother trying to complete high school, explained that day care was preferable to family care: 'I tried to rely on my mum for babysitting when I started school ... last year, but she had doctor's appointments and stuff, so then I could not go to school that day. It's hard to rely on someone. I like day care better unless I get someone who is going to do it every day.' In their assessments concerning asking for support, participants in two different households provided stark comments. According to Rick, 'There's always "I did this for you" [when my wife and I have asked for help from my mother], and we try to avoid that. It took a toll on our relationship.' Another respondent, Angie, said, 'People just get further and further into financial and emotional debt [by asking for help].' Relying on kin, without being able to reciprocate the support, often created anxiety rather than solidarity.

Accepting kin support could also mean a loss of privacy and autonomy. Richard, who was living with AIDS, received financial, instrumental, and emotional support from his elderly father and his sister. 'My father is continuously calling or dropping by. He has a key,' Richard explained. 'He is on the lease to help out with the rent [so I can't complain]. My sister works [nearby] and she phones [often] ... Robbie [my partner] went up north for three weeks. He was glad just to get away from [here] because ... my father and sister [are] driving him nuts.'

For Jerry, a sole-support father with a small child, the support he received from his parents was central to his managing, but it also infringed on his autonomy. In addition to his parents providing him with an apartment in their home, they supplemented meals and offered child care while he was trying to secure stable employment. Still, he felt invaded when his mother took a dominant role in caring for his daughter: 'She [my mother] will actually come up to our apartment, before I'm even awake in the morning, and wake Erin up and bring her downstairs for breakfast. When it happens four or five mornings a week, [I am frustrated because] this is my time with my daughter.'

Friendship networks are strong sources of support in some instances, but even in the exceptional case of housemates Sabrina and Elizabeth, Sabrina's education and training meant that her unemployment – and thus her support needs – were short-term. When Sabrina was laid off from her job in social services in the initial round of cuts in social spending in Ontario, she received social assistance. She was struggling to pay for necessities such as groceries and rent, so Elizabeth, her long-time friend and roommate, decided to increase her own share of rent and utilities, helping to cushion Sabrina's drop in income. Sabrina's parents were retired and on a fixed income, but agreed to cover her student loan. They had to forgo a cruise they were planning to celebrate a wedding anniversary. Sabrina's network of support largely offset the financial setback of losing her job, but she felt guilty about 'burdening' those she loved the most. She knew that their generous help had limits; borrowing money and relying on others for inputs into daily living was just a short-term strategy. Sabrina was well-educated and had strong professional skills, so her support network viewed her financial situation as anomalous, resulting from a provincial government bent on shrinking public services. Sabrina explained: 'I've been pretty privileged ... Elizabeth doesn't share her finances with me but she shares her car. She buys me meals out. I mean I still get these fun things that keep your spirits up that other people can't have, or don't get, you know. So I still feel really lucky.'

The support did not come without a cost, however. Sabrina's siblings, who were all financially independent, could not understand how their sister had fallen on such hard times and were upset that their parents were having to pay for her outstanding debts. Sabrina soon pieced together three part-time jobs.

Veronica had left an abusive husband and was caring for her children while receiving social assistance. Borrowing money from her mother and relying on support and barter from friends took its toll. 'I think it does [affect our relationship when I ask for money],' she said. 'My mother can't say no, or doesn't want to say no. I tend to avoid the whole issue with friends ... I'm very explicit about drawing the line.'

Veronica feared she would strain these relationships, and drew less and less on family and friends: 'As the months have gone by, I don't think that I lean on [family and friends] as much as I used to. I became very aware of how much I was, and I really don't want to.' Her decision to reduce demands on her familial and friendship networks, combined with social policy changes that reduced her access to formal support, left her increasingly alone to deal with her difficulties. She was seeking support payments from her children's father, fielding harassing letters and calls from social services, dealing with threats from an abusive ex-partner, and being served with an eviction notice. She was reluctant to talk about her troubles with her friends for fear she would exhaust their patience.

Jenny noted that most people in her support network were in similar financial positions. Although her parents wanted to help her, they did not have much disposable income. She said, 'In the past, if I was really strapped for cash, I could always call up my mom and dad and borrow a few dollars to get me through. I can't ask them for $20. They're both not working now, so they're not really in a position where they can help. They feel really bad. My dad feels terrible, and says, "I wish I could help you more." I tell him that it is not his responsibility. It's hard.'

Housing Options

Housing was the biggest cost for most participants. Many hoped to get subsidized housing, but waiting lists were long and they had to make do in the meantime. A common cost-cutting strategy was to move or to share housing. Ten households moved – sometimes often – in order to keep costs low. Financially, sharing a home worked out well, but the strains of cohabiting, intensified by the strain of little money, often damaged central relationships. Moving to a new community or part of a city to reduce housing costs also cut people off from friends and community support, an isolation made worse if their budgets could not cover transportation.

Data for Canada shows that 68 per cent of all people in Canada aged 15 or older moved at least once between 1985 and 1995. Couples with children were very likely to move (74 per cent) and to be 'better off' as a result.[14] Lone parents with children were even more likely to move (84 per cent), but only about half of these households were made better off. More than one in 10 lone parents moved in search of more afford-able accommodation (Kremarik 1999).

SHARING WITH FAMILY

Having a parent or other family member willing to share an asset such as a house greatly helped several participants.[15] Six households gained access to their current homes because of their parents. In three cases, parents split their homes so that their offspring and their families had a separate living space. In four cases, adult children moved in with par-ents to meet costs, even though their parents were not wealthy to begin with. Denzel, a young man who struggled with a series of low-paying jobs, lived for several months in a small apartment with his mother and siblings. Canadian data on three-generation households indicate that the number of these households rose 39 per cent between 1986 and 1996 (Che-Alford et al. 1999). The majority of three-generation house-holds (44 per cent) were found in Ontario. While reasons for cohabita-tion and the number of earners in households varied, in households with only one 'maintainer' (principal person who covered housing and utilities expenses), it was the grandparent in 59 per cent of cases. This underlines the effects of precarious employment on younger workers, and the unequal distribution of assets across generations.

Relying on family to offset low incomes for housing had the same potential pitfalls as borrowing, and the strategy was often not sustain-able. The details of Jackie's household and Ashley and Rosa's house-hold with sharing housing demonstrate the limitations of a reliance on family as a long-term strategy. Jackie was in her mid-thirties and lived in a medium-sized city in southeastern Ontario. She worked half time for a small not-for-profit agency, and shared a home with her three children and her mother, Edith.

When we first met in 1997, Jackie's son, Angus, was not yet a toddler. Her daughter, Kerry, was 14 years old. Jackie had divorced Kerry's father many years before because he was violent. She did not want Kerry to grow up in that environment, so she raised her daughter mostly on her own following her separation. In 1999, after a brief reconciliation with Angus' father, she gave birth to a daughter. Jackie managed on her part-time income because she received a partial day-care subsidy and shared costs with her mother.

Maintaining a good relationship with her mother was a constant struggle. She felt that she and her kids were a burden to her mother, but they had few other housing options. In 1997, Jackie and Edith were trying to maintain separate residences and live in the same house. Although they shared the kitchen, the laundry facilities, and the yard, they had separate phone lines, and Jackie, Angus, and Kerry were living in the basement while Edith used the rest of the house. In early 1998, they gave up this division when Angus was diagnosed with asthma and allergies. As a result, Jackie and Edith both had significantly less personal space and time. Jackie intensified her unpaid work as she attempted to make up in labour the income she could not contribute to the house. Jackie said, 'My mother complains about the house, that the roof needs doing, it needs painting, the furnace is old, the windows need to be replaced, the rug needs replacing. It just gets right on top of me, and I have no escape. I don't know where to channel it. I have no money or time to go work out at a gym. But I have to manage. I have to be healthy for Kerry and Angus. I have to [provide a good home].'

Jackie considered co-op housing as an option for her family. However, Jackie and her mother shared a used car. Edith had increasingly severe arthritis, and Kerry had a genetic bone condition. Jackie contributed to paying off the loan for the car, but Edith paid the insurance and maintenance. Kerry would not be able to get around the city if they moved, because Edith would keep the car and Jackie could not afford to buy and maintain one on her own.

The strategy of sharing a home in order to keep housing costs low was helpful financially, but it caused deep fractures in Jackie and Edith's relationship and was a source of constant stress for them both.

Ashley and Rosa's story shows that the more people are required to depend on just one or two others, the more their relationship is at risk. It also shows how the stigma typically associated with receiving social assistance can not only erode recipients' self-esteem, but can alienate them from their family and friends.

Ashley, a woman in her mid-fifties, and Rosa, her 33-year-old daughter, took up residence together after they both found themselves in financial straits. When it became clear neither would find employment in their southeastern Ontario town, they moved to the Greater

Toronto Area where both had full-time but low-paid employment. The situation worsened after Rosa became pregnant, and, because of complications with her pregnancy, could no longer hold down her job. Ashley then lost her job because of funding cutbacks at a community agency. Rosa applied for social assistance and was enrolled in a full-time upgrading program while Ashley continued to look for full-time employment. Out of financial necessity they decided to pool resources and move in together.

Embarrassed by their situation, Rosa and Ashley tried to keep their financial status to themselves. They were hurt by the lack of understanding of their family members, particularly Rosa's three siblings. They felt judged for their failure to find good jobs, for their sparse living quarters, and for their inability to entertain. This humiliation was compounded by public hostility to the poor and to those receiving social assistance. Yet isolating themselves from others, including other family members, only made them more dependent on each other.

As their economic situation deteriorated, their utilities were cut off, they bought cheaper cuts of meat and produce, and increasingly had to go without to make ends meet. Mother and daughter were forced to rely on each other more, pooling resources, even sharing personal belongings such as a single pair of winter boots. Their experience as they increasingly confronted the need to ask family and friends for financial aid highlights the difference between entitlements and charity. Ashley had no difficulty accepting her non-resident partner's offer to extend his employers' medical and dental coverage to her. Neither she nor her partner had to justify their request for it. In contrast, when Ashley and Rosa had to ask Rosa's siblings for help, they both felt ashamed.

Feeling burdened, resentful, and overwhelmed by their debt load, Ashley and Rosa's relationship began to fray. By the third interview, they were no longer living together, and each accused the other of not carrying her weight. Ashley describes the final days of their shared living arrangement: 'I told Rosa, I said I just, I can't take it any longer, and I couldn't take her any longer, we were just arguing and it was like very tense. She [Rosa] wasn't paying her fair share, all of my money was going, all of the food I was buying. I ended up paying most of the bills ... I didn't have the money. From about the sixth of the month I would pay all the food from there. Where the heck was her money? I don't know, I was paying all of it, and I'm not going to not buy food. If I put one thing down [in the cellar] it was gone. It was like a very stressful situation, extremely stressful.' Rosa also attributed their breakup to strained finances: 'It's almost like a married couple, when money and stuff comes into play. That's the big, that's one big argument, do you know what I mean? And it gets worse, money always gets worse. The payments ... it was just like trying to dodge, and trying not to get caught, give them a rubber cheque. I think that was the proverbial straw.'

After a bitter parting of ways, Rosa rented the basement of her sister's home. While the arrangement was mutually beneficial in terms of reciprocal child care, Rosa hid her financial situation from her sister. Her sister was oblivious to Rosa's frequent use of food banks or her need to pawn personal possessions to make the rent. In fact, her sister was so unaware of Rosa's financial situation that she asked Rosa to act as co-signer for a mortgage.

Ashley moved back to her home in a southeastern Ontario town and applied for social assistance. Her partner and her mother paid her property tax arrears, but she still feared her dilapidated home would be taken away from her if she was forced to stay on social assistance. These experiences undermined her confidence and her ability to make positive changes in her life. Family relations were fraught with conflict, and for a period of months Ashley did not have any contact with her children.

The examples of Ashley and Rosa and Jackie and her mother show the dangers of forcing people to rely on family, especially for housing. Ironically, the government policy of encouraging people to rely on family and friends instead of state services threatens to erode the very support such networks could provide.

MOVING TO CHEAPER HOUSING

When Olivia was diagnosed with breast cancer, and the household income dropped, Olivia and Gary moved to a new community in search of cheaper rent. She worried they would end up in one of the motel strips that serve as housing for many low-income people. She said, 'You really need stability, you need to know that you have a home to live in. I've been driving with Gary to go to the hospital. The route is always the same, and there are a lot of motels that run along the road we take. Invariably, the thought that goes through my mind is, We could have and still can end up in a motel along with other families that live there. That threat was a very real one.'

Unexpected illness resulting in a change in household income presented significant housing challenges to other low-income families. Richard, a white man in his fifties with AIDS, moved four times in three years in search of a combination of cheaper housing and access to support services. While the moves themselves were stressful, even more disturbing was that he could not afford adequate housing. As his health deteriorated, he was only able to get by when his elderly father offered to pay a significant portion of his rent. At the time of his final interview, Richard stated that his next move would be to an AIDS hospice where he expected to die.

SUBSIDIZED HOUSING

Josie lived in a rent-geared-to-income unit in cooperative housing. When her daughter entered a detox program, Josie took over care of her three grandchildren. When the daughter was released, she was receiving a minimal amount from social assistance and she too came to live with Josie. As a result, the co-op ruled that Josie's rent should increase to market value – from $936 a month to $1,034 (an increase of 10.5 per cent). According to Josie, once rent is deemed to be payable at market cost, it cannot then be re-subsidized, regardless of income fluctuations. Josie's efforts to help her family cost her a necessary housing subsidy.

Anne and Jenny both lived in subsidized housing, mainly because the waiting lists in their medium-sized community were not as long as those in bigger urban centres. This made all the difference; they did not have to choose between returning to an abusive spouse or moving in with already overstretched family members. But subsidized housing was hard to come by. Many, like Amy, remained on waiting lists – some up to 10 years long. Jenny notes that the bureaucratic problems related to subsidized housing make it very hard to manage, despite its financial benefits. In addition, recipients must constantly face the possibility of losing their subsidy:

> Every year when you're in subsidized housing, you renew your lease and you have to sign a copy of all your earnings. You have to have your social worker fill out this form and you send it back. All this information has to be back by such and such a date or your rent will go up to market price. If they don't have all the details, they can't assess the amount. My worker lost my form. I said: 'Excuse me, I need this or my rent's going up.' He

said, 'Well, I'm sorry we lost it, there's nothing I can do about it.' After that, conveniently, I couldn't get hold of him. He wasn't answering the phone. I'd leave messages, he wouldn't get back to me. So I had to run around trying to sort this out and it was a big hassle. Two months down the road, he sent it back to me and I thought, Oh what a joke.

RETURNING TO AN ABUSIVE SPOUSE

Anne, Veronica, and Jenny all considered returning to an abusive spouse when their financial situations became hard to bear. Jenny tried to have the charges dropped against her ex-husband after he assaulted her and their child, and permitted him to move back into her home briefly in order to gain greater income security. Veronica thought about how much easier her day-to-day life would be if she had her ex-spouse's income, despite a vicious history. Social assistance had forced her to go after her spouse for child support a few years earlier, with brutal emotional outcomes and only $100 a month in payments. She was furious because she had been put in a position of 'stoking his anger': 'Why don't you guys [social assistance] get him drunk, stand us face to face and get him to hit me, or put his arms around my neck again?' she raged. 'That's what you're doing to me. You're setting me up.' Despite a two-year court battle over child support and three abductions of her child, her level of financial and emotional stress led her to consider a reconciliation:

After I missed a bunch of days from work because of [my son] being in the hospital, I had to get a letter of explanation from my employer. [My welfare worker] wanted a letter of explanation from my doctor, from my son's doctor. She wanted medical records proving that my son was sick. And I drew the line and I almost went back with my ex-husband. I was this close, because I thought, with his income and me working part-time I could tell that woman to go to hell. But I'm trapped. That's not an option either. It's either deal with this abusive woman or deal with a previous partner, and I'm stuck in the middle. I just find she has been very militant since this whole concept of Ontario Works came in play.

Putting Together a Living: A Profile in Coping

Anne's story graphically illustrates the dynamics of getting by on a small income, raising children, and attempting to maintain an autonomous household in a leaner and meaner welfare state. Anne is a resourceful and resilient single mother who lives in a medium-sized community in southeastern Ontario. In early 1997, Anne was living in a three-bedroom subsidized townhouse on a busy street. She had four boys ranging in age from an infant to seven years old. As noted in Chapter 5, all of the children had serious problems requiring medical attention and close supervision. Anne talked with intensity about her fierce devotion to her high-needs kids, her struggle to leave an alcoholic husband, her efforts to make ends meet, and her dreams of owning a home and returning to school.

Anne's concerns with making ends meet were compounded by her worries about how she was faring as a parent. Finding herself suddenly a single parent with four young boys with serious and threatening health problems was overwhelming. In addition, she had been in a car accident several months before our first meeting, had begun experiencing panic attacks, and was being treated for an anxiety disorder. 'I was doing more yelling than talking with the kids,' she said. 'This medication for stress has helped; if the kids do something, I'm going from zero to 10, not zero to 100.' She still questioned her judgment and decisions: 'I'm still having a hard time dealing with the breakup of my marriage. I always wonder if I have done the right thing ... Should I be staying with their dad because of them or should I be on my own to make me happy? No doctor can give you something to tell you ... no one can say you did this wrong or you did that right.'

Anne's children suffer from chronic asthma, a condition their father also has. Two of her boys have severe attention deficit hyperactivity disorder (ADHD), with attendant behavioural and learning problems. Her second youngest son has a bowel condition, and her infant has an eye condition that required surgery in 1998. Her kids were in and out of the hospital on a weekly basis. Anne managed multiple medical needs and dispensed large amounts of medication: 'I got seven prescriptions from the doctor yesterday ... I've got, like, 13 different medications for four kids, three or four times a day.'

In early 1997, Anne had pulled together a good team of personal supports around her: 'I rely on Jenny, who is my neighbour and best friend. I have another friend, Shelley. We rely on each other a lot for emotional and financial support. And my sister is really good for support. I go through a lot of hard times with the kids being sick and struggling with taking care of them, especially figuring out how to get my other kids looked after while I'm at the hospital with a sick child. So I do have three people that really do support me.'

Anne also got support from professionals. She saw a psychologist to help her deal with her anxiety, and a counsellor for her children's behavioural problems. Anne had to be very resourceful and persistent to get these services: '[When I needed help with the kids after the car accident], I begged the social service agency, "Please just don't put me on a waiting list." I said, "Please help me, I need your help. My family is in a crisis. I'm losing my marbles. My patience with my kids is going. I need your help." It was very important that they didn't just shove me on a waiting list. And they didn't, thank God. I was accepted within two weeks and they were coming to the house. So that's been a massive, massive release just to know that there is professional support other than just your personal support.' She worried that she was not coping well with so many demands, but explained that she had no choice but to carry on as best she could: 'I can't run, you know. I can't just walk out the door like my husband did. Every day he went to drink and that door would close and I'd be left here crying with the kids and he wouldn't think twice. So I learned to hold in a lot of the frustrations and just learn to deal with it as best as I can. I have not always done things the right way. I don't think I've always been a good parent. I've made wrong decisions, but I'm learning. Everything's a learning experience.'

The restructuring of social services dramatically affected Anne's family. The cuts meant that both health care and social assistance departments were understaffed and overburdened; as a result, access to services was diminished and inconsistent: 'I used to be able to get certain medications covered on my drug card and now I can't. I have to pay for those medications. And my kids have chronic asthma so that's a constant expense for me. The waiting lists are phenomenal for appointments [with medical specialists or with social workers] because of the cutbacks. There used to be five intake workers. Now there's only one intake worker, so if your crisis isn't as bad as the next person's crisis, you're on a waiting list. They say, "I'm sorry, there's a waiting list due to social cutbacks." Everybody says it.'

In 1997, one of the things that made it possible for Anne to get by was her housing subsidy. In 2000, the provincial government announced that it was considering barring social assistance recipients from receiving those subsidies, what it called 'double-dipping.' Anne noted, 'If I were living in a place paying $700 a month I wouldn't even have food money.'

Social assistance resources were increasingly directed towards verification processes and surveillance in the late 1990s. Ontario established a welfare fraud hotline in 1995. The Family Benefits division had always been somewhat intrusive, but the intensified scrutiny of poor families was alarming. Anne explained how such monitoring affected her when she was in the hospital in 1997, and her ex-husband stayed in her home to care for their children: 'Somebody reported to the mother's allowance hotline that my husband was living here. I flipped. I was in the hospital! I have four children that I could not take care of! Yes he was here, but normally he isn't here at all. He was staying here to care for *his* children for the three days that I was sick in the hospital! He doesn't even pay support. It took me two years to get away from him. Did they think I'm just going to let him move back in here?' In addition to her own illness and stress, Anne had to persuade social service officials that she did not have 'a man in the house,' a frustrating and time-consuming activity that also evoked painful emotions as she confronted both the end of her marriage and her ex-husband's growing withdrawal from the children. As the year progressed, he had less and less to do with the children and then moved to another province. He returned episodically, and when he did, he questioned Anne's parenting abilities and choices. They went to court, and Anne retained custody.

In late 1997, Anne was able move to a slightly larger townhouse on a much quieter street. This meant that the kids were attending a new school. Anne's relationship with her neighbour Jenny had fallen apart, depriving both of them of an important source of support. The children's medical needs had also intensified, but, as a result of the efforts of their paediatrician, Anne began receiving Handicap Benefits for two of her children's medical conditions, and applied for benefits for her youngest son. The provision of respite money and extended drug coverage made a significant difference to her finances:

They pay for the aerochambers, they pay for all the masking, for their tubes, their machines. They pay for medication that isn't covered on my drug card. They give me a special drug card that allows me to get these medications. They allow me pull-ups for Aaron because of his bowel problem. Handicap Benefits were giving me respite money because I was a single parent with four high-need children and I never had time for them. I just functioned in the house, just the basic functions. So they were allowing respite so that I could get somebody to babysit two of them so I could spend one-on-one time with the other. But what's been happening, because they've been in the hospital so much, I've been using this respite money to pay for babysitters while they've been in the hospital.

Managing the paperwork associated with receiving extended assistance was time-consuming:

James, the baby, has now been identified as having severe asthma; he has had four hospital admissions in the last month. He's now had an application filled out for handicap benefits. I've been keeping track over the last year what I use for respite, appointments for the kids, and when they've been in the hospital. It reads asthma, ADHD, baby in hospital, baby in hospital, baby in hospital, James in hospital, Aaron had to have his CAT scan, doctors' appointments, asthma, asthma, asthma, asthma, Calum in hospital.

In early 1998, Anne managed to pull together all of the care providers who worked with her family, and was planning a case conference to coordinate appropriate responses:

We're having this big case conference, for many reasons, including because I have a problem with the Ritalin [the drug which treats ADHD]. I have two kids on ritalin, which is like a kiddy cocaine. I have Aaron on the slow release and two blue pills a day, and I have Calum on three blue pills a day. And that's a lot of medication for a six-year-old and a three-year-old to be taking ... The day care will also be there because Calum pulled the fishtail off the fish when it was swimming in the bowl, and does really bizarre attention deficit, impulsive things. This wonderful lady through the Children's Aid Society, who has been helping me keep the kids in day care, will also be there. This case conference is hopefully going to get it wide open on the table so that everybody knows everything, because right now the family services organization hears from me, Children's Aid hears from me, I talk to the doctor, but there's no communication with everybody. I'm going to have [the pediatrician] Dr Shamus's attention for two hours. This is just going to be amazing.

As a result of the case conference, Anne was able to get a Children's Aid worker to come into her home 10 hours a week in the evenings to help with homework and bath time. Because one child avoided the bus and skipped school, the worker also came in the morning to walk one of her sons to the bus.

> A Children's Aid worker was coming in. It took me months to get them to help me. They wouldn't help me. I wasn't abusing my children, so they wouldn't come in. But now she'll come in for 10 hours a week at night, from 6:00 PM to 8:00 PM. She's been working with me for a couple of months, and we are very comfortable with her. The kids all love her. And she takes them swimming and different things out of the home. They've just cut her hours. She was the one that was coming at 8:00 in the morning till 8:30 to take Aaron to the bus stop, wait for the bus, trying to coax him onto the bus. I went through three weeks where every day Aaron was leaving the school. It'd take me two hours to find him. He was terrified to go to school.

Anne's main strategy with her children was to provide a rigorous schedule and routine. Calum, who was four in 1998, needed structure 'every single second of the day or he will completely take this family over.' After dinner and homework, the kids used their ventilator machines (which took up to 40 minutes), and had baths and stories. Anne slept on the couch to keep an eye on things because Calum liked to disassemble electrical equipment and had set several fires.

Two other major events were occurring in Anne's life at the same time. She had to take her ex-husband to court for child support; his boss hid his earnings and lied for him, so that Anne had no recourse to his wages. In addition, Anne's doctor, her child psychologist, and the family service agency all recommended that Calum, her four-year-old son, be put in a foster home.

> They want to place him in a foster home because of his severe ADHD ... They just think that he needs to be in a two-parent, one-child environment. They say that the energy level in this house is so fast paced. They're saying, 'It's what you can cope with, Anne.' They [the children] have major high needs, mentally, physically, healthwise. They're saying, 'What's in Calum's best interest? Put your feelings aside.' But what do I say? 'Do you want to go live somewhere else Calum?' They ask, 'What are you doing for your kids? Is it best for your kids to be in this environment where you're just putting out fires all the time?' That's basically what I'm doing; I'm just around to take Aaron off the covers, Calum out of the fridge, turn off the burners, shut my car doors. I don't know what to do. I

have been telling their father that they want Calum to go into a home. He says, 'Oh, he's going to hate you and you'll be some worthless mother if you do that.'

Anne's sources of support as well as her confidence became seriously frayed during this period. Many of those involved in her case conference changed jobs, and there was little continuity in the programs and supports that she had pulled together for her family:

> Since the case conference I had these two people that were in charge of my whole caseload. One's on medical leave and one quit. I'm no longer working with Children's Aid. So now I'm just dealing with whoever's picking up my file. With Judy, they cut her hours back so I'm going to be more and more on my own again. I understand there are a lot of kids out there that need help because of abuse. I'm stressed out, too. I do yell at my kids and I have spanked them and I do lose my temper. I've lost the two main people in these groups that were helping me. So I'm just getting shoved onto somebody else.

In 1998, Anne's handicap benefits were suddenly decreased by $300, a 33 per cent cut. She dreaded having to go through the paperwork to determine why they had been cut and whether they could be readjusted. The letter about the cut came just as Aaron's behavioural, health, and educational problems intensified.

> Aaron was ripping his books up, throwing chairs at the teachers, leaving the school grounds. The principal was driving around looking for him. He's really bad. They can't get an extra teacher involved. They can't get, you know, an assistant teacher to spend more one-on-one time with Aaron for him to feel more comfortable in there. So that's the major problem. If they would provide that, he would be fine. That's all the doctor's recommended, an extra special pair of hands for Aaron, but with the cutbacks ... They say, 'We can't do it, so Aaron's just going to have to deal with it.' He sucks his thumb, he falls asleep in class, he doesn't take his coat off, never eats lunch. He's pretty severe ADHD, very hyper, and a pretty emotional kid from his dad going and everything else.

When we met for the last time in late 1999, Aaron had been placed in a treatment home. 'It was just becoming too much for me and for the other kids, so the doctor recommended I give this a try.' Anne was much calmer, and had begun working part-time at a retail store. For the first time in three years, she felt all right, although not financially secure: 'Right now I think I'm doing okay because I get the extra handicap benefits, [but] that's going to go down in September though. I'm going to get probably $350 a month instead of $650 because [the children's] medications changed and they're getting a little bit better. I think I am okay right now, especially now I'm working.'

Anne's coping strategies – her budgeting, receipt keeping, and tracking of multiple costs and payments – took an enormous amount of time. Staff turnover and lack of response on the part of social service workers intensified her workload. The work of social reproduction in Anne's case expanded, not just because of income fluctuations, but because of fluctuations in formal and informal supports and the amount of unpaid work time it took to coordinate and ensure support.

Coping Consequences

The supports and resources available to participant households, and low-income households in particular, were altered by a series of trends. Changes in labour market regulation and an employability approach to training and income support made access to income sources less secure. At the same time, a preference for social policy delivered through the tax system rather than through service provision, combined with a decisive attack on social assistance, meant that supports were much less accessible. Female household members in particular devised and implemented survival strategies for their families in order to maximize household resources. Participants in the study attempted to raise money by getting more paid work, selling household goods, making and selling items, bartering for goods, or going into debt. They also tried moving into cheaper housing, either alone or with others, or borrowing money from family and friends. Whatever strategies they used, participants' efforts to maximize resources directed to social reproduction were in most cases short-term and unsustainable. People who do without basic goods such as food or personal sundries face both physical and mental health problems. Those who cannot afford child care, transportation, or social events get increasingly anxious, isolated, lonely, and vulnerable. Household cohesion – including between spouses such as Kate and Carl or Christine and Dwight, who separated in part because of finances – is compromised when the expected supports are no longer accessible.

Because reciprocity is difficult for many on low incomes, household participants who borrowed money or shared homes felt indebted and their family relationships were strained. Support, whether financial, emotional, or in-kind, was often a source of division as well as of assistance.

Where household participants were able to get access to additional services and supports, they found many either had conditions attached (e.g., food banks) or required an enormous amount of time and effort to navigate and maintain. Careful budgeting was an often-cited strategy among participant households. Living on tight budgets with no margins of error, however, meant that unexpected costs were crippling. Strategies like barter were helpful, but often required substantial time, skills, or energy. The stress of just getting by, or not being able to provide the kind of care, love, and support that they wanted to, made individuals feel as though they were living on the edge.

Women's capacities to manage scarce resources and new crises were central vehicles for offsetting some of the deleterious effects of welfare state restructuring. Yet the strategies available to low-income women in participating households were not sustainable. The ability of families to cope with dramatic social service and labour market change depends on their class location, and on the variety of their social networks (or their social capital). The presence of a diversity of social networks, especially ones that consist of individuals with access to assets, higher incomes or professional skills, affect access to non-kin services and supports. Likewise, the relative strength of a familialist ideology in social and economic policy affects women's capacities to offset welfare state and labour market restructuring. The case study data show that although families are sites of cooperation and support, and communities and friends do help pick up where families cannot, reliance on these groups comes with a heavy unpaid-work and emotional burden and is not a sustainable strategy for coping with insecurity.

The result of welfare state and labour market restructuring in Ontario in the 1990s meant that women's capacities to maintain independence from labour markets (de-commodification) and from marriage (autonomous households) were undermined. Unpaid work intensified for low-income households (predominantly for women) as they managed income and social service insecurity. Some participants in this study were able to manage in the short-term; others, who were extremely vulnerable, could not cope.

7 Rethinking Welfare State Retrenchment

Not only does it [social reproduction] require physical and emotional energy, but, most important, it carries a responsibility for the survival, well-being and happiness of other people. It is unequally distributed by gender, as women are historically the ones made responsible for the dependent sections of the population (children, the old and the sick) and for adult males as well. It can be supplemented by waged work at home, waged work in public and private services and voluntary social work, but unpaid family work still has the final responsibility for harmonizing other work and/or absorbing its inadequacies.
– Picchio 1996: 89

The implementation of the Ontario neo-liberal experiment in the 1990s required that the relationship of the state to families/households and to the market be redesigned. In practice, this translated into the state retrenching its role in redistribution and social service. It became more punitive, less universal, accessible, and transparent for citizens, but vastly more accessible for private business. The labour market that was fostered by neo-liberalism intensified established patterns of insecurity and precariousness. To enact a neo-liberal welfare state, the Conservatives elevated the individual market citizen, romanticized women's familial roles, and ignored the mounting need for investments in social reproduction, which their own policies exacerbated. At decade's end, more families required multiple earners to get by, while social policy changes deepened their vulnerability to economic and social crises.

Three main conclusions emerge from the study. First, at the level of individual households, decreased support for, and increased work in, the tasks associated with social reproduction intensified the strain on women in particular to develop strategies to maintain standards of living in a context of insecure income and decreased social support. Second, the state-market-family/household relationship was reconfigured in a neo-liberal context so that the work of social reproduction was shifted across these sectors, falling to the family/household and to the private market to provide. Third, the reconfiguration of the state-market-family/household relationship signalled a shift within the gender regimes of these institutions and the broader gender order. The gender order that was consolidated is one in which the work of social reproduction is increasingly organized via women's unpaid labour in a context in which a dual earner model has come to dominate.

The examination of legislative and regulatory changes along with the experiences of members of households during a period of significant social and economic restructuring showed the struggle that many faced in meeting their subsistence needs. Meeting the needs of members of households was a task that was usually divided along gender lines. Many women worked for pay in the market (whether or not they had another wage-earner in the household who contributed to household income) and struggled to gain access to non-market income sources at the same time as they organized and performed most of the work of provisioning and caring for members of their households. Among participant households, the gender spread of low income was notable, especially as these low-income households often combined multiple-income sources and could not financially rely solely on market-based earnings.

Due to significant changes in the provision and organization of key social services, such as health care and education, increasing amounts of time were spent by male and female participant households attempting to navigate, gain access to, and maintain key supports. Especially for those with low incomes, the costs, such as additional community-based care, could not be met through the market and thus were transferred onto already overburdened women. Further, in areas such as primary and secondary education, parents whose children required additional care and services were often the same people who lacked the time or resources to attend and be part of school councils. Increased insecurity in almost all income sources (from employment, government, and other sources, including child support) coupled with decreased access to formal social supports required that multiple strategies be employed by members of households in order to meet the subsistence and development needs of their members.

The coping strategies employed by many lower-income households were not sustainable over the long term. Debt loads were high and increasing, educational and training pursuits were deferred, and relationships central to people's lives were strained by the effects of little income and time. Parents were less able in terms of time, and, in some instances, skill, to assist their children in their educational pursuits. Strategies such as selling household goods, doing without, or intensifying the amount of time spent shopping and preparing foods were stopgap measures. Social policies, such as work for welfare, intensified these problems as they geared recipients towards a low-wage labour market. The long-term effects of poor nutrition, unmet health care needs, deferred education, and high levels of stress ensure that there will be some reproduction of these conditions among children. Further, household dissolution and an absence of intra-household supports (often due to the breakdown of key kin relationships) intensified the isolation of poorer households. Some could not cope. One felt she would be better off dead; another attempted suicide. Household infrastructures and the associated capacity to engage in human development tasks such as assisting with reading are degraded in the context of decreased social spending, a neo-liberal economic orientation, and an increasingly insecure labour market. For women, who are the primary users of social services and a significant portion of workers in the insecure labour market, the cumulative effect of these series of changes degraded their abilities to perform the tasks needed to sustain household members. The capacity of lone mothers to form and maintain autonomous households was massively curtailed by the labour market and social policy changes characteristic of the Harris Conservatives.

The neo-liberal regime that emerged in the province of Ontario sharpened the contradiction between the pursuit of profit and the work of social reproduction. The state mediated this friction through mechanisms such as legislation which deregulated capital controls and privatized key sectors, and through centralization of decision-making authority for areas like health care and education. It simultaneously increased its surveillance of the poorest members of society, women in particular. The result of this mediation was to shift increasing amounts of responsibility for provisioning away from state purview and onto families/households. But because the state 'plays a constitutive role in well functioning markets – supplying an infrastructure of rights and regulations without which no orderly market is possible' (Elson

1998:199), the long-term effects of degraded household infrastructures have an effect on the state's attempt to shift costs to households. Citizens are less equipped socially, in terms of levels of skill, and, more generally, their human and social capital are poorly developed. Indeed, the experiences of Ontario households run contrary to the prevailing current policy logics about building social capital (see World Bank 1998); those who are socially and economically vulnerable have social networks with the same attributes, which cannot be called on for sustained support over the long term (see Bezanson forthcoming).

The Conservative provincial government relied on a discourse of re-familialization as it attempted to individualize problems in meeting standards of living. The family/household was assumed to absorb the shocks of economic adjustment and to be the safety net of last resort (Elson 1998:199). The capacity of this sector to compensate for malfunctions or decisions elsewhere in the economic system is not without limits; the family/household 'can be undermined by lack of resources, insecurity and demoralisation; and in return it will be unable to supply ... the demand, the labour, the intangible social assets that the public and private sectors need to reform.' (199). Demoralization results from, among other things, an assumption that little work or investment is required to maintain what Elson terms intangible social assets at the household level, including a sense of ethics, citizenship, communication, and uncodified social norms (200).

What happens at the level of individual households, then, has feedback effects to the state and market levels. The risks associated with deregulating capital are shifted downward. In the context of neo-liberal states such as Ontario, in which de-commodified entitlements were greatly reduced, the family/household sector was less able to absorb shocks – that is, was less able to be flexible and dynamic – associated with neo-liberal restructuring. As Elson (1998:205) notes, 'when people have to live from hand to mouth human energies and morale are weakened: "contingent labour" is conducive to "contingent households" which fragment and disintegrate, with costs for the people from those households and for the wider society.' The logic of neo-liberalism replicates many of the dynamics of nineteenth-century capitalism in Europe: the demand for unskilled labour and the attendant conditions of work and social reproduction produced a major social crisis which required mediation. The neo-liberal model in Ontario also produced social crises in terms of de-skilling and impoverishment.

At the level of aggregating the organization of gender relations, it is evident that the gender order in Ontario was not stable, in that the demands of social reproduction and on paid labour were mounting and incompatible. In the late 1990s, the nuclear family form with a male breadwinner model was no longer viable, except for the most wealthy. The organization of the work of provisioning and caring remained tied to women's unpaid labour in the home, but the supports for such work (a stable male income, de-commodified access to income via a relationship with a man, or universal state services) were inadequate. In this dual earner/female carer model, women's labour market participation was visible, while the work of social reproduction done in homes was less visible. The gender order that was consolidated was marked by insecure and unpredictable work arrangements, and an assumption that the family/household would internalize the conflicts resulting from these arrangements. A key feature of the gender order, then, was the family/household's alternator role, which increased the demands on women to juggle paid work and unpaid work with few additional supports. As the experiences of members of households bear out, the absence of supports and the insecurity of income sources made the arrangement ad hoc at best, and led to household dissolution at worst.

The gender order that emerged in Ontario in the late 1990s was one in which neo-liberalism predominated, creating a certain limited space for neo-conservatism. Neo-liberalism emphasizes a reduction in social spending and redistribution, less government, and fewer regulations on markets, including labour markets. It elevates market individualism over citizenship. The neo-liberal welfare state is one in which goods, services, and to a large extent labour, are increasingly privatized and re-commodified. It encourages families to absorb or purchase care work, while it simultaneously encourages men and women to become workers, ignoring the constraints posed by care work. Neo-conservative ideology elevates the nuclear family as the moral unit for social reproduction, while simultaneously removing its supports and inputs. The stories of low-income participant households show that a dual earner/female carer model for welfare states cannot address social reproduction and thus cannot be sustained.

The effects of Ontario's version of neo-liberalism share similarities with the experiences of other nations that underwent similar experiments (see Bashevkin 2002a; Daly 2001). In Canada, standards of living and the work of social reproduction are generally considered only in the context of extreme poverty. Despite overwhelming evidence of increases in the gap between the rich and the poor, and in the depth of poverty for particular groups, public policies have not caught up with reality. Trends such as labour market deregulation, deregulation of capital controls more generally, cuts in social spending, and an emphasis on individualism over collectivism are widespread. At the level of capital accumulation on a broad scale, the gender order that is consolidated by a retreating welfare state continues to place enormous demands on paid and unpaid work, with little investment in the domestic sector. Polanyi's insights about the social need to limit capital's destructive tendencies compels a rethinking of the current gender order; its reconfiguration will require states at an international level to mediate the tension between accumulation and social reproduction. If this mediation is to be successful, it will require a deeper reconfiguration of responsibility among men, women, and communities, as well as among markets and states, of responsibility for the work of social reproduction.

APPENDIX A

Low Income Cut-Offs (LICOs) 1998 (1992 Base)

Community size	500,000+	100,000– 499,999	30,000– 99,999	Less than 30,000*	Rural areas
Family size					
1 person	$17,571	$15,070	$14,965	$13,924	$12,142
2 persons	$21,962	$18,837	$18,706	$17,405	$15,178
3 persons	$27,315	$23,429	$23,264	$21,647	$18,877
4 persons	$33,063	$28,359	$28,162	$26,205	$22,849
5 persons	$36,958	$31,701	$31,481	$29,293	$25,542
6 persons	$40,855	$35,043	$34,798	$32,379	$28,235
7 or more persons	$44,751	$38,117	$38,117	$35,467	$30,928

Source: Statistics Canada (1999), cat. 13-551.
* Includes cities with a population between 15,000 and 30,000 and small urban areas (under 15,000).

Notes: According to Statistics Canada, LICOs are used to delineate family units into "low income" and "other" groups. LICOs are based on the Family Expenditure Survey. From this data, the average family expenditure on food, shelter, and clothing in Canada is calculated (as a percentage of pre-tax income). Base-year LICOs are set where families spend 20% more of their income than the Canadian average on food, shelter, and clothing (Statistics Canada, Cat. no. 13-551:8). The 1998 LICOs are included here as participants were asked to reflect questions pertaining to income covering the period 1990-1999 (most did not have complete information for 1999 due to the timing of the interviews).

APPENDIX B

Selection and Recruitment of Participants

The following provides a brief summary of the selection and recruitment process. It is adapted from McMurray's (1997: 4–5) report on the
methodology used in the Speaking Out project, which provides greater
detail.

Once the template capturing a range of household configurations and
characteristics has been established, Speaking Out asked selected community service and other organizations to identify potential participants. The research team reasoned that people might be more inclined
to make a commitment to participate in a three-year study if they were
introduced to the project by someone they knew. Agencies and organizations passed along our information to other contacts, with a snow-
ball effect.

The main criteria for selection were that households should meet some
mix of the template characteristics and that participants should be able
to communicate their day-to-day experiences. Initial demographic
information was collected and a face-to-face or telephone screening
interview was undertaken with at least one household member.
Households were selected on a rolling basis.

A $100 honorarium was paid to a household for each round of inter-
views. Interviews were tape recorded and transcribed, identifying
information was removed, and the tapes were destroyed.

APPENDIX C

Detailed Household Structure

Table 1. Household Structure 1997*

Income group	Names	Household type	Number of children/ Ages**	Age***	Gender	Geographic location	Individual characteristics
High Income	Sara & Anand	2-parent, opposite sex	2 children/ 4, 6 yrs	35 &36	Female and male	Toronto	South Asian Canadian, anglophone
Middle Income	Denise & Rick	Blended 2-parent, opposite sex	4 children/ 16, 16, 14, 13 yrs	39 & 43	Male and female	Greater Toronto Area (GTA)	White, anglophone
	Christine & Dwight	2-parent, opposite sex	1 child/ 12 yrs	35 &37	Female and male	Small SW Ontario town	White, anglophone
	Victoria	Lone parent	1 child/18 yrs	48	Female	Ottawa	White, anglophone
	Frank & Michael	Couple, same sex	None	36 & 38	Male	Toronto	White, anglophone, gay
	Angie	Lone parent	2 children/ 13, 11 yes	33	Female	Ottawa	White, anglophone
	Cheryl & Paul	2-parent, opposite sex	2 children/ 14, 11 yrs	40s	Female and male	Small SW Ontario town	White, anglophone
	Maria & Leo	2-parent, opposite sex	2 children, early teens	Early 50s	Female and male	GTA	North African, ESL
	Jessie & Mark	Couple opposite sex	None	31 & 30	Female and male	Mid-sized Northern Ontario town	White, anglophone
	Janet & Christopher	2-parent, blended opposite sex	3 resident, 2 on weekends/ 16, 14, 11, and two teenage	Late 40s	Female and male	Mid-sized Eastern Ontario town	White, anglophone

Income group	Names	Household type	Number of children/Ages**	Age***	Gender	Geographic location	Individual characteristics
	Pamela & Bert	2-parent, opposite sex	1 child &1 adult child/ 16, 26 yrs	Late 40s	Female and male	Mid-sized Northern Ontario town	White, anglophone
	Barbara & Adam****	2-parent, blended opposite sex	2 children/16, 15 yrs	Early 40s	Female and male	Small Northern Ontario town	First Nations, anglophone
	Melanie, Heather & Ron	Mixed-generation	None	50, 27, & 26	Female, Female and male	Toronto	White, anglophone
	Julie	Single	None	Early 30s	Female	Ottawa	White, anglophone, Physical disability, lesbian
	Sabrina & Elizabeth	Housemates	None	Early 30s	Female	Toronto	White, anglophone
Low Income	Jenny	Lone parent	3 children/8, 5, 1 yrs	27	Female	Mid-sized Eastern Ontario town	White, anglophone
	Anne	Lone parent	4 children/7, 5, 2, 1 yrs	26	Female	Mid-sized Eastern Ontario town	White, anglophone
	Ashley & Rosa	Mixed-generation	1 child/2 yrs	56 & 32	Female	Toronto	African Canadian, anglophone
	Olivia &Gary	2-parent, opposite sex	1 child/14 yrs	36 & 34	Male and female	GTA	White, anglophone
	Patrick	Single	None	32	Male	Toronto	White, anglophone

APPENDIX C: (continued)

Income group	Names	Household type	Number of children/ Ages**	Age***	Gender	Geographic location	Individual characteristics
	Veronica	Lone parent	2 children /6, 3 yrs	Late 20s	Female	GTA	White, anglophone
	Teresa	single	None	30	Female	Toronto	White, anglophone, lesbian, physical disability
	Sadan	Lone parent	4 children/13, 10, 7 yrs, 2 mo.	39	Female	Toronto	African Canadian, ESL
	Richard & Robbie	Housemates	None	50 & 26	Male	Mid-sized SW Ontario town	White, anglophone, gay
	Amy & Charles	2 parent opposite sex	3 children/11, 5, 3 yrs	27 &26	Female and male	Toronto	African Canadian, anglophone
	Kate & Carl	2 parent opposite sex	2 children/ 7, 2 yrs	33 & 27	Female and Male	Toronto	Kate – White Carl – First Nations, anglophone
	Liz	Single	None	53	Female	Toronto	White, anglophone
	Michelle	Lone parent	2 children/ 7, 5 yrs	Late 30s	Female	Toronto	African Canadian, anglophone
	Rosie & Bob	Couple opposite sex	1 adult child, rent paying	59 & 66	Female and male	Toronto	White, anglophone
	Denzel	Single	None	25	Male	Ottawa	African Canadian, anglophone
	Jackie	Lone parent	2 children/ 17 yrs, 8 mo.	30	Female	Mid-sized Eastern Ontario town	White, anglophone

APPENDIX C: (concluded)

Income group	Names	Household type	Number of children/ Ages**	Age***	Gender	Geographic location	Individual characteristics
	Josie & Rebecca	Mixed generation	3 children/ 5, 4, 2 yrs	Late 40s, 20s	Female	GTA	White, Francophone
	Randy & Monica	2-parent, blended opposite sex	3 children/13, 7, 5 yrs	29 & 30s	Male and female	Small SW Ontario town	White, anglophone
	Lisa & *Ray*	2-parent, opposite sex	2 children/ 14, 11 yrs	44 & 38	Female and male	Mid-sized Northern Ontario town	First Nations, anglophone
	James	single	None	26	Male	Toronto	First Nations, anglophone
	Aida & Xavier	2-parent, opposite sex	2 adult children (20s), 1 teenager	Late 40s	Female and male	Toronto	Latin American Canadian, ESL
	Tara	Lone parent	1 child/ 4 mo.	17	Female	Toronto	Latin-American/ First Nations, Anglophone
	Natalia & Antonio	2-parent, opposite sex	2 children/11, 7 yrs	Early 40s	Female and male	Toronto	Latin American Canadian, ESL

Notes: Italicization under the column "Names" indicates which household member(s) was/were the primary participants in all *four* rounds of interviews. Light shading indicates a household whose members separated and who were re-interviewed as newly constituted households.Dark Shading indicates a household whose members were interviewed once but could not be relocated to be re-interviewed.

*The number of households interviewed changed over the three years. Tara could not be located to be re-interviewed. Samantha, whose demographic characteristics were similar, was added in late 1997. Brad was interviewed in early 1998 but could not be located to be re-interviewed subsequently. Ashley and Rosa became two households and each was subsequently interviewed. The same was true of Kate and Carl. Jerry, a single father with a small child, joined in early 1998 (see Table 2 below).
** Only children who resided in the household were counted.
*** A number of participants did not want to disclose their precise ages. The majority of adult participants (56 per cent) were in the 25 to 40 age range. Thirty per cent were 41 to 55, while 5 per cent were 56 and older. Seven per cent were under 25.
**** Barbara characterized herself as a single mother with a new partner, indicating that parenting and care were not shared.

Table 2. Households That Joined after First 1997 Interview

Income group	Names	Household type	Number of children/ ages	Age***	Gender	Geographic location	Individual characteristics
Middle income	Jerry	Lone parent	1 child/ 4	26	Male	Ottawa	White, anglophone
Low income	Samantha & Nathan*	Two-parent household	2 children/ 3, 1 yr.	17 & 20	Female and male	Toronto	African-Canadian, anglophone
Low income	Brad	single	None	19	Male	Toronto	White, anglophone

Note: Dark shading indicates a household that was interviewed once and could not be re-located.

* replaced Tara.

APPENDIX D

Benchmark Questions

DAILY CONCERNS

1. Have there been any major changes in your household (demographics, crises, job loss, new job, geographic move) since we last spoke?
2. Last time we spoke you noted that *_____* was a concern for you. What is this situation now? How have things changed?
3. Can you tell me about other daily or immediate concerns?
4. Do you foresee any new concerns arising in the next little while?
5. Have there been any crises or turning points in your life since we last spoke?
6. Are there future changes in government programs or policies that concern you or that may have some impact on you or members of your household?

COPING STRATEGIES

In relation to your concerns or worries, we want to find out how you deal with them:

1. Who or what has helped you deal with the ups and downs of life since we last spoke?
2. Has your household had to do anything differently since we last spoke, to try and make ends meet?
3. Is there anything you have had to give up (money, leisure time)?
4. Where and to whom did you turn?
5. How would you rate your ability to handle the day-to-day demands in your life?

COMMUNITY

We have been discussing how your cope with difficulties. Now I'd like to get some idea of who you depend upon and who you support and help – whether that is friends, relations, neighbours, or services you use.

1. Since we last spoke, has anyone not living with you relied on you for financial support? For emotional support?

2. Who outside of your household do you rely on for financial support? For emotional support?
3. Have your sources of support changed since we last spoke?
4. What other kinds of assistance have you had to seek out since the last interview (agencies, doctors, friends, family)?
5. Have any of your relationships been affected when you have sought out support? If so, how?
6. Last time we spoke, we spent some time discussing the communities in which you live (friends, neighbourhood). Have you noticed any changes in these communities? Why?
7. Have you noticed any changes in the communities in which you live (friends, neighbourhood) since we last spoke?

THE NEAR FUTURE

1. Looking ahead for the next two years or so, what changes do you anticipate in your life?

APPENDIX E

The Speaking Out Research Process

1. Interview members of households using benchmark and policy open-ended questions. Transcribe.
2. Establish themes across the households.
3. With main report focus determined, do basic coding of interviews using interview software (NU*DIST).
4. In context of report focus, disaggregate interviews to produce more sub-coding on specific policy issues.
5. Sub-coding adds more detailed discoveries about policy across households and over time.
6. Comparison is made with external studies, reports, statistics, seeking connections between household experiences and general data.
7. Begin draft of outline for report, basic areas, general sections. Usually two authors write a report, but entire team involved in planning.
8. In each section, researchers begin connecting specific household findings and stories to other data.
9. (A) Generalize from household findings to entire province when possible, (B) use stories to illustrate the findings of larger stuidies, (C) explore the multi-dimensional effect of policy on households.
10. Clearer themes of each section and overall picture emerge. Numerous drafts of sections, feedback from entire team.
11. Hammer out final report, final agreement from households on quotes and descriptions. Those quoted in the report were sent their quote (with identifying information changed) for their verification and consent.
12. Produce, release and distribute final report through Caledon Institute of Social Policy.

Source: Neysmith, Bezanson, and O'Connell (2005:203).

APPENDIX F

Speaking Out Publications

Bezanson, K., and S. McMurray. 2000. *Booming for Whom? People in Ontario Talk about Income, Jobs and Social Programmes*. Ottawa: Caledon Institute of Social Policy.

Bezanson, K., and L. Noce. 1999. *Costs, Closures and Confusion: People in Ontario Talk about Health Care*. Ottawa: Caledon Institute of Social Policy.

Bezanson, K., and F. Valentine. 1998. *Act in Haste ... The Style, Scope and Speed of Change in Ontario*. Ottawa: Caledon Institute of Social Policy.

McMurray, S. 1997. *Speaking Out Project Description, Research Strategy and Methodology*. Ottawa: Caledon Institute of Social Policy.

Noce, L., and A. O'Connell. 1998. *Take It or Leave It: The Ontario Government's Approach to Job Insecurity*. Ottawa: Caledon Institute of Social Policy.

O'Connell, A., and F. Valentine. 1998. *Centralizing Power, Decentralizing Blame: What Ontarians Say about Education Reform*. Ottawa: Caledon Institute of Social Policy.

In 2005, a book organized around household profiles was published based on the Speaking Out Data. See Neysmith, S., K. Bezanson, and A. O'Connell. 2005. *Telling Tales: Living the Effects of Public Policy*. Halifax, NS: Fernwood.

APPENDIX G

Profiles of Participant Households Who Received Social Assistance in the 1990s

1. Participant Households Who Stopped Receiving Benefits before 1995

Name and household configuration	Level of benefits	Characteristics	Why no longer receiving social assistance?
Olivia, Gary, 1 child	Full benefits for one year while unemployed	Both adults had some post-secondary education; he immigrated to Canada from southern Europe	1994: Gary started self-employment
Denise, 2 children	Full benefits for one year after she left abusive partner	Single mother, some post-secondary	1995: started new relationship with waged man, found part-time work
Antonio, Natalia, 3 children	Full benefits for 4 years after arriving in Canada as refugees	Refugees, English as a second language, both have university degrees, he was attending college, supplemented income with cash work	1995: Antonio enrolled in college, worked part-time
Angie, ex-husband, 2 kids	Full benefits for 1 year while she returned to school, her ex-spouse was unemployed	Angie has grade 12, 2 high-health-needs kids, left spouse	1991: found full-time work after upgrading
Carl	Full benefits, then income top-up over 3 years	First Nations man, health crisis, some post-secondary	1992: part-time work, then training.
Jackie, 1 child (her 2 other children born later)	Full benefits for 2 years after marriage ended; completed university degree	Single mother, child with a physical disability, university degree	1991: part-time work after university

Jessie and Mark	Income top up; full benefits for short time over 2 years	northern household; she has post-secondary education; he has some	1995: Jessie found 2 jobs, Mark became self-employed
Monica, Randy, 3 kids	Full benefits for 3 months while his Workers' Compensation application processed	Health crisis in household; children very young; she has some high school, he has high school	1994: Randy began receiving WCB, Monica found work.
Lisa, Ray, 3 kids	Full benefits for 1 month	First Nations, he has some post-secondary education, she has some high school, northern household	1991: Ray found full-time work
Janet, 3 kids	Full benefits for 4 years while in college	Single mother, post-secondary education	1994: part-time work; self-employment, then new relationship
Barbara	Full benefits for 6 years after relationship ended, went to college	Single mother, First Nations, northen community, university degree	1991: found full-time work after school

2. Participant Households Who Stopped Receiving Benefits after 1995

Name and household configuration	Level of benefits	Characteristics	Why no longer receiving social assistance.
Ashley*	Full benefits for 3 months while waiting for EI claim	Older woman, person of colour, some post-secondary education	1998: EI self-employment
Rosa, 1 child	Full benefits for 4 years after baby was born	Single mother, person of colour, some post-secondary education, health crisis while pregnant	1999: full-time job
Patrick	Full benefits, then top-up income for 2 years	Single man, some post-secondary	1997: found part-time job

Amy, 3 kids	Full benefits, then top-up for 7 years (on and off)	Single mother, immigrant, person of colour, child with severe disability, high school	1997: college (receiving OSAP)
Kate, 2 kids (plus one part-time)	Full benefits for 9 years	Single mother, some high school, child with disability, part-time work for cash under the table	1998: benefits terminated (being investigated for fraud)
Michelle, 2 children	Top-up benefits, medical plan assistance for 9 years	Single mother, person of colour, post-secondary	1999: felt secure in full-time job, left benefits
Rosie and Bob	Medical plan assistance for 2 years	Older couple, little formal education	1997: Old Age Security benefits began
Denzel	Full benefits for 2 years	Young male, person of colour, some post-secondary education	1997: full-time job
Josie, 3 kids**	Full benefits, child care support for 1.5 years while adopting grandchildren	Francophone, high school	1996: returned to full time work
Jerry, 1 child	Child-care subsidy through Ontario Works for 1 month	Single father, some Post-secondary	1997: needed short term financial help to keep child in daycare
Sabrina	Top-up for 2 years after laid off	Post-secondary	1997: patched together 3 part-time jobs

*Was living with her adult daughter, Rosa, and Rosa's child, between 1996-1998.
** Josie's adult daughter, Rebecca, moved in with her when she finished a drug treatment program. Josie was the legal guardian of Rebecca's children. Rebecca was the primary child caregiver and received social assistance while Josie worked full time.

3. Participant Households Receiving Social Assistance Benefits, 1999–2000

Name and household configuration	Level of benefits	Characteristics
Jenny, 4 kids	Full benefits for 8 years, during and after relationship ended	Single mother, has very young children, some high school, left abusive spouse
Anne, 4 kids	Full benefits, and top-up for 8 years on and off during and after end of relationship	Single mother, kids with very high health care needs, some high school, working part-time, left abusive spouse
Veronica, 2 kids	Full benefits and top up for 9 years on and off between relationships, while working part-time	single mother, left abusive spouse, some high school, part-time work
Teresa	Full Family Benefits/Ontario Disability for 6 years	Severe physical disability, physical illness, victim of violence, some post-secondary education
Sadan, 5 kids	Full benefits for 10 years	Immigrant woman, person of colour, English as a second language, little formal education, separated from partner
Richard	Family Benefits/Ontario Disability Support and top-up for 9 years	Physically impaired, AIDS, high school
James	Homeless allowance/full benefits on and off for 9 years	Single man, First Nations, addictions, works under the table, some post-secondary
Samantha, 2 kids (partner Nathan now lives with them and they collect Ontario Works benefits together)	Full benefits for 3 years	Very young single mother, person of colour, in high school

*Two other households could be added here: Brad was a participant with whom only one interview was conducted. He worked as a "squeegee kid" and could not be located for subsequent interviews. He received homeless allowance/full benefits for about four years. Tara was another participant with whom only one interview was conducted. She was a precariously housed young single mother with whom we made contact through a shelter. She received full benefits on and off for two years, and had received some benefits when she left her foster home.

Notes

Preface

1 It is interesting to note that the very institutions that have promoted and implemented neo-liberal structural adjustment policies internationally for over two decades, such as the World Bank and the International Monetary Fund, have recently begun to seriously question the benefit of these policies for the most vulnerable populations (Wolfensohn 1998; Kanbur and Vines 2000; World Bank 2001, 2002; International Monetary Fund 2003; Wade 2004). The World Bank has, over the course of the 1990s, shifted its focus away from its Structural Adjustment Policies and replaced them with its Comprehensive Development Framework (CDF). However, Pender (2001:397) concludes that despite a new focus on poverty reduction, the CDF imposes significant conditionality on loans, and thus 'severely constrains the potential for genuine ownership of development policy.' Moreover, Bergeron (2003) finds that from a gender perspective, the World Bank 'discovered' the importance of social networks in people's capacities to manage crises. She notes that the emphasis on poor women's social capital is often opportunistic and presumes that the solution to poverty is increased market integration. The recent confirmation as World Bank president of Paul Wolfowitz, former deputy defence secretary in the George W. Bush administration and architect of the United States' war in Iraq, suggests that the bank's development framework will continue to shift to the right (Wroughton 2005).

Chapter 1: The Neo-liberal Experiment in Ontario, 1995–2000

1 This quotation is an excerpt of Harris' speech to the Kitchener-Waterloo Chamber of Commerce, 28 January 1999.

2 Harris was premier from 1995 to 2002. His former finance minister, Ernie Eves, returned from private sector work to lead the Progressive Conservative Party and the government from 2002 to 2003. The Progressive Conservatives were defeated by the Liberal Party under Dalton McGuinty in 2003.

3 Rates stayed at this level until Liberal Premier McGuinty's 2004 budget, when they rose by just 3 per cent (Trichur and Won 2004).

4 Familialistic welfare states enact public policy which presumes that the family is principally responsible for the well-being of its members, and that this responsibility must be enforced (see Esping-Andersen 1999; Zanatta 2004).

5 Minister of Women's Issues Diane Cunningham noted that many Ontarians 'were perfectly happy to leave their kids with a neighbour, or friend, or a relative while they go out to work' (*Toronto Star*, 24 October 1995).

6 In welfare state theory, Australia, Canada, the U.S., the UK, Ireland, New Zealand, and Japan are considered *liberal* welfare states (see Esping-Andersen 1990; Swank 2005). Liberal welfare states are a type of regime in which 'social provision is limited and shaped so as to preserve maximum scope for individual initiative and market forces' (O'Connor, Orloff, and Shaver 1999:9).

7 Details of the Speaking Out project are provided below. See also the appendix in this volume; McMurray 1997; Neysmith, Bezanson, and O'Connell 2005.

8 The total number of individuals and households interviewed changed slightly over the three years of the study. When adult household members separated, each was interviewed separately in their new household, thus adding to the total number of households interviewed, though this did not always increase the number of adult participants. Changes in household membership sometimes added to the number of total participants. In two cases, single adult participants could not be found to be re-interviewed, and, in these cases, new participants were sought. Many children who remained co-resident with parents over the three years became 'adults'; that is, they moved from under the age of 18 to over 18 during the course of the study. As a shorthand, I refer to 40 households as the number that participated over the course of the study because that was the number at the midway point in late 1998/early 1999. In 1997, there were 38; in 1998, 39; and in 2000, 41. Throughout the book, however, I make an effort, where appropriate, to underline the total number of individuals and households at the time of each interview (e.g., 121 members of 38 households were interviewed in 1997). See also McMurray (1997) and Neysmith, Bezanson, and O'Connell (2005).

9 Pierson (1996) argues that little welfare state dismantling occurred in Great Britain, the United States, Germany, and Sweden due in part to institutional interests that prevented dramatic restructuring. There is much debate about the extent of retrenchment in welfare states (e.g., Castles 2004). Myles and Pierson (1997) suggest that Canada and the United States experienced significant restructuring to produce an increasingly residualist and individualist welfare state rather than a universalist one. Swank's (2005) review of the OECD's *Comparative Welfare State Entitlement Data Set 1960–2000* shows that Canada's spending on social services as a percentage of GDP has declined 23 per cent since the late 1980s.

10 Pierson (1994) describes two strategies available to governments to dismantle welfare states: programmatic retrenchment and systemic retrenchment. Programmatic retrenchment entails restricting programs and cutting social spending. Systemic retrenchment involves reorienting budgetary and institutional practices that alter the overall political and policy environment in which the welfare state exists. Rice and Prince (2000:112) add a third strategy, called paradigmatic retrenchment, which refers to 'weakening or dropping support for guiding principles that serve as the basis for policy action.' Elements of all three have been implemented in Canada.

11 The virtues of flexibility and service delivery via the voluntary sector are extolled. Social programs are reoriented towards dependence on a wage and job readiness, and use a language of client-based services. The social rights of citizenship associated with Keynesian welfare states are eroded (see Cameron 2006).

12 I use the term families/households deliberately to draw attention to the diversity of household living arrangements that cannot be easily captured under the heading 'families.'

13 Porter (2003) pokes holes in the idea that the Fordist gender order was stable. Her research on women claiming unemployment insurance in Canada suggests that as early as the 1950s, women were entering the labour force in large numbers and making claims on the state as workers. The idea of a normative Fordist gender order applied to a segment of the working population, and excluded many workers of colour and many working-class women whose spousal or labour market attachments never provided for a family wage (see Williams 1995).

14 The kind of economic model that Ontario pursued between 1995 and 2000 has drawn criticism from a number of sources. Feminist scholars argued that economic theory tends to describe male norms and conceptualize market actors as asocial in their economic behaviour (Bakker 1994; Elson 1995b). They noted the failure of economics to theorize the production and

care of people. The ideal worker in a capitalist economy is one who is not constrained by externalities, such as caring for children or parents (Elson 1995a; Folbre 1999; Sen 1999). Critics of neo-liberal policies noted a range of detrimental outcomes in developing nations, such as decreased female educational attainments, increased female morbidity, and infant mortality rates (Beneria and Feldman 1992; Chant and Craske 2003). The overarching factor unifying feminist and other critiques of neo-liberal policies was that the economic model being pursued did not, and in fact could not, incorporate an analysis of the work of social reproduction. Such insights hold true for advanced welfare states undergoing processes of neo-liberal restructuring.

15 Statistics Canada's Low Income Cut-Offs were used to determine low-income status. See Appendix A for details.

16 The phrase 'living through Conservative times' is borrowed from the title of Sylvia Bashevkin's 1998 book *Women on the Defensive: Living through Conservative Times* (Toronto: University of Toronto Press, 1998).

17 It should be noted, however, that the Progressive Conservative government shifted the terrain of participation for citizens by enacting legislation that would require referenda on key issues, in particular tax increases and constitutional amendments. Notably, decisions to cut social spending or alter social programs were not subject to a mandatory referendum.

18 Sheila Neysmith (University of Toronto) and Michael Mendelson (Caledon Institute of Social Policy) were the co-principal investigators of the project and oversaw it. Anne O'Connell, Louise Noce, Fraser Valentine, and I (all PhD candidates at the time) conducted interviews, coded data, conducted policy research, and wrote all reports. Susan McMurray coordinated the project.

19 I conducted interviews with two households in Spanish; the interviews were then translated and transcribed.

20 Statistics Canada's Low Income Cut-Offs (LICOs) were used to define household income categories (see Appendix A for 1998 LICOs). LICOs vary by income, household size, and size of community. They range from $11,839 for a single person living in a rural area to $43,634 for a family of seven living in a large urban centre. Families living below these income levels are considered to be living in 'straitened circumstances' (Statistics Canada 1999). 'High-income' households were defined as those with more than double the average income for all families (average family income in 1995 was $55,247) – approximately $110,000. Households earning an income between the LICOs and $110,000 were defined as 'middle income.'

21 The households' primary source of income was easier to classify in some situations than in others. For example, it was easy when both adult house-

hold heads were employed and had no other source of income, or where the single adult member relied solely on social assistance or pension income. It was more difficult to classify when the income recipient was a full-time student who was also employed, where one adult member worked while the other received Employment Insurance (EI) benefits, or where household members received different types of social assistance.

22 It should be noted, however, that although a household was chosen for specific characteristics, this did not determine and predict how members would discuss the effects of particular policies or even which policies they would emphasize. For example, Cheryl and Paul, a middle-income professional couple with strong ties to the field of education and with children in the education system, spoke almost exclusively about health care for three of the four interviews.

23 Those children (18 years of age or younger) who participated in interviews chiefly contributed their experiences of changes in primary and secondary education policy. They were invited to participate in the entire interview process with their parents present and with parental consent.

24 For example, a household could consist of one adult who was employed and concerned about labour market issues and another who was a student and affected by education changes. Moreover, we surmised that one household member (usually a mother if there were young children present) would manage a range of needs, such as education, health, transportation, and so on. A range of policy issues pertinent to one household member might not be raised by another household member.

25 The interview process makes use of feminist insights about power relations in interview processes and among participants, and draws on interdisciplinary research on households. Hence, while multiple, intensive, semi-structured qualitative interviews were the main research tool for gathering primary data, a host of disciplinary and methodological elements informed the planning and implementation of the study.

26 Research for social change refers to a commitment on the part of the researchers to disseminate findings as widely and as accessibly as possible. One of the aims of the research was to generate public debate about timely social policy issues that affect the lives of Ontarians from a range of income backgrounds and household configurations.

27 Of the two participants who were not available for re-interviewing, one was a 'squeegee kid.' (He was at first homeless, then a precariously housed youth who derived some income from washing car windows.) The other was a single mother with whom we made initial contact through a centre for young mothers. There were also two household breakups – one involv-

ing spouses who separated and one involving a mother and daughter whose relationship unravelled – meaning two extra household interviews were subsequently carried out. See Appendix E for a description of the research process and Appendix F for a list of the publications that the Speaking Out project produced.

28 Two more households joined in early 1998. The second interview for these households consisted of questions from the first and second rounds of interview questions. Data from all rounds of interviews was thus available for 40 households.

29 The following table provides relevant data on income distribution.

Incidence of Low Income among the Population Living in Private Households, Canada and Ontario (1996 and 2001 Censuses)*

	Canada persons	Ontario persons
Income status, 2000 **	29,105,705	11,202,560
Low income	4,720,485	1,611,505
Other	24,385,215	9,591,055
Incidence of low income %	16.2	14.4
Income status, 1995	28,011,350	10,562,620
Low income	5,514,190	1,869,040
Other	22,497,160	8,693,580
Incidence of low income %***	19.7	17.7

Source: Adapted from Statistics Canada's calculations; retrieved from http://www40.statcan.ca/l01/cst01/deffamil60a.htm#1 May 2005.
*Income data from the 1996 and 2001 Censuses relate to the calendar year prior to the census year, i.e., 1995 and 2000, respectively.
** See Appendix B for LICO details.
*** The incidence of low income is the proportion or percentage of economic families or unattached individuals in a given classification below the low-income cut-offs. These incidence rates are calculated from unrounded estimates of economic families and unattached individuals 15 years of age and over.

Chapter 2: Struggles over Social Reproduction in a Neo-liberal Era

1 The third, or voluntary sector, is a another important site which mediates the tension between accumulation and social reproduction. In Canada, as neo-liberal policies have taken hold, the third sector has been called upon to take on increasing quantities of work previously provided by public services. This has reconfigured the nature of charity-based organizations as

many take on managerial and surveillance roles in social policy delivery. For a good overview, see Shields and Evans 1998.

2 Vosko (2000) uses the referent Fordist-Keynesian to make explicit both the kind of accord between capital and labour and the kind of state management of the economy. I use it here for similar reasons as it makes plain the mode of capital accumulation and its regulation in a particular period.

3 The focus on the production of people continued in much socialist thought throughout the nineteenth and twentieth centuries and was implicit in some Marxist theory. However, these currents remained marginalized.

4 Bakker (2001:1) specifies three aspects of social reproduction: biological reproduction, the reproduction of the labour force, and the reproduction of provisioning and caring needs.

5 Social reproduction can be and has been marketized to varying extents. This marketization, in the form of domestic workers or paid home care workers, for example, creates further ambiguity about the concept. These paid positions are usually precarious, poorly paid, feminized, and often racialized; putting a money value on aspects of the work of social reproduction reveals that it remains undervalued. For excellent discussions, see Katz 2001; Mutari and Figart 2003; Arat-Koc 2006.

6 Various scholars have elucidated the ways in which states and families mediate the tension between accumulation and social reproduction in different historical periods. Seccombe (1992), Ursel (1992), and Jenson (1986) offer three interesting examples of attempts to specify these relationships. Debates about what constitutes getting a living in capitalist societies, as well as elaborations of the processes of social reproduction when combined with feminist interventions about sex/gender divisions of labour, demonstrate that there is nothing inherent in the work of social reproduction assigning this work to women, and that institutional actors such as states and families/households mediate this function. Historical examinations of the organization of family/households in relation to different periods of capital accumulation usefully apply this theoretical lens, and demonstrate that the organization of production and social reproduction function differently in different periods.

7 Because capitalism requires the production of profit as well as the production of labourers, the family and the state are institutional sites where the contest between the needs of reproduction and the drive for accumulation play out. Capital follows a set of options in order to keep reproduction in step with production so that profits are not reduced. These include several imperatives: to keep the standards of living low in terms of level and composition;

to reduce the cost of wage goods and services through high productivity; to transfer the costs of reproduction to the state; and to shift them on to the family, increasing women's burden of housework (Picchio 1992:121).

8 According to Shaikh (1991:160), 'we must distinguish between *general crises*, which involve a widespread collapse in the economic and political relations of reproduction, from the partial crises and business cycles which are a regular feature of capitalist history.' Marx identified the organization principle of capitalist society as the relationship of wage labour and capital, and he formulated this fundamental contradiction between social production and private appropriation (Bottomore 1991:118; Marx (1996[1867]), vol. 1, *Das Kapital*). Most Marxist economists have identified the role of the state as a key institutional mechanism for dealing with the tendency towards crises (of both varieties) in capitalist economies. Keynesianism is associated with the highest form of state mediation to date of fiscal and monetary management; this kind of intervention indicates that even if particular states were successful in minimizing economic fluctuations, this was only achieved by staving off problems and potential crises (Bottomore 1991:118). The family is not explicitly considered in most economic theory as a mediating mechanism in the face of systemic economic crises and downturns. This omission is being rectified by the contributions and analyses of feminist economists such as Bakker (1994, 1997), Elson (1994; 1995a, b), and Picchio (1992). The systemic tendency towards crises in capitalism affirms Picchio's central argument that the tension between accumulation and social reproduction cannot be solved, but only mediated by institutional means in capitalism.

9 McKeen (2004) argues that in the 1990s in Canada, activist and lobby group discourses around poverty, and women's poverty in particular, focused on treating women as *individuals*. The shift to the right in social and economic policy, however, eliminated the *social* context of that individual focus (social individualism) and elevated the neo-liberal version. Neo-liberal individualism is unconcerned with social factors such as violence against women, child care, and so on, which frame women's access to income and supports.

10 The Canadian, and, by extension, Ontario, case is somewhat distinct from the U.S. experience as its brand of Fordism was, as Jenson (1989a:78) contends, permeable. Canada's Fordism 'was designed domestically but always with an eye to the continental economy.' As Peck (2001:223) notes, this variant of Fordism was permeable 'in the sense that international ... relations profoundly structured the country's developmental path and the structure of its accumulation system ... the wage relation remained substantially privatized, while the class compromise came to be mediated

through the institutions of federalism and the ideological project of nation building.'

11 There was no fully realized ideal 'good society' welfare state, nor was the welfare state consensus complete (Ferge 1997). The neo-liberal paradigm is also an ideal type as it varies across welfare state forms. Peck (2001) is clear that Canada is not a fully formed *Workfare* state, but rather is *workfarist*. Thus neo-liberal welfare states have variants in form and content.

12 The term *Washington Consensus* was originally coined by Williamson (1990). The term originally referred to the 'lowest common denominator of policy advice being addressed by the Washington-based institutions to Latin American countries as of 1989' (Williamson 2000). However, the term is now used to refer to neo-liberalism and globalization. One commentator suggests that it means 'liberalize as much as you can, privatize as fast as you can, and be tough in monetary and fiscal matters' (Kodolko 1998). There is some debate about whether a consensus exists among these institutions, and if it is indeed now more appropriate to refer to a post-Washington Consensus era. Nonetheless, the term Washington Consensus identifies the set of policies associated with neo-liberalism, rapid privatization, and deregulation, including moving taxation policy away from statist redistribution.

13 Not only are often well-paid positions within the formal public sector lost as states restructure and downsize their public sectors, but secondary jobs are also lost. Women are often employed in good public sector jobs and in secondary services, such as housekeeping, in the public sector. Hence, neo-liberal privatization has wide-reaching implications for women's paid work in the public sector.

14 While the state-market relationship is central to understanding shifts in regime types, it is easy to overemphasize the role of the state in mediating and securing the general reproduction of norms and social relations (Lipietz 1988). States are not neutral and are influenced by a host of factors, depending on whether or not they are democratic or authoritarian. Inclusive of these factors are lobby efforts, degrees of political mobilization, international pressures, and ideological outlooks (Picchio 1992; Aglietta 1998). States are powerful institutional players in mediating the relationships among the regime of accumulation, social provisioning, protection and regulation, and the work of caring for people, which is mostly done in households or families. An additional consideration in the context of the globalization of trade and exchange is an increasingly evident hierarchy among states, with some experiencing a virtual loss of sovereignty, while others experience a relative loss of autonomy.

15 See Little (1998) for a good review of social assistance policy in Ontario in the twentieth century. This example shows the financial insecurity and hardship of female-headed households, and the changing position of the state on women's roles as dependents and caregivers rather than workers.

16 Jessop (1994:257) notes that without significant discontinuity, it would not be *post*-Fordism; without significant continuity, it would not be post-*Fordism*. He contends that the conditions are met by post-Fordism to consider it along the same lines as Fordism.

17 See Vosko (2002) for a nuanced discussion of the feminization of labour thesis.

Chapter 3: Legislative and Regulatory Changes in Ontario, 1995–2000

1 I follow Chunn and Gavigan (2004:231) in their assessment of the criminalization and pathologization of the poor in Ontario. They note that in a neo-liberal context, 'the form of the state and its social policy has shifted; social programmes designed to ameliorate or redistribute have been eroded, laying bare a heightened state presence which condemns and punishes the poor.' Policies related to social assistance, or welfare, were the most explicit terrain of criminalization: mandatory drug testing, anonymous snitch lines for perceived welfare fraud, and a lifetime ban from receiving social assistance for those convicted of welfare fraud were among the measures that the Conservatives introduced. The restructuring of Ontario's welfare state, and the Conservatives' approach to poverty in particular, led to welfare fraud becoming 'welfare *as* fraud. Thus poverty, welfare and crime were linked. To be poor was to be culpable, or at least vulnerable to culpability' (220). Single mothers receiving social assistance held a special place in this criminalization discourse: 'welfare law,' Chunn and Gavigan remind us, 'is principally and ideologically concerned with the lives of poor women, especially lone parent mothers' (220). Even where an overt tie to criminality was not drawn, moral questions about the fitness of single mothers in receipt of social assistance raised the spectre of crime: fatherless boys with lazy mothers would end up in trouble with the law. Beyond those receiving social assistance, the homeless, and particularly young men who cleaned windshields (called squeegee-ers), were subject to the Safe Streets Act, which made this activity illegal (see Glasbeek forthcoming; Esmonde 2002).

2 Another dimension beyond privatization, which was clearly present in Ontario, was that the state itself had become marketized. The state sought to use market criteria to evaluate success, and market-efficiency models to

determine how social goods should be delivered. A striking example was the involvement of the American multinational, Andersen Consulting. The provincial government contracted this firm in an attempt to make the delivery of social assistance more 'efficient.' Experiences with Andersen in other jurisdictions, such as New Brunswick, resulted in 25 per cent of New Brunswick's social workers losing their jobs. Those who did not lose their jobs were mandated to spend no more than 4.5 minutes with each client (Mullaly 1997).

3 I use the term *extra-household* here to note that household members take up care responsibilities for non-residents, such as older parents who live in separate quarters or children not living at home. Confirming the research by Luxton and Corman (2001) and Side (1999), household members tended not to take active long-term care responsibilities for non-kin.

4 People viewed the shifting of care away from hospitals to home or community as positive in some ways, because it meant that convalescence could occur with greater comfort in one's own home. But the shifting of services outside hospitals meant that the costs were no longer covered under the Canada Health Act, so that things like drug needs were not covered as they would have been in hospitals. In addition, the Ontario government changed the ways in which home care contracts could be bid on, decreasing overall wage rates and increasing the involvement of for-profit agencies. Many household participants recognized that fewer home care services were available, and that the presence of a caregiver at home made a difference in the level of service provided.

5 Following Chunn and Gavigan, I cite Segal's analysis of single mothers.

6 While the provincial government claimed that it was reducing the size and scope of government, the concentration of executive power, coupled with extensive re-regulation of non-market sectors of the economy, indicated that the government did not decrease its scope, but rather shifted its regulatory focus.

7 Five key policy areas are covered in this chapter. They can be summarized as follows:

Area of Policy Change	Key Tools/Actions
Governance	− Introduce omnibus legislation − Impose time allocation on debate − Create commissions to make major policy decisions − Download delivery of services to lower levels of government

Education and child care	– Decrease funding to all levels of education and to child care
	– Increase standardization in public education
	– Amalgamate public school boards
	– Increase power of ministry of education and unelected commission, decrease legislative debate
Health care	– Cut and redirect funding
	– Privatization
	– Close and merge hospitals
	– Increase power of ministry of health and unelected commission, decrease legislative debate
Income support	– Cut funding to social assistance, social housing and support agencies
	– Impose new tenant act
Labour	– Weaken union rights
	– Eliminate pay and employment equity
	– Weaken worker's compensation
	– Impose new employment standards act

8 The full amount was not cut during this time period, but was spread over the next three years. In his 1996 budget, the finance minister announced plans to cut government spending on programs, staffing, and services in order to meet a balanced budget goal for the fiscal year 2000–1 (Ministry of Finance 1996). The major announcement in this budget, however, was the government's plan to cut personal income taxes by 30 per cent over three years, and to cut payroll taxes for business. Budgets for ministries were significantly reduced (the budget for the Ministry of Health was reduced by $1.5 billion over three years) and ministries were asked to find 'savings' within their existing infrastructures.

9 Two other Red Tape bills, Bill 115 regarding the Ministry of Finance and Bill 120 regarding the Ministry of Northern Development and Mines, were put forward and became law in 1997 (S.O. 1997, c. 19 and S.O. 1997, c. 40). These two bills were more in keeping with the kinds of changes generally found in omnibus legislation.

10 The eight acts were: Environmental Review Tribunal Act, S.O. 2000, c. 26, sch. F; Wine Content and Labelling Act, S.O. 2000, c. 26, sch. P; Enforcement of Judgments Conventions Act, S.O. 1999, c. 12, sch. C; Settlement of International Investment Disputes Act, S.O. 1999 c. 12, sch. D; Licence Appeal Tribunal Act, S.O. 1999, c. 12, sch. G; Ontario Lottery and Gaming Corporation Act, S.O. 1999, c. 12, sch. L; Statutes and Regulation Act, S.O. 1998, c. 18, sch. C; Ministry of Health Appeal and Review Boards Act, S.O. 1998, c. 18, sch. H.

11 Omnibus bills are common in parliamentary tradition and are typically

used by governments as an administrative mechanism to make a large
number of small adjustments without policy implications, such as correct-
ing spelling errors in a number of pieces of legislation (Bezanson and Valentine 1998:3).

12 National and provincial polling data suggest that the Canadian public is
strongly supportive of publicly funded health care (Bezanson and Noce
1999). As a political strategy, the provincial and federal governments support public health care, yet policies enacted in this area allow for creeping
privatization. In Ontario, many laboratory services have been contracted
out to the private sector, food services in hospitals are delivered by private organizations, and, in the area of home care, private sector companies have an increased role in bidding for contracts (Bezanson and Noce
1999).

13 In 1994, the Long-Term Care Act, S.O. 1994, c. 26, was enacted by the former
provincial government. This act has been amended on four occasions since
1994: in 1996, 1997, 1998, and 1999. Each was part of an omnibus bill which
amended the Long-Term Care Act, as well as other pieces of legislation
(Health Care Consent Act, 1996; Government Process Simplification Act
(Ministry of Health); Red Tape Reduction Act, 1998; and the Ministry of
Health and Long-Term Care Statute Law Amendment Act, 1999). Two regulations have been made under the Long-Term Care Act since its passage in
1994. The first, 'Conveyance of Assets' (O. Reg. 179/95) was filed in March
1995 (under the previous government) and has not been amended since.
The second, 'Provision of Community Services' (O. Reg 386/99) was filed
in July 1999. 'Provision of Community Services' has been amended twice.
The first amendment (O. Reg. 494/00) added sections dealing with eligibility for school services and maximum amount of school services. The second
(O. Reg. 677/00) added a subsection to an existing section (maximum
amount of homemaking and personal support services) and added a new
section (eligibility for personal support school services). The newly created
Community Care Access Centres are governed by independent, corporate
non-profit boards of directors. These boards are accountable, through service agreements, to the Ministry of Health (Ministry of Health 1996:3; Personal correspondence with Elaine Campbell, research officer, Ontario
Legislative Library, October 2001).

14 Bill 103 (City of Toronto Act 1997) abolished locally elected municipal governments within Metro Toronto effective January 1998 and put officials
under the control of a provincial government-appointed board of trustees.

15 During the week of 13–20 January 1997, Bill 103 (City of Toronto Act)
received second reading, and Bills 104 (Fewer School Boards Act), 109

(Local Control of Public Libraries Act), 105 (Police Services Amendment Act), 106 (Fair Municipal Finance Act), 107 (Water and Sewage Services Improvement Act), and 108 (Streamlining of Administration of Provincial Offenses Act) were introduced. Of these, 103, 104, 105, 106, and 107 received royal assent.

16 The Liberal government of Dalton McGuinty, which defeated the Conservatives in 2003, allowed rates to rise in April 2004 and has legislation before the house to restructure Ontario's electricity sector, promote the expansion of electricity supply and capacity, facilitate electricity demand management, encourage electricity conservation and the efficient use of electricity and regulate prices in parts of the electricity sector (Electricity Restructuring Act 2004). It is unclear if the Liberals will counter the Conservative initial steps to privatize Hydro.

17 A three-volume collection of memos, government publications, and internal ministry documents (mainly within the ministries of the environment and health as well as the Management Board Secretariat) were entered as exhibit numbers 398A, B, and C (Walkerton Inquiry 2001:3).

18 In August 2000, three months after the deaths in Walkerton, the province passed a regulation that, according to Paul Cavalluzzo, 'cleared up the notification protocol, so that it's clear now that labs and the owner must notify the appropriate official' (Walkerton Inquiry 2001:61) if irregularities are found. In addition, mandatory accreditation is now in place.

19 Mr Cavalluzzo suggested to the premier that the lack of regulations and the swift privatization of labs were 'consistent with your [Harris'] government's new regulatory culture' (Walkerton Inquiry, 2001:59).

20 Evidence presented at the inquiry revealed that in addition to the Red Tape Commission (governing regulatory review), the government in 1995 established a Fat Finding Commission, which sought to identify, as stated by Premier Harris, 'fat ... as unnecessary for the delivery of government programs ... we would eliminate government doing that' (7). The Ministry of the Environment was particularly hard hit in terms of budgetary cuts and staffing cuts resulting from these commissions and from the exercise of 'business plans' put in place by the Management Board Secretariat (19).

21 Numerous Acts were passed relating to balanced budgets and tax cuts, including: Balanced Budgets for Brighter Futures Act (S.O. 2000, c. 42); Responsible Choices for Growth and Accountability Act (S.O.2001, c. 8); Tax Credit and Revenue Protection Act (S.O. 1998, c. 34); More Tax Cuts for Jobs, Growth and Prosperity Act (S.O. 1999, c. 9); Tax Cuts for People and Small Business Act (S.O. 1998, c. 5); and the Taxpayer Dividend Act (S.O. 2000, c. 10).

22 In addition to tax credits for parents whose children attend private schools, this bill included further personal income tax reductions and corporate tax reductions. MPP Hardeman explained the content of the bill in the House on 26 June 2001 (Ontario Legislative Assembly): 'Amendments to the Corporations Tax Act to reduce the general corporate tax from 14 per cent to 8 per cent by 2005 will give this province the lowest combined corporate income tax rate in the United States and all of Canada. The removal of the capital tax on the first $5 million of taxable capital will eliminate the tax for more than 11,000 small and medium-sized businesses. We will also do a thorough review of all tax initiatives to ensure that they are effective.'

23 In fact, funding and services to education were cut and restructured every year between 1995 and 2000. Between 1995 and 1997, for example, schools grants were cut by 12 per cent (including junior and adult education), university grants by 15 per cent, community college grants by 16 per cent, and training program budgets by 64 per cent, for a total of $1.415 billion in cuts over two years (O'Connell and Valentine 1999).

24 Legislation changes included: Bill 34 (1996), Education Amendment Act; Bill 104 (1997), Fewer School Boards Act; Bill 160 (1997), Education Quality Improvement Act; Bill 161 (1997), Fairness for Parents and Employees Act; Bill 64 (1998), Instruction Time: Minimum Standards Act; Bill 74 (2000), Education Accountability Act; Bill 81 (2000), Safe Schools Act; Bill 132 (2000), Ministry of Training, Colleges, and Universities Statute Law Amendment Act; and various Back to Schools Acts enacted after work stoppages in different boards.

25 In 1999, a court challenge by the Equal Pay Coalition resulted in the reversal of this decision (see Childcare Resource and Research Unit 2001).

26 In 1996, the minister of health announced that the existing 38 Home Care programs (which arranged nursing visits and homemaking services) and 36 Placement Coordination Services (which managed admission into long-term care facilities) would be consolidated into 43 Community Care Access Centres (CCACs) (Bezanson and Noce 1999:18; Ontario Ministry of Health 1998; Provincial Auditor of Ontario 1998:103–234).

27 In 1999, the provincial government introduced legislation called the Safe Streets Act (S.O. 1999, c. 8), which penalizes 'aggressive panhandling.' Its full title is 'An Act to promote safety in Ontario by prohibiting aggressive solicitation, solicitation of persons in certain places and disposal of dangerous things in certain places, and to amend the Highway Traffic Act to regulate certain activities on roadways.' Thirteen homeless or precariously housed individuals were arrested on charges under the Safe Streets Act. The Canadian Civil Liberties Association represented the individu-

als, claiming that the law was unconstitutional and vague (*R. v. Banks* [2001] CarswellOnt 2757). The 13 individuals were found guilty and charged.

28 Chapters 4 and 5 present participants' experiences of this program redesign. Because social assistance is at once an income support program and a labour market program, it bridges the categories of income programs and social programs. In addition, because social assistance was viewed as one of the most significant barriers to a minimalist government, it was a central feature in policy change.

29 In *F. (S.) v. Ontario* (Director of Income Maintenance, Ministry of Community and Social Services) [2000] 75 C.R.R. (2d) 1 (124 O.A.C. 324), the Ontario Superior Court of Justice (Divisional Court) dismissed the Ministry of Community and Social Services' appeal to the Social Assistance Review Board. The review board found that the 'spouse in the house' provision (O. Reg. 409/95) was unconstitutional. The Conservative government appealed this decision. The new Liberal government abandoned the appeal on 1 September 2004 (CBC 2004).

30 Following a coroner's inquest into her death, the Liberal government reversed the province's position on lifetime bans for social assistance recipients convicted of fraud (Harries 2003). It did not, however, dismantle fraud hotlines.

31 From the perspective of a social reproduction framework, labour market policy is least likely to consider the entire process of the social reproduction of labour, focusing instead on the regulation of labour and labour power. Social policy, and social assistance policy in particular, considers the costs associated with maintaining and reproducing people: it itemizes costs for housing, suggests costs for food, provides a minimal allowance for items such as winter clothes for kids, and considers costs associated with medication and transportation.

32 The Ontario Works Act and the Ontario Disability Support Plan Act are enacted under the Social Assistance Reform Act.

33 Fudge (2001:19) notes that since the 1970s, small businesses have been the key contributors to job creation. Women are more likely than men to be found in firms with fewer than 20 employees.

34 Arat-Koc (2006) and Bakan and Stasiulus (1997) draw attention to the racialization of the paid aspects of care work. Often, the women hired as 'nannies' are live-in caregivers who come to Canada under the Live-In-Caregiver Program. Their residency and working standards are often insecure.

Chapter 4: Putting Together a Living in Ontario in the Late 1990s

1 Access to income and access to public supports and services are mutually reinforcing. For the purpose of clarity, I have separated the discussion of these into two chapters. However, social policy (such as health care or education) affects labour market experience just as labour market experience (e.g., part-time employment) affects access to programs and services (such as Employment Insurance).

2 Detailed income data was collected in 1997 and 1999; however, some participants were interviewed in early 2000.

3 Paid employment was not in all cases the main source of income over the period of the study. For example, women who gave birth and were eligible received Employment Insurance benefits as their main source of income. Yet over the course of the study, they did work for pay.

4 Detailed information on household income was gathered for 1999. However, household income sources changed over the period under study. These changes, particularly as they relate to changes in government benefit levels and job types, are explored below.

5 Statistics Canada defines employment earnings as wages and salaries as well as net income from self-employment. Government transfers include all social welfare payments from federal, provincial, and municipal governments, including Child Tax Benefits, Old Age Security and Guaranteed Income Supplements, spouse's allowances, Canada and Quebec Pension Plan benefits, Employment Insurance, Workers' Compensation, training allowances, veteran's pensions, social assistance, and pensions to the blind and persons with disabilities. Statistics Canada also includes refundable tax credits and the Goods and Services Tax credits as income, but I have chosen here not to include the GST as a government income transfer because the amounts are so small for most low-income households. Private transfers include alimony and child support payments, annuities, superannuation, scholarships, and other items not included in other categories (Statistics Canada 2000b: 146). I note here that the Ontario Student Assistance Plan is included as a private transfer, as it is in fact a loan that is repaid with interest.

6 In 1999–2000, there were 73 adults in all households, but seven were co-resident adult children who had moved from under age 18 to over 18 during the study. Two were siblings of adults who had been interviewed in three previous rounds, who began in 1999 to share housing because of a breakup.

7 The minimum wage was not unfrozen in Ontario until February 2004. At that time, the general minimum wage was raised from $6.85 per hour

(where it had been since the early 1990s) to $7.15. It is set to go up to $7.45 per hour in 2006, $7.75 in 2007, and $8.00 in 2008 (Ontario Ministry of Labour 2004).

8 The following chart lists recent developments in this area.

Employment Insurance Trends at a Glance

- In 1997, 36 per cent of the unemployed received benefits, down from 74 per cent in 1989.
- In 1996, the number of hours required for eligibility increased from 180 and 300 (depending on geographic location) to between 420 and 700 hours. New or returning labour market entrants must have worked 910 insured hours over the previous year to qualify.
- Benefits payments dropped 17 per cent between 1996 and 1998.
- The percentage of women collecting benefits dropped from 37 per cent to 30 per cent between 1996 and 1998; the percentage of men dropped from 44 per cent to 41 per cent during the same period.
- In the 2000 federal budget, the number of hours needed to qualify for sickness, maternity or parental benefits was reduced to 600 hours from 700 hours.

Sources: Torjman (2000); Human Resources Development Canada (1998); Bezanson and McMurray (2000).

9 In 1996, the federal government offered the provinces the Labour Market Development Proposal, through which they would assume more responsibility for the design and delivery of the employment measures of the Employment Insurance Act, such as targeted wage subsidies, self–employment assistance, and skills loans/grants. Local training boards will be responsible for the planning and delivery of training programs. Ontario has not yet signed a labour market agreement with the federal government, although it supports some training initiatives using both EI and provincial funds (Torjman 2000:7–8). Torjman notes that Ontario claims it is not getting sufficient funds; Ottawa is, on the other hand, concerned that Ontario will privatize the training system and contract out the training process.

10 Household participants were asked to identify their sources of income and income levels over a 10-year period.

11 The training components of the EI system underwent significant restructuring. Critics of the new emphasis on active EI – that is, geared to getting claimants into jobs – note that it is those who already have good labour market skills who can find jobs, because EI training support tends not to be individualized. Unemployed workers are now expected to contribute financially to their own retraining, often seeking grants or loans to do upgrading (Torjman 2000:22).

12 The following chart summarizes changes to Ontario benefits.

Reforms to Social Assistance, 1995–2000 at a Glance

- Benefits for all except the aged and disabled were cut by 21.5% in October 1995.
- The Social Assistance Reform Act (1997) created two streams: Ontario Works (which included a component work for welfare) and Ontario Disability Support.
- New eligibility restrictions increased barriers to qualification and appeal rights were restricted.
- The 'spouse in the house' rule was reintroduced by the provincial government. This meant that a social assistance recipient could be cut off benefits if found to be living with someone of the opposite sex with whom she/he was suspected of having a relationship.
- A verification process, called the consolidated verification process, was required by regulation. It increased scrutiny of social assistance recipients' income, assets, relationships, and other information, and increased administrative reasons for deeming recipients ineligible for assistance.
- Recipients were barred from accessing Ontario Student Assistance Program loans and attending post-secondary institutions while receiving social assistance.
- Labour market participation became the immediate goal of the program, and included everyone receiving Ontario Works except mothers with very young children.
- After 12 months, a lien (for up to the full amount of benefits received after that date) could be placed on a recipient's home, to be repaid if and when the home was sold.

Source: Bezanson and McMurray (2000).

13 They were unable to locate the majority: 60 per cent left for what they termed 'unknown reasons' (e.g., incorrect/disconnected telephone numbers, changes of address and refusals), which indicates that many recipients saw no benefit in keeping in touch with the ministry.

14 The following chart highlights the benefits and restrictions of the program.

Ontario Disability Support Program, 1997 at a Glance

- Persons with a disability are eligible to receive income support under ODSP if they pass a needs test (assessing their income, assets, needs, and circumstances) and a test for eligibility.
- The test for disability has a higher threshold than that for Family Benefits.
- The needs test pertaining to assets is more generous than under the previous system.
- Benefits are higher than under Ontario Works. A single person with a disability receives a maximum of $930 a month.
- ODSP recipients are exempt from mandatory employment placements and community participation.
- Many decisions under ODSP cannot be appealed, including decisions with respect to employment supports.

Source: Bezanson and McMurray (2000:25).

15 Important features of the program are listed below.

Canada Child Tax Benefit (CTB) at a Glance

Characteristics
- The CTB is an income-tested program that pays its maximum amount to lower-income families/households and a diminishing amount to non-poor families/households, excluding those with high incomes.
- A federal, non-taxable benefit is paid on a monthly basis (on behalf of all eligible children under 19 across Canada) to the parent who is the primary caretaker to the child.
- Eligibility for and amount of benefit is based on net family/household income, as calculated on the annual income tax return.
Benefit Amounts
- In 2001–2002, the first tier paid a maximum of $1,117 per child under 18. A supplement of $77 per year was provided for large families (3 or more members) to $220 per year extra for children under age 7 for whom a child-care expenses deduction was claimed.
- Within the first tier, maximum payments go to families/households with net incomes under $32,000 and are reduced incrementally above this level.
- The second tier, the National Child Benefit Supplement (NCBS), is directed only to low-income families/households. In 2001–2002, the NCBS paid a maximum of $1,255 for the first child, $1,055 for the second child, and $980 for each additional child, decreasing gradually above net family/household income of $21,744.
- Together, the CTB and the NCBS amount to $2,372 for one child, $2,172 for the second child, and $2,175 for each additional child.

Source: Adapted from Battle and Mendelson (2001).

Chapter 5: Interactive Effects of Social Policy Change on Households

1 As noted in Chapter 1, the 1990s was a decade marked by a significant reorientation in federal-provincial finance and regulation relations. In the early part of the decade, the Canada Assistance Plan (CAP) was dismantled and replaced with the Canada Health and Social Transfer (CHST). The CHST effectively eliminated cost-sharing for social assistance and social services. The federal government cut the total cash transfer to the provinces by a third in 1995, and although the 2000 health care agreement between the first ministers and the federal government promised to restore transfers for health care, federal cuts have had a significant effect on the provinces' ability to deliver health care services (Browne 2000:23–26).
2 As noted in Chapter 3, the legislative initiatives that affected health care in the province spanned a number of areas and significantly weakened civic participation in the process of change. Changes to labour legislation, including public sector dispute resolution, laid the groundwork for

contracting out and privatization (Browne 2000; Bezanson and Noce 1999).

3 Community-based care encompasses a range of services and supports. Home care services are most often associated with community-based care, but this sector also includes homemaking services, professional services (nurses, physiotherapists), day programs for seniors, supportive housing, Meals On Wheels, attendant services for people with disabilities along with more formal long-term care services such as nursing homes, and for people who require 24-hour, on-site nursing services. Community Care Access Centres (CCACs) coordinate access to services for people at home and provide some long-term care facility placement (Government of Ontario 1998; Bezanson and Noce 1999).

4 After 1995, provincial spending on long-term care increased, but over the same period, hospitals lost a significant amount of funding ($575 million in 1997–1998), which put increased pressure on the long-term care system. Cutting hospital funding and beds without having long-term care services available led to far fewer resources, and, for many families/households, a crisis in accessing care that was evidenced by very long waiting lists for long-term care services. The government also cut back on many of the services covered by OHIP, allowing doctors to charge fees for letters or forms requested by third parties such as employers, and to bill patients directly for items such as casts and tensor bandages.

5 These findings are consistent with the research on health care done by Pat Armstrong (1999).

6 The writing of household profiles was a collective effort, involving at different stages all members of the Speaking Out project. See Neysmith, Bezanson, and O'Connell (2005); Bezanson and McMurray (2000), Bezanson and Noce (1999), O'Connell and Valentine (1998), Noce and O'Connell (1998), and Bezanson and Valentine (1998).

7 The labour market orientation in social assistance reforms also results in women who are receiving social assistance being forced to provide in-home child care (Bashevkin 2002).

Chapter 6: Coping Strategies of Low-Income Households

1 For a discussion of gender and autonomous households in welfare states, see Orloff 1993; O'Connor, Orloff, and Shaver 1999; and Esping-Andersen 1999.

2 Children had almost no power in household financial decisions. When household participants were asked if all household members were aware of

all income, most replied that adult members were aware but that children were not. This is an important area of further investigation.

3 In part, these results demonstrate the limitations of the 1996 Statistics Canada Census questions on unpaid work, which did not capture the variety, much less the extent of unpaid work activities. Those interviewed had enormous difficulty conceptualizing domestic labour as *time*, and struggled to answer the Census questions.

4 Canadian data indicate that in 1998, 64% of the hours spent on informal caregiving were carried out by women, due mainly to women's primary responsibility for unpaid child care (Zukewich 2003:15).

5 Despite some indication that men are taking on more traditionally 'female' unpaid work, men in Canada in 1998 spent the largest amount of their unpaid time on repair and maintenance work. For women, meal preparation, cleaning, and care work took up the bulk of their time (Hamdad 2003).

6 Other studies bear this out. See for example, Pahl 1989; Finch and Mason 1993).

7 Mother's Allowance was the name often used to refer to the previous social assistance program, Family Benefits.

8 Ellen Ross's study of nineteenth-century women in London shows that they used the same strategy to get by: women pawned good clothes on Monday, used the money throughout the week, and then took Friday's pay to redeem the clothes in time for church on Sunday. Ross traces the intricate flow of a tiny amount of money as people borrow and lend to get by (Ross 1993).

9 According to the Statistics Canada Survey of Financial Security in 1999, for every $100 of assets, Canadian family units have $16 in debts. For some types of families, this amount was much higher. Lone-parent families owed $29 for every $100, and two-parent families with children owed $23 (Statistics Canada 2001).

10 This strategy of going after former social assistance recipients for overpayments emerged in a number of household stories. While I could not find documentation confirming an escalation in the employ of collections agencies, anecdotally it appears that the Harris government attempted to use this avenue to increase provincial revenues.

11 This echoes Raddon's (2002) findings that men's skills in local exchange networks were often overvalued while women's were undervalued. Gendered definitions of skill and value permeated the gift or exchange economy and led to many women withdrawing from exchange networks because they felt they could not reciprocate.

12 In Canada in 1996, the average Census family spent $1,663 on gifts of

money, and on contributions to persons outside their household (Statistics Canada 2003). Given the increases in personal out-of-pocket expenses (shown in Chapter 5) needed to offset the retrenchment of the welfare state and the erosion of services and supports, these contributions would need to be substantially higher to offset new costs.

13 The Statistics Canada General Social Survey (1994) found that 57% of married Canadians turn to their partners for support. Fifteen per cent stated that they would turn to a friend, 10% to a relative and 6% to a professional. Among unmarried Canadians, 48% turn to friend, 16% to parents, 20% relatives and 6% to a professional (McDaniel, S.A., C. Strike, and Statistics Canada 1994).

14 The survey acknowledges the subjectivity of the concept 'better off.' Better off was defined by what people perceive to be important at any given stage in life.

15 According to Statistics Canada, the median net worth of Canadian families in the 55 and older age range was over $200,000 in 1999, compared to under $100,000 for those 35 to 44 and $81,000 for the population as a whole (Statistics Canada 2001). This means that parents in this study were more likely to have access to assets like a home than were their children. However, for those family units with incomes under 30,000 (44% of family units in Canada), median net worth was less than $15,000.

References

PRIMARY SOURCES

Statutes

Balanced Budget Act. S.O. 1999, c. 7, Sch. B.

City of Toronto Act. S.O. 1997, c. 2.

Economic Development and Workplace Democracy Act. S.O. 1998, c. 8.

Education Quality Improvement Act. S.O. 1997, c. 3.

Employment Standards Act. S.O. 2000, c. 41.

Employment Standards Improvement Act. S.O. 1996, c. 23.

Family Benefits Act. O. Reg 409/95.

Fewer Schools Boards Act. S.O. 1997, c. 3.

Government Process Simplification Act (Ministries of the Solicitor General and Correctional Services). S.O. 1997, c. 39.

Government Process Simplification Act (Ministry of the Economic Development, Trade and Tourism). S.O. 1997, c. 36.

Job Quotas Repeal Act. S.O. 1995, c. 4.

Labour Relations and Employment Statute Amendment Act. S.O. 1995, c. 1, sch. A.

Nutrient Management Act. S.O. 2002, c. 4.

Ontario Property Tax Assessment Corporation Act. S.O. 1997, c. 43.

Ontario Works Act. O. Reg 134/98.

Ontario Works Act. S.O. 1997, c. 25.

Prevention of Unionisation Act (Ontario Works). S.O. 1998, c. 17.

Public Sector Labor Relations Transitions Act. S.O. 1997, c. 21.

Responsible Choices for Growth and Accountability Act (2001 Budget). S.O. 2001, c. 8.

Safe Drinking Water Act. S.O. 2002, c. 32.
Savings and Restructuring Act. S.O. 1996, c. 1
Social Assistance Reform Act. S.O. 1997, c. 25.
Social Housing Reform Act. S.O. 2000, c. 27.
Sustainable Water and Sewage Systems Act. S.O. 2002, c. 29.
Taxpayer Protection Act. S.O. 1999, c. 17, Sch. A.
Workplace Safety and Insurance Act. S.O. 1997, c. 16

Cases

Falkiner v. Ontario [2002] (Ministry of Community and Social Services, Income
   Maintenance Branch), 59 O.R. (3d) 481; O.J. No. 1771 (Ont. C.A.), online QL
   (OJ)
Rogers v. Sudbury (2001) 57 O.R. (3d) 460 (Ont. Sup. Ct. J.)

Debates

Ontario Legislative Assembly. Debates. 37th Parl., 1st sess., 23 Nov. 2000. http:
   //www.ontla.on.ca/hansard/house_debates/37_parl/session1/L107/htm
Ontario Legislative Assembly. Debates. 37th Parl., 2nd sess., 26 June, 2001.
   http://www.ontla.on.ca/hansard/house_debates/37_parl/session2/
   L036A.htm
Ontario Legislative Assembly. Debates. 37th Parl., 2nd sess., 18 Oct. 2001.
   http://www.ontla.on.ca/hansard/house_debates/37_parl/session2/
   L053A.htm

SECONDARY SOURCES

Acker, J. 1988. Class, Gender and the Relations of Distribution. *Signs* 13 (3):474–
   497.
Aglietta, M. 1998. Capitalism at the Turn of the Century: Regulation Theory
   and the Challenge of Social Change. *New Left Review* 232 (November/
   December):41–90.
Amin, A., ed. 1994. *Post-Fordism: A Reader.* Oxford: Blackwell.
Arat-Koc, S. 2002. From 'Mothers of the Nation' to Migrant Workers: Immigra-
   tion Policies and Domestic Workers in Canadian History. In *Rethinking Canada: The Promise of Women's History,* edited by V. Strong-Boag, M. Gleason,
   and A. Perry. Toronto: Oxford University Press.
Arat-Koc, S. 2006. Whose Social Reproduction? Transnational Motherhood and

the Challenges to Feminist Political Economy. In *Social Reproduction: Feminist Political Economy Challenges Neo-liberalism*, edited by K. Bezanson and M. Luxton. Montreal and Kingston: McGill-Queen's University Press.

Armstrong, P. 1996. The Feminization of the Labour Force: Harmonizing Down in a Global Economy. In *Rethinking Restructuring: Gender and Change in Canada*, edited by I. Bakker. Toronto: University of Toronto Press.

Armstrong, P. 1997. Restructuring Public and Private: Women's Paid and Unpaid Work. In *Challenging the Public Private Divide: Feminism, Law and Public Policy*, edited by S. Boyd. Toronto: University of Toronto Press.

Armstrong, P. 1999. *The context for Health Reform*. Toronto: National Network on Environments and Women's Health.

Armstrong, P., and H. Armstrong. 1986. Beyond Sexless Class and Classless Sex: Towards Feminist Marxism. In *The Politics of Diversity*, edited by R. Hamilton and M. Barrett. London: Verso.

Armstrong, P., and H. Armstrong. 2004. Thinking It Through: Women, Work, and Caring in the New Millennium. In *Caring for/Caring About: Women, Home Care and Unpaid Caregiving*, edited by K. Grant. Aurora, ON: Garamond.

Armstrong, P., and M.P. Connelly, eds. 1999. *Feminism, Political Economy and the State: Contested Terrain*. Toronto: Canadian Scholars' Press.

Aronson, J. 1998. Lesbians Giving and Receiving Care: Stretching Conceptualizations of Caring and Community. *Women's Studies International Forum* (21):5.

Aronson, J., and S.M. Neysmith. 2001. Manufacturing Social Exclusion in the Home Care Market. *Canadian Public Policy* 27 (2).

Bakan, A., and D. Stasiulus. 1997. Foreign Domestic Worker Policy in Canada and the Social Boundaries of Modern Citizenship. *In Not One of the Family*, edited by A. Bakan and D. Stasiulus. Toronto: University of Toronto Press.

Baker, M., and D. Tippin. 1999. *Poverty, Social Assistance, and the Employability of Mothers: Restructuring Welfare States*. Toronto: University of Toronto Press.

Bakker, I. 2001. Neoliberal Governance and the Reprivatization of Social Reproduction. Paper read at the Gender, Political Economy and Human Security Conference, York University, Toronto. 5 October.

Bakker, I., ed. 1994. *The Strategic Silence: Gender and Economic Policy*. London: Zed Books.

Bakker, I., ed. 1997. *Rethinking Restructuring: Gender and Change in Canada*. Toronto: University of Toronto Press.

Bakker, I., and S. Gill., eds. 2004. *Power, Production and Social Reproduction: Human In/security in the Global Political Economy*. London: Palgrave Macmillan.

Barrett, M. 1980. *Women's Oppression Today: The Marxist/Feminist Encounter.* London: Verso Editions.

Bashevkin, S. 1998. *Women on the Defensive: Living Through Conservative Times.* Toronto: University of Toronto Press.

Bashevkin, S. 2000. Rethinking Retrenchment: North American Social Policy during the Early Clinton and Chrétien Years. *Canadian Journal of Political Science* 33 (March):7–36.

Bashevkin, S. 2002a. *Welfare Hot Buttons: Women, Work, and Social Policy Reform.* Toronto: University of Toronto Press; Pittsburgh, PA.: University of Pittsburgh Press.

Bashevkin, S. 2002b. *Women's Work Is Never Done: Comparative Studies in Caregiving, Employment, and Social Policy Reform.* New York: Routledge.

Battle, K. 2001. *Ottawa Should Expand the Child Tax Benefit.* Ottawa: Caledon Institute of Social Policy.

Battle, K., and M. Mendelson. 2001. *Benefits for Children: A Four Country Study.* Ottawa: Caledon Institute of Social Policy.

Becker, G.S. 1985. Human Capital, Effort and the Sexual Division of Labour. *Journal of Labor Economics* 3 (1).

Beechey, V. 1979. On Patriarchy. *Feminist Review* 3:66–82.

Beneria, L. 1987. Introduction; Theoretical Framework. In *The Crossroads of Class and Gender,* edited by L. Beneria and M. Roland. Chicago: University of Chicago Press.

Beneria, L. 1999. The Enduring Debate over Unpaid Labour. *International Labour Review* 138 (2):287–309.

Beneria, L., and S. Feldman., eds. 1992. *Unequal Burden: Economic Crisis, Persistent Poverty and Women's Work.* Boulder, CO: Westview Press.

Beneria, L., and M. Roldan. 1987. *The Crossroads of Class and Gender.* Chicago: University of Chicago Press.

Benston, M. 1997 [1969]. The Political Economy of Women's Liberation. In *Materialist Feminism: A Reader in Class, Difference, and Women's Lives,* edited by R. Hennessy and C. Ingraham. New York: Routledge.

Bergeron, S. 2003. The Post-Washington Consensus and Economic Representations of Women in Development at the World Bank. *International Feminist Journal of Politics* 5 (3):397–419.

Bezanson, K. Forthcoming. Gender and the Limits of Social Capital. *Canadian Review of Sociology and Anthopology.*

Bezanson, K., and S. McMurray. 2000. *Booming for Whom? People in Ontario Talk about Income, Jobs and Social Programmes.* Ottawa: Caledon Institute of Social Policy.

Bezanson, K., and L. Noce. 1999. *Costs, Closures and Confusion: People in Ontario Talk about Health Care.* Ottawa: Caledon Institute of Social Policy.

Bezanson, K., and F. Valentine. 1998. *Act in Haste ... The Style, Scope and Speed of Change in Ontario.* Ottawa: Caledon Institute of Social Policy.

Bottomore, T., ed. 1991. *A Dictionary of Marxist Thought.* 2d ed. Oxford: Basil Blackwell.

Braedley, S. 2006. Someone to Watch You: Gender, Class and Social Reproduction. In *Social Reproduction: Feminist Political Economy Challenges Neo-liberalism,* edited by M. Luxton and K. Bezanson. Montreal and Kingston: McGill-Queen's University Press.

Brodie, J. 1995. *Politics on the Margins: Restructuring and the Canadian Women's Movement.* Halifax: Fernwood.

Brodie, J. 1996. Changing State Forms and Public Policy. In *Women and Canadian Public Policy,* edited by J. Brodie. Toronto: Harcourt-Brace.

Brodie, J. 1997. Meso-Discourses, State Forms and the Gendering of Liberal-Democratic Citizenship. *Citizenship Studies* 1 (2).

Browne, P.L. 2000. Unsafe Practices: Restructuring and Privatization in Ontario Health Care. Ottawa: Canadian Centre for Policy Alternatives.

Burman, P. 1996. *Poverty's Bonds: Power and Agency in the Social Relations of Welfare.* Toronto: Thompson Education.

Cagatay, N., D. Elson., and C. Grown. 1995. Introduction. *World Development* 23 (11):1827–1836.

Cameron, B. 2006. Social Reproduction and Canadian Federalism. In *Social Reproduction: Feminist Political Economy Challenges Neo-liberalism,* edited by K. Bezanson and M. Luxton. Montreal and Kingston: McGill-Queen's University Press.

Canada Mortgage and Housing Corporation. 2003. *CMHC Rental Market Survey.* Ottawa: CMHC.

CBC. 2004. *Ontario Drops 'Spouse in the House' Appeal* 2004 [cited September 3, 2004]. Available from www.cbc.ca/story/canada/national/2004/09/02/spouse_ont040904.thml.

Canadian Centre for Policy Alternatives. 2003. *Investing in Quality Child Care.* Ottawa: CCPA.

Carroll, W.K., and M. Shaw. 2001. Consolidating a Neoliberal Policy Bloc in Canada, 1976 to 1996. *Canadian Public Policy* 27 (2):195–217.

Castles, F. 2004. *The Future of the Welfare State: Crisis Myths and Crisis Realities.* New York: Oxford University Press.

CBC Newsworld Live. 2001. *Live Reporting of the Walkerton Commission, 29 June 2001.* Toronto: Canadian Broadcasting Corporation.

Chant, S., and N. Craske. 2003. *Gender in Latin America*. New Brunswick, NJ: Rutgers University Press.

Che-Alford, J. Hamm, B. Hamm, and S. Canada. 1999. Under One Roof: Three Generations Living Together. *Canadian Social Trends* (Summer/cat. no. 11–008):6–9.

Childcare Resource and Research Unit. 2001. *Early Childhood Education and Care in Canada 2001: Summary*. Toronto: CRRU.

Chunn, D., and S. Gavigan. 2004. Welfare Law, Welfare Fraud and the Moral Regulation of the 'Never Deserving' Poor. *Social and Legal Studies* 13 (2):219–243.

Clarke, J. 2004. Dissolving the Public Realm? The Logics and Limits of Neo-Liberalism. *Journal of Social Policy* 33 (1):27–48.

Clarke, L. 2000. Disparities in Wage Relations and Social Reproduction. In *The Dynamics of Wage Relations in the New Europe*, edited by L. Clarke, P. Gijsel, and J. Jannssen. London: Kluwer Academic.

Cohen, M.G. 1994. The Implications of Economic Restructuring for Women: The Canadian Solution. In *The Strategic Silence: Gender and Economic Policy*, edited by I. Bakker. Ottawa: North-South Institute.

Connell, R.W. 1987. *Gender and Power*. Stanford: Stanford University Press.

Connell, R.W. 1990. The State, Gender and Sexual Politics. *Theory and Society* 19:507–544.

Connell, R. W. 1995. The History of Masculinity. In *Masculinities*. Cambridge: Polity Press.

Connell, R.W. 2002. *Gender*. Cambridge, UK: Blackwell.

Cook-Reynolds, M., and N. Zukewich. 2004. The Feminization of Work. *Canadian social trends* 72:24–29.

Corrigan, P., and R.D. Sayer. 1985. *The Great Arch: English State Formation as Cultural Revolution*. Oxford: Blackwell.

Cossman, B., and J. Fudge, eds. 2002. *Privatization, Law and the Challenge to Feminism*. Toronto: University of Toronto Press.

Crompton, R., ed. 1999. *Restructuring Gender Relations and Employment: The Decline of the Male Breadwinner*. Oxford: Oxford University Press.

Dalla Costa, M., and S. James. 1975. *The Power of Women and the Subversion of the Community*. Bristol: Falling Wall.

Daly, M. 2001. *Care Work: The Quest for Security*. Geneva: ILO.

Daly, M., and J. Lewis. 2000. The Concept of Social Care and the Analysis of Contemporary Welfare States. *British Journal of Sociology* 51 (2):281–298.

Daly, M., and K. Rake. 2003. *Gender and the Welfare State: Care, Work, and Welfare in Europe and the USA*. Cambridge, UK: Polity Press.

Day, S., and G. Brodsky. 1998. Women and the Equality Deficit: The Impact of Restructuring Canada's Social Programs. Ottawa: Status of Women Canada.

Delhi, K. 1998. Shopping for Schools. *Orbit* 1:29–33.

de Wolff, A. 2006. Bargaining for Collective Responsibility for Social Reproduction. In *Social Reproduction: Feminist Political Economy Challenges Neo-liberalism*, edited by K. Bezanson and M. Luxton. Montreal and Kingston: McGill-Queen's University Press.

Dore, E., and M. Molyneux, eds. 2000. *Hidden Histories of Gender and the State in Latin America*. Durham, NC: Duke University Press.

Ellingsaeter, A.L. 1998. Dual Breadwinner Societies: Provider Models in the Scandinavian Welfare States. *Acta Sociologica* 41:59–73.

Elson, D. 1994. Micro, Meso, Macro: Gender and Economic Analysis in the Context of Policy Reform. In *The Strategic Silence: Gender and Economic Policy*, edited by I. Bakker. London, Zed Press.

Elson, D. 1995(a). Gender Awareness in Modelling Structural Adjustment. *World Development* 23 (11).

Elson, D., ed. 1995(b). *Male Bias in the Development Process*. 2d ed. Manchester: Manchester University Press.

Elson, D. 1998. The Economic, the Political and the Domestic: Businesses, States and Households in the Organisation of Production. *New Political Economy* 3 (2).

Elson, D., and N. Cagatay. 2000. The Social Content of Macroeconomic Policies. *World Development* 28 (7):1347–1364.

Engels, F. 1990 [1884]. *The Origin of the Family, Private Property and the State*. New York: Pathfinder.

Esmonde, J. 2002. Criminalizing Poverty: The Criminal Law Power and the Safe Streets Act. *Journal of Law and Social Policy* 17:63–86.

Esping-Andersen, G. 1990. *The Three Worlds of Welfare Capitalism*. Oxford: Polity Press.

Esping-Andersen, G. 1999. *Social Foundations of Post-Industrial Economies*. New York: Oxford University Press.

Evans, P. 1996. Single Mothers and Ontario's Welfare Policy: Restructuring the Debate. In *Women and Canadian Public Policy*, edited by J. Brodie. Toronto: Harcourt-Brace.

Evans, P., and G. Wekerle. 1997. *Women and the Canadian welfare State: Challenges and Change*. Toronto: University of Toronto Press.

Fast, J.E.; J. Frederick; N. Zukewich, and S. Franke. 2001. The Time of Our Lives. *Canadian Social Trends* 63:20–23.

Ferge, Z. 1997. The Changed Welfare Paradigm: The Individualization of the Social. *Social Policy and Administration* 31 (1):20–44.

Ferguson, S. 1999. Building on the Strengths of the Socialist Feminist Tradition. *Critical Sociology* 25 (1):1–15.

Figart, D., E. Mutari, and M. Power. 2003. Breadwinners and Other Workers: Gender and Race-Ethnicity in the Evolution of the Labor Force. In *Women and the Economy: A Reader,* edited by E. Mutari and D. Figart. New York: M.E. Sharpe.

Finch, J. 1989. *Family Obligations and Social Change.* Oxford, UK and Cambridge, MA: Polity Press.

Finch, J., and D. Groves. 1983. *A Labour of Love: Women, Work, and Caring.* London; Boston: Routledge & K. Paul.

Finch, J., and J. Mason. 1993. *Negotiating Family Responsibilities.* London and New York: Tavistock/Routledge.

Finch, J., and J. Mason. 2000. *Passing On: Kinship and Inheritance in England.* London and New York: Routledge.

Folbre, N. 1999. Care and the Global Economy. In *Background Papers. Vol. 1, Human Development Report 1999.* New York: United Nations Development Program.

Folbre, N., and T. Weisskopf. 1998. Did Father Know Best?: Families, Markets and the Supply of Caring Labor. In *Economic, Values and Organization,* edited by A. Ben-Ner and L. Putterman. Cambridge, MA: Cambridge University Press.

Fox, B. 1980. *Hidden in the Household : Women's Domestic Labour under Capitalism.* Toronto: Canadian Women's Educational Press.

Fraser, N. 1997. After the Family Wage: A Post-Industrial Thought Experiment. In *Justice Interruptus: Critical Reflections on the 'Postsocialist' Condition.* London: Routledge.

Fraser, N., and L. Gordon. 1997. A Geneaology of Dependency: Tracing a Key-word of the U.S. Welfare State. In *Justice Interruptus: Critical Reflections on the 'Postcosialist' Condition.* London: Routledge.

Friedman, M. 1964. *Capitalism and Freedom.* Chicago: University of Chicago Press.

Fudge, J. 1997. Little Victories and Big Defeats: The Rise and Fall of Collective Bargaining Rights for Domestic Workers in Ontario. In *Not One of the Family,* edited by A. Bakan and D. Stasiulus. Toronto: University of Toronto Press.

Fudge, J. 2001. Flexibility and Feminization: The New Ontario Employment Standards Act. *Journal of Law and Social Policy* 16:1–22.

Fudge, J., and B. Cossman. 2002. Introduction. In *Privatization, Law, and the Challenge to Feminism,* edited by B. Cossman and J. Fudge. Toronto: University of Toronto Press.

Fudge, J., and L. Vosko. 2001. Gender, Segmentation and the Standard Employment Relationship in Canadian Labour Law and Policy. *Economic and Industrial Democracy* 22:271–310.

Gardiner, J. 1997. *Gender, Care and Economics*. London: Macmillan.

Gill, S. 1995. Globalisation, Market Civilisation and Disciplinary Neo-Liberalism. *Millennium: Journal of International Studies* 24 (3):299–423.

Glasbeek, A. 2006. My wife has endured a torrent of abuse: Gender, Safety, and Anti-Squeegee Discourses in Toronto, 1998–2000. *Windsor Yearbook of Access to Justice.*

Glenn, E.N. 1992. From Servitude to Service Work: Historical Continuities in the Racial Division of Paid Reproductive Labor. *Signs: Journal of Women in Culture and Society* 18 (1):1–43.

Glenn, E.N. 2000. Creating a Caring Society. *Contemporary Sociology* 29 (1):84–94.

Gordon, L. 1994. *Pitied but Not Entitled: Single Mothers and the History of Welfare, 1890–1935.* New York: Free Press.

Government of Canada. 2004a. *Employment Insurance (EI) Compassionate Care Benefits*. Government of Canada, 2004-05-05 [cited 06–16–04 2004].

Government of Canada. 2004b. Speech from the Throne. Ottawa: Government of Canada. 5 October.

Government of Ontario. 1998. Government invests $1.2 billion to improve long-term care in largest-ever expansion of health services. Toronto: Government of Ontario.

Government of Ontario. 2001. *Helping People Off Welfare into Jobs*. Toronto: Queen's Printer for Ontario.

GPI Atlantic. 2000. *Work and Life: Balancing Paid Work, Unpaid Work and Free Time*. Paper read at the Health, Work and Wellness Conference. Toronto. 24 October.

Graefe, P. 2004. *The Social Economy and the American Model: Relating New Social Policy Directions to the Old*. Paper prepared for the 7th Globalism and Social Policy Programme Seminar, The Rise and Fall of the International Influence of US Social Policy, McMaster University, Hamilton, ON. 11 September.

Grant, K., C. Maratunga, P. Armstrong, M. Boscoe, A. Perderson, and K. Willson, eds. 2004. *Caring For/Caring About: Women, Home Care and Unpaid Caregiving*. Toronto: Garamond.

Grover, C. 2005. Living Wages and the 'Make Work Pay' Strategy. *Critical Social Policy* 25 (1):5–27.

Hamdad, M. 2003. *Valuing Households' Unpaid Work in Canada, 1992 and 1998: Trends and Sources of Change*. Paper read at the Statistics Canada Economic Conference. May.

Haraway, D. 1991. *Simians, Cyborgs, and Women: The Reinvention of Nature.* New York: Routledge.

Harries, K. 2003. End Welfare Ban, Jury Urges. *Toronto Star.* 17 December, A23.

Hayek, F.A. von. 1963. *Individualism and Economic Order.* Chicago: University of Chicago Press.

Health Services Restructuring Commission. 1998. *Change and Transition: Planning Guidelines and Implementation Strategies for Home Care, Long-Term Care, Mental Health, Rehabilitation and Sub-Acute Care.* Toronto: Health Services Restructuring Commission.

Hermer, J., and Mosher, eds. 2002. *Disorderly People: Law and the Politics of Exclusion in Ontario.* Halifax, NS: Fernwood.

Hobson, B., and R. Lister. 2002. Citizenship. In *Contested Concepts in Gender and Social Politics,* edited by B. Hobson, J. Lewis, and B. Siim. Nothampton: Edward Elgar.

Hulchanski, J.D. 2003. *Housing Policy for Tomorrow's Cities.* Ottawa: Canadian Policy Research Network.

HRDC. 1996. *Employment Equity Data Report.* Ottawa: Human Resources Development Canada.

HRDC. 1998. *1997 Employment Insurance Monitoring and Assessment Report.* Ottawa: Human Resources Development Canada.

Humphries, J. 1998. Towards a Family-Friendly Economics. *New Political Economy* 3 (2):223–241.

International Monetary Fund. 2003. *World Economic Outlook.* Washington, DC: IMF.

Jenson, J. 1986. Gender and Reproduction: Or, Babies and the State. *Studies in Political Economy* 20:9–46.

Jenson, J. 1989a. 'Different' but not 'Exceptional': Canada's Permeable Fordism. *Canadian Review of Sociology and Anthropology* 26(1).

Jenson, J. 1989b. The Talents of Women, the Skills of Men: Flexible Specialization and Women. In *The Transformation of Work,* edited by S. G. Wood. London: Unwin Hyman.

Jessop, B. 1993. Towards a Schumpeterian Workfare State? Preliminary Remarks on Post-Fordist Political Economy. *Studies in Political Economy* 40 (Spring):7–39.

Kabeer, N. 2003. *Gender Mainstreaming in Poverty Eradication and the Millennium Development Goals: A Handbook for Policy Makers and Stakeholders.* London: Commonwealth Secretariat.

Kanbur, R., and D. Vines. 2000. The World Bank and Poverty Reduction: Past,

Present and Future. In *The World Bank: Structure and Policies*, edited by C. Gilbert and D. Vines. Cambridge: Cambridge University Press.

Katz, C. 2001. Vagabond Capitalism and the Necessity of Social Reproduction. *Antipode* 33 (4):709–728.

Kodolko, G. 1998. *Economic Neoliberalism Became Almost Irrelevant in Transition*: The Newsletter about Reforming Economies 9(3):1–6.

Kremarik, F., and Statistics Canada. 1999. Moving to Be Better Off. *Canadian Social Trends* Winter (cat. no. 11-008): 19–21.

Kwong, J.C., I.A. Dhalla, D.L. Streiner, R.E. Baddour, A.E. Waddell, and I.L. Johnson. 2002. Effects of Rising Tuition Fees on Medical School Class Composition and Financial Outlook. *Canadian Medical Association Journal* 166 (8):1023–1028.

Land, H. 1980. The Family Wage. *Feminist Review* 6:55–77.

Laslett, B., and J. Brenner. 1989. Gender and Social Reproduction: Historical Perspectives. *Annual Review of Sociology* 15:381–404.

Lewis, J. 1992. Gender and the Development of Welfare Regimes. *European Journal of Social Policy* 2 (3):159–173.

Lewis, J. 1996. The Boundary between Voluntary and Statutory Social Service in the Late Nineteenth and Early Twentieth Centuries. *Historical Journal* 39 (1):155–177.

Lewis, J. 2001. Older People and Health – Social Care Boundaries in the UK: Half a Century of Hidden Policy. *Social Policy and Administration* 35 (4):343–359.

Lewis, J., and G. Astrom. 1992. Equality, Difference, and State Welfare: Labor Market and Family Policies in Sweden. *Feminist Studies* 1 (Spring).

Lipietz, A. 1988. Reflections on a Tale: The Marxist Foundations of the Concepts of Regulation and Accumulation. *Studies in Political Economy* 26 (Summer):7–36.

Little, M. 1998. *'No Car, No Radio, No Liquor Permit': The Moral Regulation of Single Mothers in Ontario, 1920–1997*. Toronto: Oxford University Press.

Little, M. 2005. *If I Had a Hammer: Retraining That Really Works*. Vancouver: UBC Press.

Luxton, M. 1980. *More Than a Labour of Love: Three Generations of Women's Work in the Home*. Toronto: Women's Press.

Luxton, M., ed. 1997. *Feminism and Families: Critical Policies and Changing Practices*. Halifax: Fernwood.

Luxton, M. 2006. Friends, Neighbours and Community: The Role of Informal Caregiving in Social Reproduction. In *Social Reproduction: Feminist Political Economy Challenges Neo-liberalism*, edited by K. Bezanson and M. Luxton. Montreal and Kingston: McGill-Queen's University Press.

Luxton, M., and J. Corman. 2001. *Getting By in Hard Times: Gendered Work at Home and on the Job*. Toronto: University of Toronto Press.

MacKinnon, J. 2003. *Minding the Public Purse: The Fiscal Crisis, Political Trade Offs and Canada's Future*. Montreal and Kingston: McGill-Queen's University Press.

Madore, O. 2001. The Canada Social Health Transfer: Operation and Possible Repercussions on the Health-Care Sector. Ottawa: Library of Parliament.

Marsland, D. 1996. *Welfare or Welfare State? Contradictions and Dilemmas in Social Policy*. London: Macmillan.

Martin, B. 1993. *In the Public Interest? Privatisation and Public Sector Reform*. London: Zed Books.

Marx, K. 1996 [1867]. *Das Kapital: A Critique of Political Economy*. Translated by E.B.F. Engeles and C.B.S. Levitsky. Washington, DC: Regnery.

McCain, M., and J.F. Mustard. 1999. *Early Years Study*. Toronto: Publications Ontario.

McCulloch, J. R. 1954 [1854]. *A Treatise on the Circumstances which Determine the Fate of Wages and the Condition of the Labouring Classes*. New York: Kelley.

McDaniel, S.A., C. Strike, and Statistics Canada. Housing Family and Social Statistics Division. 1994. *Family and Friends, General Social Survey Analysis Series 9*. Ottawa: Statistics Canada.

McDowell, L. 1991. Life without Father and Ford: The New Gender Order of Post-Fordism. *Transactions of the Institute of British Geography* 16:400–419.

McGraw, T. 1984. *Prophets of Regulation*. Cambridge, MA.: Harvard University Press.

McKeen, W. 2004. *Money in Their Own Name: The Feminist Voice in Poverty Debate in Canada, 1970–1995*. Toronto: University of Toronto Press.

McKeen, W., and A. Porter. 2003. Politics and Transformation: Welfare State Restructuring in Canada. In *Changing Canada: Political Economy as Transformation*, edited by L. Vosko and W. Clement. Montreal and Kingston: McGill-Queen's University Press.

McMurray, S. 1997. *Speaking Out Project Description, Research Strategy and Methodology*. Ottawa: Caledon Institute of Social Policy.

Michalski, J.H. 1999. *The Assets of Canadian Families 1997: A National Survey of Clients Accessing Family Service Agencies*. Ottawa: Canadian Policy Research Networks.

Ministry of Community and Social Services (Ontario). 1998. *Survey of Individuals Who Left Social Assistance, Final Report*. Toronto: Ministry of Community and Social Services.

Ministry of Community and Social Services. 1999. *Policy Directives: Ontario Works Dir.7.0–4*. Toronto: Queen's Printer for Ontario.

Ministry of Community and Social Services. 2000. *Making Welfare Work: Report to Taxpayers on Welfare Reform*. Toronto: Queen's Printer for Ontario.

Ministry of Finance. 1996. *Your Budget, Your Future: 1996 Ontario Budget Highlights*. Toronto: Queen's Printer for Ontario.

Ministry of the Attorney General. 2002. Report of the Walkerton Commission of Inquiry. Toronto: Publications Ontario.

Mosher, J. 2000. Managing the Disentitlement of Women: Glorified Markets, the Idealized Family, and the Undeserving Other. In *Restructuring Caring Labour: Discourse, State Practice and Everyday Life*, edited by S. Neysmith. Toronto: Oxford University Press.

Mosher, J., and J. Hermer. 2002. *Disorderly People: Law and the Politics of Exclusion*. Halifax, N.S.: Fernwood.

Mosley, P. 2004. Pro-Poor Politics and the New Political Economy of Stabilisation. *New Political Economy* 9 (4).

Mullaly, R.P. 1997. *Structural Social Work: Ideology, Theory, and Practice*. 2d ed. Toronto: Oxford University Press.

Mutari, E., and D. Figart, eds. 2003. *Women and the Economy: A Reader*. New York: M.E Sharpe.

Myles, J., and P. Pierson. 1997. Friedman's Revenge: The Reform of 'Liberal' Welfare States in Canada and the United States. *Politics and Society* 25 (4):443–472.

Neysmith, S., K. Bezanson, and A. O'Connell. 2005. *Telling Tales: Living the Effects of Public Policy*. Halifax, NS: Fernwood.

Noce, M.L. 2004. *Support Networks and Welfare State Restructuring: The Experiences of 40 Ontario Households*. Toronto: Ontario Institute for Studies in Education.

Noce, M.L., and A. O'Connell. 1998. *Take It or Leave It: The Ontario Government's Approach to Job Insecurity*. Ottawa: Caledon Institute of Social Policy.

Noel, A. 1995. The Politics of Workfare. In *Workfare: Does It Work? Is It Fair?*, edited by A. Sayeed. Montreal: Institute for Research on Public Policy.

Nussbaum, M.C. 1999. *Sex and Social Justice*. Oxford, UK: Oxford University Press.

Nussbaum, M.C. 2000. *Women and Human Development: The Capabilities Approach*. Cambridge, UK: Cambridge University Press.

OAITH. 1998. *Falling Through the Gender Gap: How Ontario Government Policy Continues to Fail Abused Women and Their Children*. Toronto: Ontario Association of Interval and Transition Houses.

Oakley, A. 1974. *The Sociology of Housework*. New York: Pantheon.

O'Connell, A., and F. Valentine. 1998. *Centralizing Power, Decentralizing Blame:*

What Ontarians Say about Education Reform. Ottawa: Caledon Institute of
   Social Policy.
O'Connor, J.S. 1992. Gender, Class and Citizenship in the Comparative Analy-
   sis of Welfare State Regimes: Theoretical and Methodological Issues. *British
   Journal of Sociology* 44 (3).
O'Connor, J., A. Orloff., and S. Shaver. 1999. *States, Markets, Families: Gender,
   Liberalism, and Social Policy in Australia, Canada, Great Britain, and the United
   States*. Cambridge: Cambridge University Press.
OECD. 2001. *Starting Strong: Early Childhood Education and Care*. Paris: Organi-
   zation for Economic Cooperation and Development.
OECD. 2004. *Early Childhood Education and Care Policy: Canada*. Paris: Organiza-
   tion for Economic Cooperation and Development.
OECD Directorate for Education. 2004. *Early Childhood Education and Care
   Policy: Canada Country Note*. Paris: OECD.
Ontarians with Disabilities Act Committee. 1998. ODA Blueprint Brief.
   Toronto: ODAC.
Ontario Federation of Labour. 1999. *The Future of Work in Ontario: Discussion
   Paper*. Toronto: Ontario Federation of Labour.
Ontario Federation of Labour. 2000. Submission by the Ontario Federation of
   Labour on the consultation paper, Time for Change: Ontario's Employment
   Standards Legislation. Toronto: Ontario Federation of Labour.
Ontario Ministry of Health. 1996. *Government Announces New Directions for
   Primary Care*. Toronto: Queen's Printer for Ontario.
Ontario Ministry of Education and Training. 1998. *Backgrounder: Changes to Stu-
   dent Assistance for 1998–99, 13 February*. Toronto: Ministry of Education and
   Training. (Ontario).
Ontario Ministry of Health. 1998. Community Care Access Centres. Toronto:
   Queen's Printer for Ontario.
Ontario Ministry of Labour. 2004. *Minimum Wage*. Ministry of Labour 2004
   [cited October 10 2004]. Available from http://www.gov.on.ca/LAB/
   english/es/factsheets/fs_wage.html.
Ontario Ministry of Municipal Affairs and Housing. 1997. Speech by the
   Honourable Al Leach, Minister of Municipal Affairs and Housing, to the
   Association of Municipalities of Ontario.
Ontario Secondary School Teachers' Federation. 1998. Issues in Ontario Educa-
   tion. In *Background Paper on Bill 34*. Toronto: OSSTF.
OSSN. 2000. *Five Years Later: Welfare Rate Cuts Anniversary Report*. Toronto:
   Ontario Social Safety Network.
Orloff, A.S. 1993. Gender and the Social Rights of Citizenship: The Compara-

References 221

tive Analysis of Gender Relations and Welfare States. *American Sociological Review* 58 (June):303–328.

Pahl, J.M. 1989. *Money and Marriage*. New York: St Martin's Press.

Parsons, T. 1956. The American Family: Its Relation to Personality and the Social Structure. In *Family, Society and Interaction*, edited by T. Parsons and F. Bales. London: Routledge and Kegan Paul.

Peck, J. 1996. *Work-Place: The Social Regulation of Labor Markets*. New York: Guildford Press.

Peck, J. 2001. *Workfare States*. New York: Guildford Press.

Pender, J. 2001. From 'Structural Adjustment' to 'Comprehensive Development Framework': Conditionality Transformed? *Third World Quarterly* 22 (3):397–411.

Peters, S. 1996. *Examining the Concept of Transactions as the Basis for Studying the Social and Economic Dynamics of Families*. Ottawa: Canadian Policy Research Networks.

Philipps, L. 2000. Taxing the Market Citizen: Fiscal Policy and Inequality in an Age of Privatization. *Law and Contemporary Problems* 63 (4).

Picard, A. 1999. Pay Equity Threatens Non-profit Home Care. *Globe and Mail*, 5 April, A7.

Picchio, A. 1992. *Social Reproduction: The Political Economy of the Labour Market*. Cambridge, UK: Cambridge University Press.

Picchio, A. 1996. The Analytical and Political Visibility of the Work of Social Reproduction. New York: UNDP.

Picchio, A., ed. 2003. *Unpaid Work and the Economy: A Gender Analysis of the Standards of Living*. London: Routledge.

Pierson, P. 1994. *Dismantling the Welfare State?: Reagan, Thatcher, and the Politics of Retrenchment, Cambridge Studies in Comparative Politics*. Cambridge, MA: Cambridge University Press.

Pierson, P. 1996. The New Politics of the Welfare State. *World Politics* 48:143–79.

Pierson, P. 2001. *The New Politics of the Welfare State*. New York: Oxford University Press.

Porter, A. 2003. *Gendered States: Women, Unemployment Insurance, and the Political Economy of the Welfare State in Canada, 1946–1997*. Toronto: University of Toronto Press.

Prince, M.J. 1999. From Health and Welfare to Stealth and Farewell: Federal Social Policy, 1980–2000. In *How Ottawa Spends 1999–2000*, edited by L. A. Pal. Toronto: Oxford University Press.

Progressive Conservative Party of Ontario. 1994. *The Common Sense Revolution*. Toronto: Progressive Conservative Party of Ontario.

Provincial Auditor of Ontario. 1998. *1998 Annual Report of the Provincial Auditor of Ontario to the Legislative Assembly.* Toronto: Queen's Printer for Ontario.

Quershi, H., and A. Walker. 1989. *The Caring Relationship: Elderly People and Their Families.* London: Macmillan Educational.

Raddon, M.B. 2002. *Community and Money: Caring, Gift-giving and Women in a Social Economy.* Montreal: Black Rose Books.

Reed, P., and K. Selbee. 2001. Volunteering and Giving: A Regional Perspective. *Statistics Canada: Canadian Social Trends*:1–3.

Regimbald, A. 1997. The Ontario Branch of American Conservatism. In *Mike Harris' Ontario: Open for Business, Closed to People,* edited by D. Ralph, A. Regimbald, and N. St-Amand. Halifax: Fernwood.

Rice, J.J. 1995. Redesigning Welfare: The Abandonment of a National Commitment. In *How Ottawa Spends: A More Democratic Canada?,* edited by S. D. Phillips. Ottawa: Carleton University Press.

Rice, J.J., and M.J. Prince. 2000. *Changing Politics of Canadian Social Policy.* Toronto: University of Toronto Press.

Ross, E. 1993. *Love and Toil: Motherhood in Outcast London 1870–1918.* London: Oxford University Press.

Sainsbury, D. 1996. *Gender, Equality and Welfare States.* Cambridge: Cambridge University Press.

Seccombe, W. 1974. The Housewife and Her Labour under Capitalism. *New Left Review* 83.

Seccombe, W. 1992. *A Millennium of Family Change: Feudalism to Capitalism in North Western Europe.* London: Verso.

Segal, L. 1999. *Why Feminism?: Gender, Psychology, Politics.* New York: Columbia University Press.

Sen, A. 1993. Capability and Well-Being. In *The Quality of Life,* edited by M. Nussbaum and A. Sen. Oxford: Clarendon Press.

Sen, A. 1999. *Development as Freedom.* New York: Knopf.

Shaikh, A. 1991. Economic Crises. In *A Dictionary of Marxist Thought,* edited by T. Bottomore. Oxford: Blackwell.

Shields, J., and B.M. Evans. 1998. *Shrinking the State: Globalization and Public Administration 'Reform.'* Halifax: Fernwood.

Shragge, E., ed. 1997. *Workfare: Ideology for a New Under-Class.* Toronto: Garamond.

Side, K. 1999. Government Restraint and Limits to Economic Reciprocity in Women's Friendships. *Atlantis* 23 (2):5–15.

Silvera, M. 1989. *Silenced: Talks with Working Class Caribbean Women about Their Lives And Struggles as Domestic Workers In Canada.* Toronto: Sister Vision Press.

Smith, A. 1969 [1776]. *Adam Smith Today: An inquiry into the Nature and Causes of the Wealth of Nations*, edited by A. H. Jenkins. Port Washington, NY: Kennikat Press.

Sparr, P., ed. 1994. *Mortgaging Women's Lives: Feminist Critiques of Structural Adjustment*. London: Zed Books.

Stack, C., and L. Burton. 1993. Kinscripts. *Journal of Comparative Family Studies* 25 (2):157–170.

Statistics Canada. 1998. *Caring Canadians, Involved Canadians: Highlights from the 1997 National Survey of Giving, Volunteering and Participating*. Ottawa: Statistics Canada.

Statistics Canada. 1999. *Income in Canada*. Ottawa: Statistics Canada.

Statistics Canada. 1999. *Overview of the Time Use of Canadians in 1998*. Ottawa: Statistics Canada. Available from http://www.statcan.ca:80/english/freepub/12F0080XIE/12F0080XIE.pdf.

Statistics Canada. 2000a. *Women in Canada*. Ottawa: Statistics Canada.

Statistics Canada. 2000b. Information and Insights for the Nonprofit Sector: Building a Knowledge Base. *Issues 1–3* Statistics Canada.

Statistics Canada. 2001. Survey of Financial Security. *The Daily*. 15 March, 2001.

Statistics Canada. 2003. *Survey of Family Expenditures 1996 (Reweighted)*. Cat. no. 62M0001UCB. Ottawa: Statistics Canada.

Statistics Canada. 2004. Paying for Higher Education. Ottawa: Statistics Canada.

Statistics Canada. 2005. Child Care. In *The Daily*, 7 February. Ottawa: Statistics Canada.

Statistics Canada General Social Survey. 1994. *Family and Friends*. Cat. no. 11-612E, no. 9. Ottawa: Statistics Canada.

Swank, D. 2005. Globalisation, Domestic Politics, and Welfare State Retrenchment in Capitalist Democracies. *Social Policy and Society* 4 (2):183–195.

Taylor-Gooby, P. 2004. Open Market and Welfare Values: Welfare Values, Inequality and Social Change in the Silver Age of the Welfare State. *European Societies* 6 (1):29–49.

Teeple, G. 1995. *Gloablization and the Decline of Social Reform*. Toronto: Garamond.

Tilly, L.A., and J. Scott. 1978. *Women, Work and Family. New York: Holt, Rhinehart and Winston.

Todaro, M.P. 1994. *Economic Development*. 5th ed. New York: Longmann.

Torjman, S. 2000. Survival-of-the-Fittest Employment Policy. Ottawa: Caledon Institute of Social Policy.

Toronto Star. 1995. No bologna for Harris, his dad says. 24 October, A4.

Toronto Star. 1996. Nothing sacred in review – Harris. 5 April, A1.

Toynbee, P. 2003. *Hard Work: Life in Low Pay Britain*. London: Bloomsbury.

Transport Canada. 2000. *Transportation Policy in Canada*. Ottawa: Transport Canada.

Trichur, R., and C. Won. 2004. Ontario Welfare, Disability Benefits Get First Increase in 11 Years. *Canadian Press*, 18 May.

Tyyksa, V. 2001. Advocacy Ignored: Child Care Policy in Ontario in the 1990s. In *Changing Child Care: Five Decades of Child Care Advocacy and Policy in Canada*, edited by S. Prentice. Halifax: Fernwood.

Ungerson, C. 1997. Social Politics and the Commodification of Care. *Social Politics* (Fall):363–381.

Ursel, J. 1992. *Private Lives, Public Policy: 100 Years of State Intervention in the Family*. Toronto: Women's Press.

Vogel, L. 1984. *Marxism and the Oppression of Women: Towards a Unitary Theory*. New Brunswick, NJ: Rutgers University Press.

Vosko, L. 2000. *Temporary Work: The Gendered Rise of a Temporary Employment Relationship*. Toronto: University of Toronto Press.

Vosko, L. 2002. *Rethinking Feminization: Gendered Precariousness in the Canadian Market and the Crisis in Social Reproduction*. Toronto: Robarts Centre for Canadian Studies.

Vosko, L. 2003. Gender Differentiation and the Standard/Non-Standard Employment Distinction: A Genealogy of Policy Interventions in Canada. In *Social Differentiation: Patterns and Processes*, edited by D. Juteau. Toronto: University of Toronto Press.

Vosko, L. 2006. Crisis Tendencies in Social Reproduction: The Case of Ontario's *Early Year's Plan*. In *Social Reproduction: Feminist Political Economy Challenges Neo-Liberalism*, edited by K. Bezanson and M. Luxton. Montreal and Kingston: McGill-Queen's University Press.

Vosko, L., and W. Clement, eds. 2003. *Changing Canada: Political Economy as Transformation*. Montreal and Kingston. McGill-Queen's University Press.

Wade, R.H. 2004. Is Globalization Reducing Poverty and Inequality? *World Development* 32 (4):567–589.

Walby, S. 1997. *Gender Transformations*. London: Routledge.

Walby, S. 2004. The European Union and Gender Equality: Emergent Varieties of Gender Regimes. *Social Politics* 11 (1):4–29.

Walker, A. 1992. The Strategy of Inequality. In *The Social Effects of Free Market Policies*, edited by I. Taylor. London: Harvester Wheatsheaf.

Ward, K., ed. 1990. *Women Workers and Global Restructuring*. Ithica, NY: ILR Press.

Wellman, B. 1989. *The Place of Kinfolk in Personal Community Networks*. Toronto: Centre for Urban and Community Studies, University Of Toronto.

Wellman, B. 1999. *Networks in the Global Village: Life in Contemporary Communities*. Boulder, CO: Westview Press.

Wellman, B., and R.D. Hiscott. 1983. *From Social Support to Social Network.* Toronto: Centre for Urban and Community Studies, University of Toronto.

Wellman, B., and S. Wortley. 1988. *Brothers' Keepers: Situating Kinship Relations in Broader Networks of Social Support.* Toronto: Centre for Urban and Community Studies, University of Toronto.

Williams, F. 1995. Race/Ethnicity, Gender, and Class in Welfare States: A Framework for Comparative Analysis. *Social Politics* (Summer).

Williams, F. 2002. In and Beyond New Labour: Towards a New Political Ethics of Care. *Critical Social Policy* 21 (4):467–93.

Williamson, J. 2000. What Should the World Bank Think about the Washington Consensus? *World Bank Research Observer* 15 (2):251–264.

Williamson, J., ed. 1990. *Latin American Adjustment: How Much Has Happened?* Washington, DC: Institute for International Economics.

Wolfensohn, J. 1998. Rethinking Development: Principles, Approaches and Projects. *Annual World Bank Conference on Development Economics.*

Woolley, F. 2001. The Strengths and Limits of the Voluntary Sector. *ISUMA: Canadian Journal of Policy Research* 2 (2):21–27.

World Bank. 1998. *The Initiative on Defining, Monitoring and Measuring Social Capital.* Washington, DC: World Bank.

World Bank. 2001. *World Development Report 2000/2001: Attacking Poverty.* Washington, DC: World Bank.

World Bank. 2002. *Globalization, Growth and Poverty: Building an Inclusive World Economy.* New York: Oxford University Press.

Wroughton, L. 2005. Wolfowitz Confirmed as New World Bank President. *Reuters News Wire*, 31 March.

York, G. 1992. Family Life: Not Enough Money, Too Much Stress. *Globe and Mail* 3 (June), A1, A4. Quoted in Fudge and Cossman 1981.

Young, B. 2001. Globalization and Gender: A European Perspective. In *Gender, Globalisation and Democratisation*, edited by R.M. Kelly, J. Bayes, M. Hawesworthy, and B. Young. London: Roman and Littlefield.

Zanatta, A.L. 2004. Are We Moving from the 'Familiastic' Model to an Uncontrolled Private 'Defamilialisation' of Care Work in Mediterranean Countries? Paper read at Welfare State Restructuring: Processes and Social Outcomes Conference, 2–4 September. Paris.

Zipp, J.F., A. Prohaska, and M. Bemiller. 2004. Wives, Husbands and Hidden Power in Marriage. *Journal of Family Issues* 25 (7):933–959.

Zukewich, N. 1998. Work, Parenthood and the Experience of Time Poverty. In *Days of Our Lives: Time Use and Transitions over the Life Course.* Cat. no. 89-584-MIE. Ottawa: Statistics Canada.

Zukewich, N. 2003. Unpaid Informal Caregiving. *Canadian Social Trends* (Autumn/cat. no. 11-008):14–18.

Index

Picchio, A., 126, 161
Pierson, P., 185nn9, 10
playing, 26
Polanyi, Karl, 166
policy-making process. *See* Harris government; legislation
political economy, 39
post-Second World War, 30, 32, 36
poverty: below line, 90; gap between rich and poor, 165–6; solutions to, 4. *See also* criminalization of poor
power: balance between women and men, 27, 189nn6, 7; of capital, 36; centralized, 9, 40, 49; of government executive, 48, 55, 193n5; in households, 15, 19, 26, 130–1; in interviews, 187n25; of school boards, 106; in social reproduction, 25
Prevention of Unionization Act, 59, 61–2
private schools, 52–3
private sector: government responsibility for, 8; growth, 3; responsibility transferred to, 42. *See also* privatization
private transfers, explanation of, 199n5
privatization: balanced budgets as, 52; in child care, 54; of government agencies, 46, 61; of health care services, 55, 92–4, 195nn12, 13; legislation for, 48; in neo-liberal model, 40–2; of public goods and services, 32, 50, 191n13, 196n19; of services, 63; of social reproduction, 11, 32; Walkerton Inquiry, 50–1. *See also* Harris government
production of people, 24, 189n3, 198n31

Progressive Conservative, 3, 13. *See also* Harris government
property tax assessments, 49, 195n15
provincial spending cuts, 79. *See also* Harris government
provincial transfers. *See* government transfers
public income transfers, 3. *See also* government transfers
public sector: changes in provincial spending in, 78; cuts to, 5, 79; job cuts in, 98, 191n13; participation in health care, 92–4; promises to cut, 3
Public Sector Labour Relations Transition Act, 61

race: in care work, 37–8, 44, 198n34; in commodification, 44; hierarchies of, 23; in restructuring, 37, 125; in social assistance, 115; wages ascribed by, 33
Reagan government, 10
Red Tape Commission, 51, 61, 196n20
Red Tape Reduction Acts, 47–8, 51, 194nn8, 9, 195n13
refamilialization, 164. *See also* familialization
referenda, 186n17
regulation of capital, 29
regulation of industry, 33–4
religious schools, 52–3
rent controls, 45, 57
replacement workers, 61
research models, 16, 187nn25–6
responsibility of individuals, 3–4, 23
Responsible Choices for Growth and Accountability Act, 52
restructuring: budgets (government),

12–13, 41, 62–4, 78–9, 182n7,
185n10; in child care, 104–5,
193–4nn6, 7; of community sector,
125; debate of depth of, 185n9;
in education, 46, 52–5, 104–6,
197nn22, 23; of Employment
Insurance (EI), 200–1n11; gender
roles in, 37; general results of, 161;
of health care services, 46, 48, 55–6,
99, 104, 202n2, 203n4; effect on
low-income households, 3–6, 13,
124–5, 159–60; manufacturing in,
5; models of, 45; of municipalities,
46; race in, 37, 125; reconsidered,
183n1; of social assistance, 198n28,
200n12; of social services, 154–9; of
third sector, 8, 42, 49, 125, 127; effect on women, 124, 190n9
*Rogers v. Greater Sudbury (City)
Administrator of Ontario Works,* 58

sample size, 14
Savings and Restructuring Act, 46,
48, 55, 61
school boards, 49, 53–4, 106
security, 36, 76
sexual orientation of participant
households, 18–19. *See also* participant households
Sheep and Wool Marketing Act, 47
shelters, 122
single mothers: access to education,
112; and Canada Child Tax Benefit,
88; coping with high-needs children, 152–9; cost of children, 124;
criminalization of, 42; effect of cuts
to education, 106; as employable,
59; food as negotiable expense,
135–6; government supports, 56;
over-represented in low-income

households, 13; paying for social
assistance, 141; time spent on
unpaid work, 128; as undeserving
of social assistance, 44–5; vulnerability of, 80; workload of, 128
skills, 22; social reconstruction of, 26;
value of, 204n11
snitch lines, 42
social assistance: access to, 114–20;
access to drugs, 94; accusations of
cheating, 42; allowance calculations, 84; cheating of, 44; collection
of overpayment of, 141, 204n10;
cost of redesigned, 10; effects of
cuts on recipients of, 138–9,
159–60; cuts to, 4, 63; downloaded
to municipalities, 46; drug testing, 115; federal-provincial cost-
sharing, 8; fraud charges, 46, 58,
115, 192n1, 198n30; generosity or
stigma, 19; income of participants,
80; intertwined with child care,
111; labour market orientation of,
204n7; medical assistance, 141;
perceptions of recipients of, 119;
reasons for leaving, 84–5, 201n13;
reforms to, 46, 56–60, 79, 83;
restructuring of, 198n28, 200n12;
statistics of cuts to, 56; statistics
rates, 184n3; student loans, 117; for
students, 112. *See also* Ontario
Works
Social Assistance Reform Act, 60,
200n12
social housing, 4, 122–3, 146. *See also*
housing
social norms, 26
social policy: access to services,
199n1; dealing with poverty, 166;
employability in, 8; ignoring